CONSCIOUS
GARDENING

ALSO BY MICHAEL J. ROADS

Nonfiction

Stepping . . . Between . . . Realities
THROUGH THE EYES OF LOVE, Journeying with Pan BOOK ONE
THROUGH THE EYES OF LOVE, Journeying with Pan BOOK TWO
THROUGH THE EYES OF LOVE, Journeying with Pan, BOOK THREE
TALKING WITH NATURE—JOURNEY INTO NATURE
JOURNEY INTO ONENESS
INTO A TIMELESS REALM
THE MAGIC FORMULA
MORE THAN MONEY—TRUE PROSPERITY
THE ORACLE
A GLIMPSE OF SOMETHING GREATER

Fiction

GETTING THERE

MICHAEL J. ROADS

CONSCIOUS GARDENING

Practical and Metaphysical Expert
Advice to Grow Your Garden
Organically

SIX DEGREES PUBLISHING GROUP
PORTLAND · OREGON · USA

SIX DEGREES PUBLISHING GROUP
5331 Macadam Avenue, Suite 258
Portland, OR 97239 USA

ISBN: 978-1-942497-05-9
U.S. Library of Congress Control Number 2015932462
Digital Edition ISBN: 978-1-301351268
Cover photo: Tracey Roads

Previous soft cover edition published by Findhorn Press, 2011.

Sales: This book is distributed by Ingram Content Group to major retail booksellers and independent bookstores. Additionally, special sales of Michael J. Roads books may be purchased by contacting:
office@michaelroads.com
RoadsLight pty ltd, PO Box 778, Nambour, QLD, 4559, Australia
www.michaelroads.com

Publisher's Note: This book is written in Australian English. The metric unit measures converted to US standard unit measures are approximate. For exact conversions, consult a metric/standard conversion chart.

Enquiries: Publisher@SixDegreesPublishingGroup.com
www.SixDegreesPublishing.com

Published in the United States of America
Printed Simultaneously in the United States of America,
the United Kingdom, and Australia

1 3 5 7 9 10 8 6 4 2

DURING THE TIME between writing this book and its publishing, my late wife, Treenie, died. I took time out to recover.

Now, in the way of life, I am again very happily married. To my surprise, I fell in Love with a long-term friend, Carolyn. I dedicate this book to these wonderful ladies, both of whom have given me so much Love and brought so much richness into my life.

∾

CONTENTS

ACKNOWLEDGEMENTS

Throughout my life, I have met people who have enriched the garden of my soul, fertilising me with the goodness of their intent. To all those people who fertilise life with their Love and care, a sincere thank you. You are the gardeners who reap the greatest harvest.

Despite marriage to my beloved Carolyn, in some ways I am also married to the Spirit of Nature. To me, marriage is when souls connect, rather than just physical bodies, and I have long felt a soul connection to Pan, the very essence of Nature. To Pan, my guide and teacher, 'Thank you' seems totally inadequate, but he knows the content of my heart . . . and that *is* adequate.

INTRODUCTION

M Y LOVE AFFAIR with gardening began at around the age of six. I well remember the day that my father came home from his work with a dozen tomato plants. To my delight, he gave me six of them to grow and care for. I was very proud. This seemed a huge responsibility to me and I took it very seriously. Together we set the plants in two rows, six in his vegetable garden and six in my little patch. I was a schoolboy, and every afternoon when I came home I would race down to my garden patch to see if the tomato plants were growing. To my disappointment, I could not see a difference from the previous day, so I would carefully dig up the plants to have a look at the roots, and then replant them.

A few weeks later, my six tomato plants were shrivelling and dying, while Dad's were growing strong and healthy. Tearfully, I showed him my plants. He was very puzzled. "I can't understand it. The plants were all the same when we set them; it doesn't make sense," he said.

"I dig them up every day when I get home to see if the roots are growing," I said miserably, "but they never are."

Dad's face broke into a smile. "Ah! That's the problem, Michael.

Once you set a plant you should never dig it up to check the roots. You have to trust Nature that the roots are growing and all is well." He then proceeded to give me a lesson about how plants grow best without too much human interference.

For some reason it all 'clicked' with me. Rather than being put off by such a disastrous beginning to gardening, it impressed into me that there is something mystical and mysterious about Nature. I fell in love with Nature, plants, gardens and gardening. Since then my passion for gardening has expressed itself in England and in various parts of Australia, ranging from cool temperate Tasmania to warm temperate New South Wales, and now to subtropical Queensland.

I wrote the first book on organic gardening written in Oz for our conditions, *A Guide to Organic Gardening* in Australia. A small, humble little book, it took my wife Treenie quite a while to convince me, a school dropout, that I could indeed write such a book. When it rapidly became a best seller, nobody was more surprised than me, or more pleased and proud than Treenie. I followed it a couple of years later with *A Guide to Organic Living.* This, too, became a best seller. This was back in the mid-1970s, and of course, both are long out of print.

Much later, at the end of the 1980s, I decided to update my knowledge of organic gardening and the soil, and I wrote *The Natural Magic of Mulch.* Despite only average sales, I was personally very pleased with it. I have never judged the quality or value of a book by its sales figure. I was so pleased, in fact, that just as we transplant many of our garden plants, so I have transplanted a few chapters from *The Natural Magic of Mulch* into the pages of this book. Even years later I cannot improve or add much more to my words on 'The Living Soil,' nor on the 'How and Why of Natural Fertilisers.' I consider those chapters an excellent example, in their concise and precise way, of describing in simple terms the complex interactions of soil nutrients and minerals.

Equally, I have found no need to change the more basic common knowledge in the chapters that deal with vegetable growing, fruit trees, making compost, and lawns, although this has all been expanded.

For me, true gardening is not about techniques, or even just the accumulation of knowledge. Just as a wild tree has to reach its maturity before it bears fruit—modern hybrids bear fruit long before they have the strength to support them—so also a gardener has to reach a certain maturity before his or her gardening knowledge becomes *gardening wisdom*. And this, truly, is a profound transition. This book, more than anything, is an addition to *The Natural Magic of Mulch*. It explores areas that very few gardening books care to go. It is very easy to be labelled as 'alternative' or 'radical' or 'strange' once you step beyond the narrow borders of 'normality.' Personally, I have spent so many years divorced from what is considered 'normal' that it no longer bothers me.

By the time *The Natural Magic of Mulch*—also out of print— was published there were many 'organic' gardening books on the market, and belatedly, I realised mine was handicapped by the word 'mulch.' During a publicity tour, I was astonished to learn that many people had no idea what mulch is. Today, no self-respecting gardener could fail to know, but twenty years ago it was a very different story. After around two decades of excellent TV gardening education, the change has been both positive and dramatic.

I remember when I was publicising my first organic gardening book in 1976, I was ridiculed by quite a few radio interviewers at that time. Even some of the newspaper interviews made fun of the 'radical English migrant who enthuses over the alternative organic gardening theory.' Interestingly, twelve years later when I was publicising *The Natural Magic of Mulch*, some of the same people said things like, "Well, of course, any intelligent person knows that organic is better, it's more natural." When I asked them where those intelligent people had been hidden when I publicised my first book, they just smiled condescendingly.

None of this is a grumble, it's just an indicator that times change, and hopefully, so do we. That is why I am writing this book. Just as we get settled into fully embracing organic gardening, so I want to once again *stretch* those people who are more open-minded into new areas of thought, exploration, and experience. As I learned at six years of age, we set our plants and allow Nature to take over. But what happens? I'm sure that a soil scientist would have their explanations, and many people could describe the biological processes that are involved in root and plant growth — but there is something beyond all this.

Nature is not 'just' a set of biological processes. A flower is not 'just' the sex programme of a plant. Science may say I am wrong, but a more holistic exploration of Nature reveals insights into Nature that literally cannot be described in words. Nature is physical, yes, but Nature is also metaphysical. Meta, meaning beyond—more than being physically limited to no more than physical processes. Are you and I no more than physical? Few would argue that we are, indeed, more than physical. There is the spiritual self, the emotional self, the intellectual self, the intuitive self—we are far more than is apparent. So also is Nature. So is every garden. And when the open receptive self becomes involved in the open receptivity of Nature—and this can happen beautifully in a garden—then you stand on the cusp of CONSCIOUS GARDENING.

–Michael J. Roads, Queensland, Australia

GETTING TO
KNOW EACH OTHER!

HAVING READ THE INTRODUCTION—and if you have not, you should—you will realise that this book is about more than 'all that meets the eye'. It is also about that which the eye does not, and mostly cannot, see. This does not mean that it is impossible to see the seldom seen; it means that if you want to see that which is hidden from 'normal' observation it requires more than normal attention, awareness, and acceptance.

This will be mostly a 'chatty' book. I'm a chatty type of person. Oh, incidentally, the Oz I refer to in this book is, of course, Australia. I am writing this as though you and I are chatting about the potential of a garden, rather than me writing another gardening book, regardless of you. I'm going to assume that you already know a fair bit about gardening and, a big assumption, that you are open-minded and receptive to new ideas and speculation about Nature and the nature of gardens. To be reading this, you will need to be!

Everything that I write in this book is from my experience. All of it! I was an Organic Farming consultant for a few years, travelling into four different states of Oz, so I gleaned a lot of knowledge and experience of the land and different soil types. I was very good at what I did, and my knowledge of soil and soil nutrients was essential, but I learned to use far more than just that knowledge during those years.

THE SPIRIT OF THE LAND

When I walked over the land, I could feel an energetic resonance vibrating around me that varied from farm to farm. This energetic resonance is always on the farm; it does not travel with or is personal to me! It varies from farm to farm because the farmers are different. Where the farmer—this includes his or her spouse or partner—is attuned to the land in a sympathetic way, the land is affected. You cannot separate the energy of the farming family from their farm. This does not mean that if the farmers 'love' their land things will automatically go well for them; it means that this connection with the land enables a two-way growth to take place.

Seldom, however, is this connection actively looked for, recognised, or acknowledged. I call this energetic resonance the *Spirit of the Land*. There are thousands of farms across the Western world today where that energetic resonance is absent. On millions of hectares (acres) the agricultural abuse of agribusiness is so aggressive, so erosive, and the land is so denatured, the Spirit of the Land has withdrawn.

This does not mean that crops will not grow on such land. They will, with their forced and manipulated high yields, but there is a spiritual quality missing from the food. The energetic spiritual quality, born from the natural synthesis in the partnership between a caring, aware human and the living soil, becomes null and void. Agribusiness has no awareness of the land as living, no spiritual substance; the end product is all about money.

All that comes from this unholy relationship with the land is a produce with its required chemical nutrients forced into it. The spiritual essence of something you cannot measure in any laboratory, something that will not yield to scientific enquiry, is missing. The consumers of this food are unwittingly the losers.

THE EXPRESSION OF POTENTIAL

This Spirit of the Land was the area of enquiry that drew me like a bee to honey. Here was a nebulous 'something' that could never be scientifically proven. This was the hidden promise that held me poised, trembling as a dewdrop on the edge of a leaf in the morning sun. Too heavy a hand and the dewdrop falls, never again to be reconstituted in its own unique formula of that particular moment in time.

Once when I was walking the land of an 'aware' farmer who had engaged me as a consultant, he walked at my side, chattering endlessly about his land. I'd had his soil tested in a laboratory, and having translated this into terms that relate to organic farming, I knew a lot about his physical soil, its imbalances, problems, and potential. As I half-listened to him I was getting ever more frustrated, because I wanted to *listen* to the Spirit of the Land. In perfect timing, his wife waved to him from the distance, indicating that he was wanted on the phone. No mobiles in those days! With an apology to me, he departed. Perfect, now I could attune with his land.

As I walked it came into my incredulous awareness that where I walked on the land, in my footsteps, the pH was beneficially changing. I need to add that this land was on the alkaline soils of the Darling Downs in SE Queensland, and the pH was very high. I did some careful soil tests for the pH with my expensive and accurate pH tester. Directly under my footsteps the change was greatest, the pH measuring pH 8.0. The further I went from my footsteps, the higher the pH. At twenty-five metres the pH was 8.5, at a hundred metres pH 9.0.

'So what?' you might say. Let me briefly explain. Neutral is pH 7.0. This land had a pH 9.7. Bearing in mind that pH 9.0 is a hundred times more alkaline than neutral, and pH 10.0 a thousand times, this indicates that the land was nearly eight hundred times more alkaline than neutral. In our present knowledge and understanding of the physical qualities of the soil, the change in pH where I walked, simply by walking on the land was impossible. But it happened. And that happening had a huge affect on me. I realised on an intuitive level that the relationship this aware farmer had with his land fostered the potential for this to happen, and my relationship and love for the land brought that potential to fruition.

That experience also connected me with some of the farmer wisdom of my late father. So often he told me, "The best fertiliser the land can ever receive is the footsteps of the farmer." How right he was. Only the aware and conscious farmer walks his or her land simply for the love of it.

METAPHYSICAL CONNECTIONS

My experience with the land could not be denied. You can doubt it if you so choose, but because it was my experience I could neither doubt nor deny it. Oddly, it led me toward the time when I would stop being an Organic Farming consultant, revealing to me the lonely path that my soul longed to follow. And follow it I did. It is to where this led me, from where this book comes. This path led me to Self-discovery, eventually leading to my wife and I travelling the world, teaching other people about Self Realisation, and what I now term as the Metaphysics of Nature.

Why am I telling you all this? Because I want you to get a feeling for the person I am. In this way we can consciously connect in this book, and you will receive far more than the sum of the words you read. Just as we can make a metaphysical connection with Nature, so can you and I.. If this holds no appeal for you, it is time to pass this book on to someone else.

Equally, if you stay with me, then on a deeper level I can get to know you, for any real and true connection is a two-way flow.

Look deeply into a flower, connect with it in its total essence, then tell me that this is no more than the sex act of the plant. To believe that is to suggest that the sex act between people is devoid of any deeper meaning or potential. As we know, the sex act itself means nothing, unless it conveys the spirit of love, of care, of wanting to connect on a deeper than physical level. This, then, depends on the consciousness of the people concerned in the act of sex. So too with a plant. There is a consciousness involved. This is not a human consciousness, but there is awareness and intelligence involved. Not human awareness or human intelligence, but the awareness and intelligence of Nature. And this is where the speculation of the human intellect cannot go. It is a journey for the aware consciousness.

While I accept that normal observation of a flower reveals nothing of what I am suggesting, when you *metaphysically connect* with the flower you become aware of, and experience, a far greater-than-physical reality. Cynicism and scorn leaves a person forever isolated on the outside, while an openness to deeper inquiry can, indeed, be very revealing. I believe it was Cleeve Baxter who wrote a book 'proving' that plants have emotions. No one is suggesting that these are human emotions, but his experiments indicate there is a definite connection between plant and human emotion. Enough that one can recognise, connect with, and flow into the other.

ONENESS OR SEPARATION?

Our modern isolationist education suggests and indicates that all life is separate. It suggests that I am separate from you, that you are separate from your family. Interestingly, our physical senses support this. We can see the spaces of physical separation. We were taught this, yet we are also told of the 'web of life' where everything is connected. We are now told that this web of connection is so significant that the passage of a running bear in Alaska might have an effect on the flight of a mob of kangaroos in Oz. So which do we believe? We can see separation. This makes it very believable. Can we see the web of connection? Hardly! Does this mean that we disbelieve? Or are we supposed to believe in both opposing views and just muddle along with it?

It gets complicated, doesn't it? Yet, it is not complicated at all.

We need to accept that our five physical senses are the four walls and the ceiling of the prison we live in. We believe that if we cannot see it, it is not there. We believe this, knowing how incredibly limited human vision is. We cannot see with X-ray vision, or into the ultraviolet or infra-red spectrum of vision. Equally, compared with a wolf our sense of smell is almost non-existent. Apparently a wolf has a ten thousand times greater sense of smell than we do. Compared to most wild animals, our hearing is as dim as our sight, and our sense of touch is literally forgotten. Certainly we have developed our taste buds for gourmet food, but if that food was a poison to us, we would not have a clue until we were very sick. By comparison, a dingo used to be extremely difficult to poison. The instant its stomach recognised a poisonous substance, and that was within seconds, the contamination was rejected so fast the animal was safe. Hence, the development of such fast and terrible poisons as 1080 in agriculture.

Put simply, if we stay within the evidence of our physical senses, we stay within our own limits. If, on the other hand, we can dare to venture into the metaphysical potential that we all contain, then our personal universe can expand into experiencing the Oneness of all life.

This is what I want us to explore. I choose to do it in the simple, humble setting which I so love, a garden, doing what I am still learning to do, Conscious Gardening.

SPIRITS OF NATURE

One of the problems people are faced with is a subconscious need to conform. School uniform, the need to blend in, lack of self-confidence, a fear of standing apart, following fashion trends, or its counterpart, defiant fashion, all this and much more ensures that from our early childhood we will stay within the confines of an overall consensus reality. It is a comfortable place, even if stagnant. Imagine attending a Garden Club meeting anywhere in Oz, or elsewhere, and listening to a speaker talking about Nature

Spirits, using words like fairies! With a few possible exceptions, the audience would go from surprise to ridicule. How many people would be open and comfortable listening to such a talk? Very few. Unfortunately, most people like to stay within their safe comfort zones . . . and not just personal comfort zones. It includes the overall conformity of what other people believe and accept as reality. Our resistance to the 'unknown' is based in a deep subconscious fear, thus creating a fast and automatic rejection.

But not all people. I travel a lot, and I 'do' talk about Nature Spirits, and in all the countries I visit I get quite large audiences. Not people who are weird, but people in all the occupations you could think of, from high court judges to lawyers, psychologists, doctors, musicians, therapists, business people, and more. All open to the metaphysical world that lies hidden in the heart of a physical reality.

So . . . are there fairies at the bottom of your garden?

AN INNER AWAKENING

I have learned to accept that most gardeners never seem to transcend the purely physical side of gardening. Not that there is anything wrong with this, but it often puzzles me that the pure and vibrant energy of a loved garden is unable to open the inner doors of the many, rather than only the few. I also accept that the garden itself cannot open those inner doors, it is the *conscious* garden lover who does that, but the stimulation and impulse from the garden can be so very powerful.

Often I have pondered why this inner 'awakening' is so selective. I have known passionate gardeners who regard me with scepticism and suspicion. Why? Simply because I got more deeply involved in the energies of Nature than they. Looking back over the years of my ever-deepening connection with Nature, I am sure that one of the essential ingredients is a deeply 'romantic' nature. I have no idea when it began, but somewhere over the years my love affair with Nature naturally developed into a mystical romance.

At some point in our relationship it seemed natural that an energy which could create such intriguing beauty as one finds in the plant kingdom, had other qualities to offer on other dimensions of natural expression. And so it proved to be.

Why is most of humanity so very limited in their outlook on life? If we look at the human package we call self in a mirror, we must surely realise that within the skin package there is an incredible biological diversity that not only creates energy, but which also maintains something we call life.

Not a scientist on this planet understands how all this works as a synchronised whole. Probably because the mystery of life is so vast, humanity basically looks at life as being physical even when all religions accept that we are spiritual Beings. Instead of humanity accepting that physical form expresses the spiritual energy we call life, we have come to believe that physical form 'is' life. It seems not to occur to most people that all life is the expression of spirit.

How can one look in the mirror at this 'self' package and not realise that beyond the physical body something else is looking back at us? Some other aspect of Self that is both the physical self, and something intimately and vastly greater. For me, this Mystery was so huge it consumed my life. I needed to know the Self I Am. However, it actually began the other way around. First, I was intrigued by the intelligent energy we call Nature, only later did my fascination with the Mystery of Self begin.

AN EXPRESSION OF INTELLIGENCE

Nature does not play mind games. Nature is an expression of intelligence, but it does not express this intelligence on an intellectual level. This is where I, along with a surprising number of other people, part with the majority of humanity. We are able to connect with this non-intellectual intelligence in a holistic way, allowing it to translate into a very different life picture. We have connected with the deeper, quintessential *knowing* buried in the human psyche. At this level we have always been aware of our oneness with Nature. As a gardener, while I enjoy the huge range of plants we are able to grow, I *love* the deeper intelligence that expresses through that overwhelming diversity of physical forms we call Nature.

However, we each walk our own path, and because mine is open to ridicule, I have had the moments when I wished that my path had stayed physical, never straying into the realms of metaphysical reality. I can become a proficient gardener, knowing pretty well all I need to know about the physical side of gardening, yet the metaphysical side of gardening and Nature opens endlessly before me. Neither does this make me a better gardener than a person who stays entirely with the physical. Attention to detail is often the factor of excellence in the garden, and a full physical focus is required for this. Like the majority of gardeners, I do what I do because I love it.

This love, this passion for the garden, is not rare among gardeners. Far more rare is taking that passion to a higher level. Every garden lover knows that their passion for gardening is not physical. It is certainly an emotion, but passion goes far deeper than emotion. Most people would agree that passion is a powerful spiritual movement, a feeling of deep inner intensity. Surely it becomes obvious that the spirit of the gardener is *moved* by the spirit of the garden, by the Spirit of Nature.

The missing ingredient in so many gardeners—and this is an observation, not a criticism—is to be conscious of the meeting of self and Nature while working in the garden. Stop working for a few precious moments. Sitting on a garden seat it is so much easier to attune with, or connect with Nature. There is less distraction. In those quiet pristine moments you feel a subtle connection with the garden which is both rare and precious. Of course, this implies that work is a distraction. And for most gardeners, it is. But it does not have to be this way!

2

'BEING WITH'
OR 'DOING TO'

S OUNDS LIKE AN ODD CHAPTER, doesn't it? Let me explain what it
means by telling you a true story. Come to that, all my stories
in this book are true! Also, I need to tell you that my garden is the
setting for most of this book.

My wife and I have a reasonably large and magnificent garden,
situated on the top of a rocky mountain ridge. Although I have
lived here for nearly twenty years, the garden was created only
about ten years ago. Before that I had a few banana plants, some
pawpaws, and a couple of custard apple trees scattered on the edge
of the bush, and not much else. (For overseas readers, what we in
Oz call 'bush' can be anything from dense rain forest, to sclerophyll
forest, to open scrubby trees, to just about anything that is growing
unattended. Our 'bush' is sclerophyll, mostly hilltop trees having a
stiff, firm leaf.)

It was during those earlier years that my old friend, Peter
Cundall, of TV's Gardening Australia fame, called in to do a
segment for the show. I remember him bending down under a
young Poinciana tree and scooping up a handful of soil. "Just look
at this soil," he exclaimed to the cameras. "It's the most bloomin'

terrible soil I've ever seen. It's totally impoverished." He then went on to talk about the soil-building benefits of mulch. He was right. You should see the soil now, Peter, after another decade of mulch.

Anyway, soon after this we had the house extended, doubling its size. Because the extension was to be a double story we had to have a bulldozer push away a hill from the end of the house. They literally went down to bedrock. All this soil, both top and sub soil, was pushed into a huge heap. Removing all the scrubby undergrowth, but leaving all the mature gum trees, I then had a bobcat come in to lay and terrace the soil over the whole area to be used as a garden. This, then, was the foundation of our present garden. Not an introduced rich, fertile, quality soil, but about two percent topsoil and about ninety-eight percent subsoil all of a very poor quality.

PONDS FOR PONDERING

I am a lover of water. Not so much in swimming pools, even though we have one, but in ponds and rivers. This leads to my fascination with fish and reptiles. I Love 'em! Because of our location on a mountain ridge, there are no rivers or streams flowing up to, or through our garden. Pity! I tried a bore for water, but no luck. However, I still wanted, even needed, the presence of water. So I created ponds in the garden. We have the House Pond that our son Russell dug many years ago. This is a small pond situated quite near our lounge, home to rainbow fish and red swordtails. Then there is the Frog Pond, which is basically a large, circular poly-tank, about 70 cm (over 2 feet) deep. Devoted to frogs, with water and marginal plants growing in it just for the frogs benefit, it actually stands on the soil, rather than is buried in it, thus preventing any entry to the water by cane toads. This is *Bufous marinus,* a large South American toad foolishly introduced into Oz to control cane beetles in the sugar cane industry, subsequently becoming a major ecological disaster. A female cane toad lays around forty thousand eggs at a time. The eggs, tadpoles, and tiny toadlets are all poisonous to fish, reptiles, and other animals.

In addition to these ponds, there is the Tropiquarium. This started life as a good-sized bird aviary, built for Tracey, our daughter. When she left home, I decided to convert the inside space into a pond, while all around it is festooned with orchids, large flowering Anthuriums, and pitcher plants—*Nepenthes*. Tracey and I are now licensed to keep and breed Eastern water dragons, *Physignathus lesueuri*, which peacefully cohabit with the goldfish in the pond. I really enjoy them!

I have one other pond, the Big Pond, and having set the scene it is time to get to that particular story. A couple of years ago, when I returned from one of our annual seminar and *Retreat* tours, I noticed that a fairly large area of our lawn had died in the drought. I knew why. Grass needs at least 30 cm (1 foot) depth of soil in which to grow. It will stay alive in shallower soil until it comes under stress, and drought or flood will deliver that stress. Because we are on tank water I never water our lawns. I explain the meaning of tank and town water in Chapter 6 (page 83). In the area of dead lawn, the soil depth was inadequate, just a few centimetres (inches).

PREPARATIONS

Rather than being upset by the weed infested area of dead lawn, I was pleased. It provided the perfect opportunity and location to create yet another pond. And this one would be special, different in some way. Knowing that bedrock was only a little way down, I reasoned that I would build a pond that was contained by a wall. Not only would this be ideal for keeping cane toads out, but it would look good and provide a comfortable pond-edge seating.

I bought a truck load of salt and pepper coloured granite, in an aggregate ranging from fist sized up to a large bucket size, and plenty of sand for mixing concrete. I was already on familiar terms with my old concrete mixer. Next, I laid out a water hose in the desired size and shape of the pond, then decided it was not big enough. After enlarging it, I dug out all the topsoil, carting it away in a wheelbarrow. Yikes! Suddenly it looked huge. Realising that I was committed, I continued digging out subsoil until I reached the soft rock that overlaid the bedrock.

I hired a jackhammer, and next day, with Russell sweating on the jackhammer and me shovelling and wheeling away the rocks, we continued until we reached bedrock. Just as a matter of interest, the temperature reached 35°C (95°F) that day. Phew! Talk about a weight loss and fitness programme!

The hole was only about 60 cm (2 feet) deep and pretty rugged, and I knew I would lose some of that depth in a thick covering of sand. I prepared my footings, then began the task of laying the foundations of the granite wall. It was only then I realised that I had never built any type of wall before, never mind one with every size and shape of granite rocks possible. Undaunted, I continued, finally laying granite rocks in a bed of wet concrete around the complete circumference. Little did I know that I had just finished the easy part.

When I began the next layer, the conditions were changed. I no longer had a nice trough in the soil filled with thick concrete in which to lay the granite. Now I had to get the wet concrete to hold onto the rounded curves and slopes of the previous layer of granite and, at the same time, try and lay a heavy, uncooperative, uneven chunk of granite onto a rocky, uneven surface, and then to finally get it to sit there until the concrete was firmly set. All this repeated over and over.

The wet concrete slid off the granite, the granite lumps toppled or slid with the cement, and all in all I learned that this was a skill I did not have. But . . . I persisted. Russell came and helped now and then, and another young friend, Kirkland, who had attended a few our Retreats, also came and helped me for a few days. It was Russell who told me that I had to get my levels pegged, so that I would know the height level I was aiming for. That was a shock! My eye told me that it was already reasonably level, but the true levels indicated that the wall would need to be much higher at one end than the other.

BEING CONSCIOUS

The real gift Russell and Kirkland gave me was two-fold: one, their willingness to help me, and two, their unavailability beyond those first few important days at the beginning. Mostly, I had to do it by myself. At first I made hard work out of it, but gradually I began to focus on what I was doing. The first thing I realised from this focus was that I had not been focussed. I had been fretting and grumbling, blaming the granite for the stress and difficulty of the situation. To help with the graphics as you imagine all this, I had more than a dozen wheelbarrow loads of granite in heaps all around the pond. By this time I had learned that each time I laid a piece of granite it had to be fairly carefully selected for size and shape. It had to fit, no matter how roughly.

To do this I would wander from heap to heap of granite, hoping to find the right piece. But, with aware focus all this changed. With deliberation and attention I held my thoughts and focus consciously on what I was doing. I released the idea that this was difficult, that I did not know what I was doing, that the granite was uncooperative, and brought my whole concentration onto what I was doing, moment by moment as I did it.

The result was astonishing. As I practised *being conscious* in the moment with what I was doing, everything became easier. I no longer had to search for the next piece of granite. I would look up and my eyes would fall straight onto the 'perfect' piece. The concrete stopped slipping and sliding off the underneath layer as I laid a lump of granite, and the granite would somehow fit easily and firmly into place. Now, building the pond had become easier, even enjoyable. Somewhere around halfway a visitor asked me if I was building a swimming pool. "Yes," I replied, "for fish!"

The hard work became a flow of energy. Instead of rapidly losing energy labouring with the heavy granite, I could feel the energy of granite helping me. Instead of working through resistance, I was working with assistance. I moved from an impatience to finish the job, to relishing every moment that it lasted. So attuned did I become there were times when I would be ready for the next piece of granite and I would *know* that the perfect piece was in a heap at the far end, buried under a wheelbarrow load of granite. And on investigation, it would be so. This is the way it continued, day after day, until the pond was finished, needing only the clay pavers that would cap and seal the edge, trapping and hiding the pond liner. Russell laid those pavers. It was something he wanted to do.

Adjust Your Thinking

Now for a *s-t-r-e-t-c-h* moment. During my years of metaphysical exploration, I have learned that linear time is a measure of physical, biological time. Beyond this, in a greater reality, all time occupies the same space. In other words, the past and the future are one with this present moment, now. I call this the timeless realm.

As I finished laying the last piece of granite, with a feeling of deep satisfaction I stepped a few metres back to look at the whole pond. In that metaphysical moment, a clear and powerful insight gripped me. The moment of finishing and the moment of beginning the pond were both the same moment in that greater timeless reality. I had the *knowing* that every block of granite already knew its place in the pond wall. When I came consciously into the moment, I entered that greater reality, the timeless realm of the moment. In that state of 'being conscious' everything changed. *I moved into the flow of energy that is always present. I became one with the energetic resonance of the garden, the granite, and the finished granite pond wall. I moved from the isolated me 'not knowing' how to proceed, to the conscious me 'knowing' the procedure of the pond wall already completed.* In other words, by 'being conscious', the me that had learned by finishing the pond wall took over from the me that was struggling and fretting with building it.

This is what I mean by 'being with' not just 'doing to'. While I was 'being with' what I was doing, it flowed easily, but when you are simply 'doing to' with thoughts scattered every which way, you are not connected in a conscious way with your task. Nor are you connected with the available energy that accompanies that task.

No Need to Weed

Take weeding a garden as an example. If the weeding is no more than a necessary chore, and you dislike the work, thinking about anything other than what you are doing, then you have little connection with your garden. You are there on a physical level only, yet the garden is there wholly. If you dislike weeding you need to realise that it is you who are responsible for them being there. After all, what is a weed? It is no more than a plant growing in a time and place where you do not want it. You are the determining factor, not Nature. For Nature there is no such plant as a weed.

So change your method of gardening. Personally, I have no desire for weeds, so I do not grow them. The weeds that grow in my garden take me a few hours a year to deal with. I am a mulch gardener, and mulch very capably suppresses the germination and growth of weeds. Of course, we often plant our own weeds. In the early stages of creating our garden I planted a large type of shrub that was very tough, with lovely yellow flowers. I have no idea what it was.

For a couple of dry years all went well, then we had a wet year. As though by magic, seedlings of this hitherto harmless shrub sprouted up everywhere, not only throughout the garden, but liberally scattered throughout the surrounding bush. Every year, up to the present time, I have to walk the bush looking for the odd stray shrub that is hiding, biding its moment to make another takeover bid for the bush.

Beware of such plants. Their beauty is no compensation for the work they cause. Where I live, the powder puff plant, *Calliandra*, is another such plant. The pink one, no problem, same for the red, but the white one sows a carpet of seedlings beneath its branches every year. Yet I have spoken to gardeners in a nearby district with white *Calliandras* that never have that problem. However, it is our own garden we have to deal with, so we have to accept the way things are on our particular piece of land.

NOURISHING ENERGY

A garden is a place of energy. Either you are feeding that energy, and in turn being nourished by it, or you are dismissive of such things. In this case, you are a stranger to your own garden. I have known so-called gardeners who were strangers to the Spirit of their garden, just as many farmers have no connection with the Spirit of the Land. What a loss.

The garden should be your meeting place with Nature—a place where you shrug off the cares of everyday life, relaxing into the welcoming energy that you are helping to create. A garden is not just a garden. A garden is a deliberate synthesis of human creativity and Nature. The big difference between a gardener and a farmer is that the farmer has to make a living from the land, and this creates a pressure on both the farmer and the land. The gardener is under no such pressure. He or she has the opportunity to transcend the level of 'must' and 'need' and is able to relax into a receptive mode of *being with* the garden.

If you are with your children, or grandchildren, and ignore them, merely being in their presence but without communication or any aware connection with them, you get nothing out of this. Nor do they. As a man with six grandchildren, if I want to enjoy them I have to be consciously connected with them, engage them, talk to them. Equally, if I am with friends, I talk to them and give them my attention. This is the very essence and substance of any meaningful relationship.

Why should it be any different with a garden? When I go into my garden, I talk to it. I talk to the plants, more on a silent mental level than verbally, but they receive the *intent* of what I say. The plant kingdom does not have ears, they are not going to converse with us through a mouth, but they are able to receive and transmit communication.

THE CONNECTIONS OF LIFE

Since the passing of my late wife, Treenie, I have married again. Her name is Carolyn, from Ohio, USA. She is very enthusiastic about her garden. I often hear her chattering away to the various plants that fill the hanging baskets she so enjoys. And hers is real baby talk! "Look at you, sweet thing. Aren't you just so beautiful. Do you want your water then? Oh, look at you, your flowers are just so cute." You get the idea, it goes on and on. Add to this the strange fact that after twenty or so years of having a garden and growing plants, she still remains blissfully ignorant about the 'how to' of gardening or the plants.

For Carolyn, *being with* is the most natural thing in the world, while 'doing to' is nowhere near so interesting. Without any real knowledge of what she is doing, she grows the most magnificent hanging baskets of flowers. And the same goes for the garden. She connects so fully with the energy of the plants she grows that she intuitively follows the correct procedure for their well-being. If you were to tell Carolyn that plants are just plants, without intelligence or consciousness, she would have her doubts about your own intelligence.

Why talk to a pet dog or cat? It certainly cannot talk in any human language, but it can communicate. Physically this happens with a meow and some purring, or a bark and tail wagging, all while looking at us. Okay, happily, plants do not bark or purr, but to the person who loves them there is a connection powerful enough to feel. And just as with our pets, this connection with our plants is very therapeutic and beneficial for us.

GARDEN THERAPY

I have three sons and a daughter. Russell is interested in plants and gardening, as is Tracey. With my other sons, a garden is something you look at, but you do not do! For a couple of years Russell had his Body Stress Release (BSR) practice based in one of the sunny rooms in our house. If his clients had to wait, they would usually sit on the garden bench facing one of the beautiful aspects of our garden. They only waited indoors if it was raining. More often than not, the person waiting would follow one of the paths and go for a slow wander around the garden.

Russell often told me that the people who wandered the garden were far more relaxed and receptive to his BSR than the ones who had no interest or connection with the garden. Our garden has a very powerful energy, but I have learned that this energy is received in different ways by different people, according to their needs. Your garden may be offering this, it certainly has the potential. It all depends on your relationship with the garden. Garden energy certainly has the ability to heal, but not if the gardener is in conflict with their garden. And this is all too common. This healing energy is one of those metaphysical aspects that, beyond the awareness of the average gardener, either grows and flourishes or is never able to take root and thrive. Again, it comes from the synthesis of gardener and garden, and can be neither forced nor coerced into growth. Everybody who has a garden knows the therapeutic value of just sitting on the garden seat, and relaxing. There are two ways of doing this; you can sit tight and tense, the weight of your worries and stress still with you, or you can *be with* the garden, allowing the energy of your garden to ease the burden. Why is it so difficult for so many people to simply relax? All you have to do is come into the moment. Sitting in your garden open to its energy, the mind quiet, your muscles relaxed, is your natural way to release stress. People get so 'uptight', so caught up in their personal drama, so involved in making something out of nothing, so locked into their heads, that real relaxation has become rare instead of regular.

Any gardener who has a large garden, as I do, will know that there is always something that needs doing in the garden. When some of these gardeners sit down, they sit and think about what they should be doing or what needs doing. This is not relaxation. This is sitting in the garden thinking. I have spoken to some of these people and they tell me that they have no idea how to stop thinking, especially worry thoughts.

Focusing on Infinity

You need to realise that we are creatures of thought. Thinking is not the problem; it is the negative focus of our thoughts that creates and maintains stress and depression. To battle thinking is to battle yourself. However, there are ways that your thinking can be slowed down and emptied of all conflict. If you have a pond in your garden, place a seat close to it so that you can gaze into the water. I will use this setting as a metaphor, for this can be done sitting quietly indoors simply using your imagination.

Imagine that the pond is the moment. Your whole attention is given to the pond. As you focus on the pond, a group of wild ducks come flying in, heading for the water. You neither deny the ducks nor do you change your focus away from the pond. The ducks are thoughts, coming to distract your attention away from the pond, the moment. Allow the ducks to come skimming over the water while you remain engaged with the pond. If you keep your attention on the pond, the ducks will simply skim the surface and continue on with their flight. However, if you give your attention to the ducks, telling them you do not want them, asking them to go away, then they will settle into the water, disturbing and fouling it.

You get the idea? Pond is the moment, ducks are your thoughts. Allow the ducks to fly into the moment, but do not engage them. With practice, there will be fewer and fewer ducks skimming across your pond. And do not be disheartened if the ducks insist in paddling around the pond, dirtying it; it takes a while. Just persist, but do not make it a battle. It is all about focus, attention, and perseverance. If you decide that a quiet and peaceful mind is worth having, then you will accept that this is a skill to be learned over a period of time—a skill that will beneficially affect you, your garden, your family, and indeed, your whole life.

GROWING TROUBLE

Conflict in a garden is all too easy to generate. I remember planting a couple of *Bauhinia galpinii* shrubs in a garden bed near one of our car ports, leaving them basically unattended for the next five years. When it finally proved difficult to find the entrance to the car port, I was forced to take stock of these two shrubs. They now covered an area twenty metres (yards) long, by ten metres wide, at an average height of four to five metres! I had no previous experience with this shrub. According to the books, this variety of *Bauhinia* grows to approximately two metres in height, and the same in width. The reality was very different. I was literally growing hard work. It took me days to cut, prune and clear away. By then I was so fed up with the plants that I got rid of them! One such shrub regularly pruned is manageable, but even then you need to like pruning when a shrub can make metres of growth annually.

A lawn is a similar situation. Many people pay to water and fertilise the lawn so they can then pay to have it cut and pay to have the clippings taken away. How crazy is this! Mind you, these are garden owners, or renters, they are not gardeners. Okay, so you have kids and they need a lawn to play on. That's good, most kids seem to want only to play on computers and PlayStations these days. Statistics indicate they spend 48% of their leisure time on them! However, apart from the family who needs a lawn for social reasons, there are many thousands of garden owners that unthinkingly pay to grow it, pay to cut it, and pay to get rid of it. In America there must be tens of thousands of streets where this is the reality for the majority of gardens. And they even water and fertilise it, just to make it grow faster!

Another 'growing trouble' scenario is when people visit a garden centre and fall in love with a tiny tree that has a label showing the picture of the most beautiful flowers you could imagine. A tree that when fully grown has the potential to wreck the foundations of the house, or block out the sunlight for much of the day—and the flowers will eventually be so high in the air you need binoculars to see them! Despite all the gardening education on television, this is still quite a common occurrence. Resist. Most garden centres give good advice these days, but if they should tell you, "Yes, it can grow large but it is easily pruned each year," back off. It is not easily pruned each year. It is laboriously and grudgingly pruned each year until the year it gets missed. Believe me, eventually you will have a huge and very expensive problem that you, personally, have grown.

POTTED PLANTS

As a person who loves plants, I have a modest collection of my own. Nothing elaborate or too demanding because I spend several months on tour each year, and other plant carers can get nervous with fickle plants. The winter requirements of potted *Adeniums* is quite challenging enough. People are unable to grasp it when you say, "No water once the leaves drop off." "But they are not cactus," they say. While most people accept that cactus can live for long periods without water, that ability is not extended to other plants. They seem to think that all other potted plants need water most days of the week.

Many people search for plants that are exotic, different, and I can understand this, but often the most different are overlooked simply because they are common, plentiful, and inexpensive. Take the Venus fly trap, *Dionea musculipa*, as a perfect example. You can buy them in almost any garden centre in most western countries, at plant stalls in some country markets, and even in many of the supermarkets.

To me, the humble Venus fly trap is the most astonishing plant on the planet. It can move fast and effectively. Every time I watch a Venus fly trap close its cellulose toothed trap with such smooth precision, I marvel. How incredible! This is vegetation, not some disguised animal. The dramatic wilting action of the sensitive plant, *Mimosa pudica,* is amazing to watch, especially when you walk across a lawn in the tropics that is infested with it, but it does not compare with the Venus fly trap. And it is so easy to grow. All you need is a mix of peat and perlite, stand its pot in a dish of water with plenty of morning sun, and it simply grows, offering this marvel of the plant kingdom.

On the other hand, maybe it is all in the eye of the beholder. Maybe I see such an astonishing plant because I don't take it for granted. People do, you know. One glance, and for many people the Venus fly trap is ignored. Been there, seen that! We all too easily develop a casual subconscious relationship with Nature, even with our own garden. If you want a relationship with Nature that takes you into the miraculous, then you have to be fully and consciously present. You have to be with it. Only in this way are you open to the deeper levels of the subtle, unseen, hidden, metaphysical Nature.

AN INSIGHT FROM NATURE

Let me give you an example of this. In 2004, Treenie and I were in the Bavarian Alps where we were attending our International Roadsway Gathering. One afternoon I was walking across the uncut lawns of short, rough mountain grass surrounding Castle Elmau, the hotel where we were staying. As I walked I noticed some deep blue flowers at my feet and, squatting in the wet grass, to my utter delight and astonishment I was surrounded by hundreds of clumps of gentians, *Gentiana clusii.* I could hardly believe it. Of all the many beautiful cold climate plants, gentians are my favourites. I had tried to grow them when I lived in England, but they are lovers of high altitude and seldom lived more than a year or so for me.

For the next hour I devoured them with my eyes and heart. Just how one plant can trigger so much more delight than another I am not sure, but gentians certainly do it for me! As I gradually got cramped, I whispered to the gentians, "How beautiful you are. Much as I would love to grow some like you, you would never survive in the subtropics where I live." I felt an instantaneous connection take place between the consciousness of gentians and my own consciousness. Now, I could *inner see* the gentian energy. To my astonishment, the gentian's field of energy was hot, very hot, the last thing I would have expected.

Then, into my *inner vision* I saw some of the subtropical plants that I grow in my garden, and they were cool, really cool. I could now *inner see* many fully tropical plants with a very cold energy, to other plants that had an extremely flexible energy field, neither hot nor cold, but able to easily adapt to the climatic conditions. I marvelled at this. How obvious and natural when it is shown to you. All plants that need extreme cold have a very hot energy, while the reverse is also true. While there is a gradient to this hot/cold energy field, once you are away from the extreme plants there is a huge range of plant species that have the ability and flexibility to grow in a very wide range of climatic conditions.

All this was new to me, yet I accept it as a reality. You might think that this is very naive of me. We are taught that such matters must be scientifically proven before we can embrace anything new, but like Nature, I prefer to get on with living my life and accepting my reality. I trust my experience, my ability to discern, my intelligence, and the inherent abilities of a metaphysical Nature.

CHAPTER

3

THE MIRACLE OF MULCH

To DESCRIBE MULCH as a miracle of Nature is not an overstatement. Indeed, it would be impossible to overstate its importance. So, for any people who still ask, "What is mulch?" we need only look at the natural ecosystem in a forest.

Wherever you live, the forest nearest you will reveal the same natural miracle, whether it is a cold, deciduous forest or a warm, steaming rain forest. The leaves, twigs, branches, mosses, lichens, and fungi in the trees, as well as the understory, continually fall to the ground, forming a natural biomass which we call mulch. Even the trees eventually fall, adding their mass to the accumulated debris that litters the forest floor. Animals, birds, and insects die, adding their bodies to the forest litter, plus the faeces of all the creatures that live in the forest. Within this mess of decomposing material proliferates a seething mass of microscopic organisms, all adding their bodies to the 'stew-pot of life' that carpets the forest floor. To an observer, it may appear as a mass of dead vegetation, but the dead vegetation is a pot in which a stew of microscopic life lives, simmers and multiplies.

This mulch is life supportive—an enriching, natural system where the recycling of all organic waste ensures the continuation of natural fertility within the soil. But this recycling programme is not confined to the forests. Wherever vegetation is growing, the cycle of birth and death continually feeds organic matter back into the soil.

FARMING IGNORANCE

Basically, ignorance means to ignore. When farmers and gardeners ignore natural cycles of fertility, attempting to replace them with chemical stimulants, the attendant problems of a sick and distressed system signal their demise. This becomes very obvious in agriculture.

The natural mulch and its organisms are vital to a forest. When bulldozers invade the forest, spinning on locked tracks and gouging the soil as they push and pull the felled trees onto huge carriers, they destroy far more than the trees. As the natural mulch is churned aside, large areas of soil are exposed to the weather. No longer sheltered by trees or the protective layer of mulch, the soil is pounded by the teeming rain and washed along bulldozer tracks and, gradually, gully erosion begins.

When trees in the bush are ripped from the soil by huge bulldozers using massive ball-and-chain techniques, the roots are revealed. In many species a single or few anchor roots plunge deep into the subsoil, while feeder roots fan out around the tree just below the soil surface. In other species above (or below) ground buttress roots stabilise the tree, while roots that seek the vital nutrients and moisture remain close to the surface. This indicates that the trees of the forest depend on the leaf litter and the soil just below the surface for the majority of their life-sustaining nutrients.

On a few large farms I have walked through 50-hectare (120-acre) tracts of forest that were dying. The forests had been degraded by sheep, the understory and biomass completely eaten away, the soil literally exposed. Slowly but surely, the system was dying. In each case the farmer thought that having a group of trees together was enough. They did not realise that a forest is a whole ecosystem, not just a collection of trees. These were not 'conscious farmers' connected to the Spirit of the Land. They had never observed that a thriving forest is a wholistic system. No matter what crops you are growing or animals grazing, it is possible to address all the requirements of a wholistic system and put them in place on the farm. The rewards far exceed the effort.

Once again, it is a matter of energy. The farm that has a vital and dynamic system creates an energy that is transmitted to the consumers of the produce of this land. Unfortunately, the opposite is also true!

MULCH IN THE GARDEN

For optimum energy in our own gardens—remembering that this energy equates as health—we need to create a wholistic system, one that is self-sustaining. Few gardeners can achieve this. While it is certainly possible, it is highly improbable that a garden will be self-supportive. This is the objective of most permaculture gardens, to feed the family and provide all the required fertility for the soil. It requires a certain dedication and specialisation, and is an admirable combination of self-sufficiency and gardening. For most of us, however, we will have to fine-tune the garden: supply fertility, prevent erosion, feed the essential soil microorganisms, keep the soil warm and sheltered in winter and cool in summer, and constantly feed it with nourishing organic matter. How do we do all this? In a word—mulch.

Organic gardening and mulch go hand in hand. This is the way of Conscious Gardening. Being conscious of the soil and its needs, being conscious of life and assisting that life to proliferate for the benefit of all.

Mulch is truly miraculous. It keeps the soil comparatively

warm in the winter, yet cool in the summer. It prevents the lashing rainstorms and hail from washing the best topsoil out of the garden, and it stops the scorching sun from over-drying the topsoil, thus slowing the oxidation of the precious nutrients from the soil in the high heat of summer. What better way to protect the crowns of slightly tender perennials when frost digs its icy fingers into the soil, than to have a buffer of mulch? What better way to protect dormant spring bulbs from the heat of summer sun? What better way to retain the vital soil moisture? What better way to feed a living soil, than to have a layer of mulch? What better way to end the chore of weeding than by mulching? Anyone who says that mulch will not suppress and stop weeds is not using enough mulch. For weed control, deep mulch is the key factor.

Mulch is to the soil as water is to a fish; they need each other! In all Nature only a desert lacks mulch, and that's not exactly a gardening paradise. Beaches are mulched by the tidal waves bringing up seaweed, but of course, this is the way Nature creates an oxygen rich decay to be returned to the sea for its enrichment.

> *Mulch is to the soil as water is to a fish;*
> *they need each other!*

Mulching is the method I use in my garden. For a number of years I used about 200 bales of sugar cane each year, then with the collapse of the sugar industry, I switched over to municipal waste mulch. Now, I mulch some of the garden with 50 to 75 bags of mushroom compost—avoiding native plants because of the lime content—then over this I put a layer of municipal waste mulch. I buy about 20 cubic metres of this each year, a couple of truck loads. And yes, I apply it thickly.

The municipal mulch is rich, holds moisture beautifully, and has an excellent soil building capacity. These are qualities I need.

Categories of Mulch

Mulch is not 'just' mulch. There are many different types of mulch available to us, and our choice should always be based on what is needed, rather than choosing just any mulch. Before choosing any mulch become familiar with the CN (carbon/nitrogen) ratio chart in Chapter 4, 'The Living Soil' (page 61) so you know how the mulch you choose will relate to the soil life. Be really conscious of your choice and why you are choosing it.

Cover Mulch

Cover mulch is primarily for just that reason, to cover the soil. This does not mean to feed the soil. All thick, coarse, heavy mulches can be called cover mulches. This includes all bark and shredded wood types, wood shavings and all the varied pine bark mulches. I also include sawdust in this category, for while it is fine, it is also a dense cover and very slow to break down.

All these mulches are basically used to conserve moisture, protect the soil, suppress weed growth, and last a long time. These mulches are ideal for ornamental trees and large shrubs. Of these mulches, sawdust needs a further explanation.

Sawdust

First and foremost, the older and more decayed the sawdust you use, the better. Sawdust is extremely dense and can become compacted after even moderate rainfall. During a dry spell, if a heavy shower dropped 25 mm (1 inch) of rain in your garden onto a mulch 150 mm (6 inches) deep in sawdust, it is doubtful that a single drop would penetrate far enough to reach the soil; the sawdust would absorb all the rain.

A thick sawdust mulch in these conditions is not a good choice. However, if that sawdust was mixed in equal parts with very coarse wood shavings, or bark, then the rain is far more likely to percolate down to the soil. For reasons like this, it is important that you are familiar with your climatic conditions, and with what mulch you need to use, and why.

Depth of mulch also has to be considered with cover mulches. You need only use 60 mm (2–3 inches) of sawdust to act as a long-term mulch in a shrubbery. Its very density acts as a good insulator, and a thinner layer would allow for rain penetration. However, if you went for the more popular chipped pine bark, then at least 150 mm (6 inches) in depth would be required. It is open and coarse, so rain can easily trickle through pine bark, but, almost as easily, moisture can evaporate back up through it.

FEEDER MULCH

There are many places in the garden where coarse, or slow to decay, mulches are totally unsuitable. Unlike a cover mulch, feeder mulches are chosen to breakdown reasonably quickly, thus feeding the soil life and promoting rapid fertility while also offering soil protection and smothering weed germination and growth. Again, check the CN ratio to see why this is so. One of the very best feeder mulches is alfalfa (lucerne) hay, but any old hay is excellent. Most hay has plenty of nitrogen-rich plants in it, such as clover and trefoil, the more the better.

I recommend a feeder mulch for all vegetable gardens, flower beds, roses—they love mushroom compost—all berry and small fruits, and, in fact, most fruit trees. Very large fruit trees, such as mature mango trees or mature macadamia nut, would certainly benefit, but it would be expensive to cover that amount of root system. If you have several trees like this a load of sawdust spread under them would be beneficial, with a few buckets of blood and bone added.

Straw is an excellent feeder mulch. It matters not whether it is wheat, barley, oats or rice; it is all very good. It is slower to break down than hay, but with grass clippings mixed in, the decay can be speeded up. Any of the straws or hay, old or new, make a very good mulch.

∾

COMMONLY USED MULCHING MATERIALS

Having looked at cover and feeder mulches, let us now consider some of the materials available. As a gardener, there is going to be a huge difference in whether you are a country, suburban, or city gardener. A city gardener is likely to look at a packaged commercial product, while a suburban gardener can vary. Some will go in the country direction, seeking old hay and straw, while others will head for the nearest garden centre. The country gardener, who is often likely to have a larger garden, will most likely get their mulch supply in the countryside. With a number of farming friends, they will know just where to go.

HAY AND STRAW

A feeder mulch. I mention these two examples of feeder mulch together because the availability and use is very similar. For suburban gardeners, local garden centres often sell bales of straw and/or hay for mulching, or, failing this, you will probably find a produce merchant in a nearby country town who will sell bales of hay or straw at a reasonable price. Price usually depends on the vagaries of the weather, with drought creating very high prices. Quite a few farmers now cut any old pasture or rubbish land to provide mulching bales for a mulch hungry market. Baled pea and bean straw is also excellent, along with sugar cane bales where available.

Some gardeners are frightened to use hay or straw because of the potential of introducing weeds into their garden. This is understandable, but is easily dealt with. To use hay or straw, thoroughly shake the hay or straw out as you spread it onto the soil, so that all the weed seeds fall out.

In this way all the weed seeds are buried and will not grow provided that you make the mulch deep enough. Generally, no seed will grow if it is buried more than eight times its own depth, so use a 30 cm (1 foot) layer of hay or straw. The seeds will germinate, then die, unable to reach the light. The only exception to this is seeds the size of potatoes. It is a mistake to try and spread a bale out to cover as big an area as possible. This is not an economical way of utilising hay or straw, or any mulch. If it is too thinly spread to be a mulch, the weed seeds will grow, and the sparse mulch will make it very difficult to hoe them. I never use hay or mulch at less than 30 cm (1 foot) deep, and very rarely does a weed emerge.

MUSHROOM COMPOST

Category: feeder mulch. In a word, mushroom compost is excellent. However, keep this away from Oz natives because of the lime content. The pH 7.0 is not too high for Oz natives, but they dislike the available lime. In many of our acid soils mushroom compost is excellent at bringing a bit more balance into the soil. I will probably use this in greater amounts each year, because the soil life simply loves it. On a warm, wet evening you can hear this glorious 'munching in the mulch' as they feast to their hearts content! It is generally very available, either from one of the many mushroom farms not too far from you, or from the garden centres.

If you need a feeder mulch and cannot get hay, use mushroom compost. Many gardeners prefer it. It breaks down quickly—but not too quickly—and is around 15:1 on the CN ratio scale. Use it liberally. By the way, every time it rains for a few months after I have spread it, I get baskets of mushrooms. We have a job to keep up with eating them, and I'm a mushroom fan.

The only place to be cautious with mushroom compost is if you have strongly alkaline soil. Even then, mushroom compost is mostly a neutral pH. Personally, I would use it anywhere.

PINE BARK AND WOOD CHIPS

Category: cover mulch. There are so many types of pine bark mulches now it is a bit confusing. There are flat ones, curly ones, coloured ones, fragrant ones, all from the barks of different types of pine trees. This is probably one of the cheapest of the general mulches, and is the most commonly used in all the wrong places. I shudder when I see strawberries growing in pine bark mulch. Availability is easy—you can even buy it in the supermarket. It is not a super mulch, but used in the right place, it does its job.

Pine bark is very good protection against heat and hail. You can use it liberally around all acid loving plants, including mature azaleas, but do not expect that this is in any way feeding the plants. Its advantage is that it is light, easy to spread, and lasts a long time. Use it quite thickly, about 30 cm (1 foot) deep. Another advantage is that it can be walked on without consolidating or compacting the soil. This is always a plus. Make sure the bark you use is well matured. Do not use it fresh from under pine trees as some barks contain resins that can inhibit plant growth.

Wood chips are used in virtually the same situations as bark, and for the same reasons. Wood chips may last even longer than bark and are undoubtedly a good long-term mulch, but beware, in many warmer areas of Oz wood chips can attract termites to the vicinity of your house.

NEWSPAPER AND CARDBOARD

Category: cover mulch. Although this can breakdown fairly quickly in warm wet weather, it contains no nutrients with which to feed the soil. If there is one material in our modern age of waste that is over abundant, it is paper. Office paper from computer printouts and faxes, wrapping paper, including cardboard, but without any doubt, newspapers contribute more paper waste than the others combined. Enter the mulching gardener!

I much prefer newspaper to be shredded or crumpled before

it is used as a cover mulch, but not all gardeners agree with this. However you use your newspaper, open flat or crumpled up, cover it with another mulch. A newspaper simply opened at the centre and laid flat on the soil could easily prevent a shower with over 25 mm (1 inch) of rain from reaching the soil. But if it was covered in a thin layer of lawn clippings, or straw, or even sawdust, the effect would be very different. Use it wisely.

A number of years ago I bought a large, inexpensive, second-hand paper shredder. This electric machine would inhale a newspaper and disgorge the shredded material. For quite a few years this was my mulch of choice. If you wonder if it looked odd, not really; it soon took on a weathered mulch look. I used this to really boost the organic content of our soil. It was cheap and effective. When I spread the shredded paper over the soil, I also spread a liberal amount of poultry manure over it. Sometimes I used poultry manure from a local poultry farm, other times I used one of the commercial pelleted products.

The very high carbon (C) content of newspaper needs to be balanced with the high nitrogen (N) content of the poultry manure. This improves the overall CN ratio. Newspaper certainly soaks up a lot of rain, but once the rain gets through it stays there. Some people asked me if the printing ink and chemicals were harmful to the soil, but it has been my experience that a vibrant, organic soil rich in micro-organisms has no problems with it.

Basically, what I have said about newspaper also applies to most cardboard. It has the advantage that if you lay several layers out flat and cover it with some other absorbent mulch, it is a very good way to rid yourself of some weed patches. Not all perennial weeds can be eliminated this easily, but many can, and it costs nothing to try. All the annual weeds that I have ever come across will succumb to smothering. In this way they recycle their own nutrients back into the soil.

MUNICIPAL WASTE MULCH

Category: cover and feeder Mulch. This mulch comes from the more enterprising shire councils where all garden waste is either collected from the households separately—and this is the ideal—or segregated at the tip and then composted. The composting is generally done in huge windrows, with the garden debris watered and turned on a regular basis to create a quick, aerobic breakdown. Some councils even spray a solution of super-enzymes into the organic waste, speeding up and improving the quality of decay. Currently, this is my choice of mulch.

I apply this to my soil annually, but in our present dry weather there is usually some that has not broken down and decayed by the end of each year. I put it on in midwinter, when it is cool for heavy work, although pushing the wheelbarrow up my garden slopes is the only real effort required. Each year I add another 20 cm (8 inches) to the garden. By now I can no longer define where the soil profile ends and the old, rotting mulch begins. It is integrating very nicely.

Personally, I would not use this mulch for the vegetable garden. It is ideal for the rest of the garden, but for vegetables only the best will do. I would always choose a mulch with a very high nutrient value for the soil, for in the end the nutrients we consume in our vegetables come from the soil. Mushroom compost would have to be ideal for this.

In my case, I buy my municipal waste mulch delivered in truck loads from a local landscaping company. All these business now sell mulch of many types. If you choose this type of mulch, contact your local council regarding its availability.

FRUIT, VEGETABLE, GARDEN, AND KITCHEN WASTE

Category: feeder mulch. Caution required. Although this is an excellent mulch, it is not for every situation. The isolated country garden, maybe, but in the suburbs or cities, no way. The rotting vegetables and fruit can cause an unpleasant smell and attract flies while repelling neighbours!

In all seriousness, if you had a big supply from a fruit and vegetable shop and you have a country garden, this could be applied in quite copious amounts to the soil. It breaks down rapidly, is very high in nutrients, and apart from the occasional smell, is a very good feeder mulch. You may have a lot of tomato and pumpkin weeds later in the year, but by leaving a few that could be to your advantage.

Generally, the only way I would recommend this type of mulch is by putting them into your compost bin. And then you are really in business. All fruit, vegetable, kitchen and most garden waste can make excellent compost. This is a top quality compost/mulch.

LEAVES AND LEAF MOULD

Category: feeder mulch. If the autumn leaves from deciduous trees are simply swept or raked up and spread in the garden, then watered well, this will make a good feeder mulch. There is some argument about this, but anything that is good enough to grow the forests of the world—mainly fallen leaves—is good enough for an organic garden. If the leaves are from drought stricken eucalyptus or evergreen trees, then they will be tough and very high in fibre. This is the time when you make leaf mould.

Equally, you can make leaf mould from the leaves of normal deciduous trees. Pile them as high as you can in a corner of the garden, or in an out of the way area, and leave them to Nature. Generally after a year or so in a heap, you have a delicious crumbly mix that the earthworms are going to love. Remember to give them an occasional watering in dry weather to keep the decay going well. It may also be a good idea to make a container, perhaps from some old corrugated iron, or wood.

Leaves tend to blow around easily, so keeping them damp and contained for a while is important. But please, don't discard leaves, or send them to the tip. They really are an excellent mulch and are very high in essential mineral nutrients.

STONES, PEBBLES, GRAVEL, AND ROCKS

Category: a cover mulch only. I have an area in front of my house which is hot and dry in the summer, with full sun on it, and shaded and dry all winter. Not a happy place for plants. I have covered all this soil in river pebbles, and in certain places I have put a few large pots of red forever flower, *Euphorbia millii samonoa*. As the name implies, these flower all year round. There is also a Bottle palm, *Hyophorbe lagenicaulis*, and a ponytail, *Beaucarnea recurvata*. An unexpected problem arose with the pebbles. During the heat of the summer sun on the pebbles became so hot that they heated the side of the house, the windows radiating the heat indoors. To overcome this I have planted some frangipani, *Plumeria*, cuttings. Because frangipani are deciduous they will provide summer shade, while allowing full access to winter light. The frangipani cuttings were well over two metres tall when I took them. There are only a few other types of shrubs or small trees that would grow from such large cuttings.

I use no weed mat or plastic under the pebbles, and we get no weeds. Generally a good depth of stones, pebbles or gravel will keep the soil cool, the weeds away, and the moisture in the soil, but be aware of the various disadvantages that can arise. Some perennial weeds can and will grow through them, compelling the use of chemical sprays.

Be aware of what works for you. A bed of perfectly white pebbles may look very nice when they are initially laid as a backdrop to green plants, but when a few years of algae have discoloured them, they look horrible. If you are going for this type of mulch, think it through first. If the white pebbles are in a hot, dry sunny position all year round, they should remain white, but place them in a shady, damp location and you are in trouble.

With regard to rocks, these are one of my favoured 'mulches' in the garden. You will probably have noticed that even in dry weather, there is usually moisture under a large, well-embedded rock. I use a large rock—but one that I can move around on a sack barrow—to place close to a young tree when I plant it. They like each other! A tree with a rock will invariably thrive better than a tree without.

Be careful with the weight of the rock. Do not hurt yourself. I have a few that are basically immovable, but usually my rocks are in the vicinity of between 20 and 50 kilograms (45 to 110 pounds). One rock that Russell and I, aided by Treenie and Tracy, moved a centimetre at a time with two crowbars and a lot of grunt, weighed well over half a tonne. It took quite a time, but it is amazing what enough determination and effort can accomplish. Standing by the Big Pond, that rock is just magnificent.

ANIMAL MANURES

Category: feeder mulches. These are for the suburban and country gardeners. Use with caution, and make sure that the manure is old and mature before it goes on the soil.

POULTRY MANURE

Mostly sold in a dried pellet form, this is generally known by some commercial brand name. When it is fully processed it has little smell . . . until it gets wet! Obviously the pellet form has no application as a mulch, but when you can get poultry manure from a poultry farm, generally dried in bags, this can be used as a mulch. Sometimes it is possible to get a truckload of fresh poultry manure for large gardens, but extreme caution must be used.

Fresh poultry manure is a fast, hot manure and should always be composted. If you had a plentiful supply, and a huge garden, you could mix it with sawdust and then leave it in a heap for a year. This would be a very good mulch. Always use it 'on' the soil, never dig it in.

HORSE/STABLE MANURE

This is easily obtained if you live in a 'horsey' area. Stables sometimes advertise it free for the taking. Generally not at all smelly, sometimes even pleasant smelling, this is one of the finest materials for a mulch. The one big drawback is that if the horses have access to pasture, any seeding weeds or grass they eat will leave the seeds in their manure. Horses that are stabled only do not have this problem. If the horses have outside access, I advise that all horse manure is very well composted. The heat will cook the weed seeds.

COW MANURE

This is generally sold processed in bags, but I—and many other gardeners—have walked the pasture picking up dried cow 'pats' and popped them into sacks to take home. I recommend that you get the farmers permission first! Unlike a horse with a single stomach, the cow has four with which to process and digest its food. The result of this is almost zero viable weed seeds. However, having said this, old cow pats often become liberally sprinkled with weed and grass seeds over the weeks as they dry out in the pasture, so you could collect some that are a serious source of new garden weeds. Basically, this all comes down to experience.

SHEEP MANURE

This is not really a mulch, but wonderful stuff to throw over the garden with other mulches. In Oz, sheep manure is generally collected from beneath the slatted floors of holding pens at shearing time, then dried and sold. They already are pellets! Long lasting and slow to act, it is valuable in both flower and vegetable gardens. Goat manure is similar to sheep, but is more likely to be mixed with straw or sawdust from the goat dairies.

PIG MANURE

This is a slow, cold manure and should always be composted. I knew a person who dug fresh pig manure into their soil, then grew his vegetables on it. His lettuce tasted like pig manure, and a boiled cabbage stunk throughout the whole house. As I have said, all animal manures—especially pig—should be composted and added to other forms of mulch. This adds the beneficial bacteria, enzymes, and nutrients they contain following the journey through the gut.

A golden rule: The more mixed the mulches are, the better their nutrient value to the living soil.

∽

EASILY AVAILABLE MULCHES

I recently checked in a large Garden Centre to see what mulches they had. All these are available in 50 to 70 litre bags, blocks, or bales.

- **Pine Bark**
  - chipped
  - very acidic, not my choice

- **Tea Tree Mulch**
  - shredded
  - It has an attractive forest floor appearance, and is ideal for Oz native plants.
  - A good choice.

- **Cypress Mulch**
  - shredded
  - Its main attraction is that it reduces the risk of termites in your mulch.
  - This works.

- **Easy Wetta Mulch**
  - shredded

- This claims to be a natural organic mixture with soil wetting granules added.
- A good gimmick.

- **Water Saver Mulch**
  - chipped
  - This is a mixture of pine bark and poultry manure pellets.
  - They are best in combination.

- **Mushroom Compost Mulch**
  - crumbly
  - This is an excellent way to promote healthy bacteria in the soil.
  - Very good.

- **Lucerne Mulch**
  - shredded
  - As a leguminous plant this will add nitrogen to the soil as it breaks down.
  - Very good.

- **Sugar Cane Mulch**
  - shredded, in a high compression bale. This is made from harvested sugar cane.
  - Very good.

Mixed Farm Manure/Much
  - crumbly
  - Basically, this is a mixture of cow and poultry manure.
  - Quick to break down, but very good.

- **Coir**
  - Made from coconut husks, this comes in a block. Place the block in a tub, water it, and it swells to a crumbly mixture many times its original size. This then makes a good mulch, especially for large pot plants. Moist coir added to your potting mix is an excellent way to retain moisture. I have begun to use it for this purpose with very good results.

All these commercial mulches are very good for the average size suburban garden. For people with a large garden the landscape specialists are a better place to go for bulk supplies. Please, do not use any form of plastic sheeting as a mulch, it reduces the energy of the soil quite dramatically.

∽

So, there it is, a list of materials most of which will improve your soil conditions. With the possible exception of pine bark, all these mulches will bring earthworms into your garden. If you need proof, simply lift up some of the damp and decaying mulch and introduce yourself. They will be there to greet you. They also love the damp under pebbles and rocks.

You can extend this list according to your own locality and your personal ingenuity. Chasing the visiting circus elephants with a large bucket is a wonderful exercise! Just as those living near a commercial macadamia farm can often get a bulk supply of the tough nut shells, so other people in other countries have equally unique opportunities to recycle some organic matter back into the soil. Basically, if the product has grown, put back on the soil it will help facilitate more growth.

Always be aware of the soil. It is a living, breathing organism, and like it or not, the soil has consciousness. I am not saying that the soil is self-aware, I am saying that the planet Earth is conscious, and that if we treat the planet and the soil with respect, then the planet will respect us. This applies to the whole human race, and to each one of us as individuals. No movement has ever begun with, or come from, the masses; it begins with each one of us, one by one, until a certain momentum in consciousness is reached. Your conscious relationship with both the earth as soil, and the Earth as a planet, takes place in your garden.

THE LIVING SOIL

I N A BOOK THAT IS DEVOTED to conscious gardening, I decided that I would give the living soil its due and honoured consideration. It is too important to dismiss without a very caring and conscious approach. Just as I have to be fully conscious as I write this book, so too I want to encourage a conscious approach to gardening and the soil. After all, soil is the very nucleus of any garden.

In a single handful of good organic soil there are literally billions of microscopic life forms. The soil is a living, teeming complex of micro fauna and flora. If this was not so, and the soil was as dead and inert as some people believe, then we would have a dead sterile planet. We would not be here. The only way a planet can sustain life as we know it is by having a living soil.

I feel a certain reverence for the soil, for that vast abundance of life about which I know so little. My past experience as an organic farming consultant taught me that we cannot ignore the Spirit of the Land without turning a deaf ear to our own soul.

In this chapter we will consider the make-up of a living soil, and in simple terms describe how it operates on a most fundamental level. By understanding the carbon/nitrogen (CN) ratio of our soil and the various mulches, we can more easily choose the best mulch for our particular needs. By taking the trouble to correct and balance the pH of the soil—and understand why we need to do this—we can grow our crops and favourite plants in the way we always hoped would be possible.

A conscious approach to the soil as a living organism—*organic gardening*—and acquiring a *feeling* for it, is to grasp the basic principle of growing plants. A plant can only grow in accordance with the soil that supplies its needs. An impoverished soil means impoverished plants. When we really understand this principle we have the ability to successfully grow plants anywhere in the world. Instead of needing to learn techniques from other people we are able to devise our own, simply because we understand the underlying principles of soil health and function, and the plants' dependence on this.

To be able to accept the soil as a *living organism*, we have to realise that soil is far more than 'just' soil. A cake is made up of many ingredients, so also is the soil. Ideally, when the cake is cooked, only the correct proportions of ingredients will result in a perfect cake; so also, to meet the requirements of growing our chosen plants, we often need to adjust the ingredients of the soil. Assuming that the soil base is the mineral component, we will look at the other basic ingredients which make a dynamic living soil.

- Organic matter—from dead and decaying plant material, also dead animal tissue and manure of all kinds.
- Humus—the ideal plant food resulting from the final breakdown of organic matter.
- Living organisms—the 'soil life' from the micro to the macro.
- Air—yes, the soil life breathes and needs plenty of oxygen.
- Water—fills the pore space between soil particles and is essential to soil life and plant growth.

If you are one of the many people who do not know the difference between organic matter and humus, now is your opportunity to learn. We will take these one at a time.

ORGANIC MATTER

Where any plants are grown there is a dependence on organic matter in the soil to provide for the formation of humus. Without organic matter, there can be no formation of humus. No matter what the soil type we own or grow our plants in, whether fine clay, coarse sand or a much more manageable loam, a vital percentage of its content is organic matter. A soil without organic matter is inert. It is impossible to overstate the value and importance of organic matter in the soil. Despite Nature's ability to adapt certain plants so that they thrive under the extreme conditions of arid desert sand, the vast majority of plants require adequate amounts of organic matter in the soil.

Soil life feeds on organic matter; the formation of humus depends on organic matter. The fertility of the soil depends on the recycling of organic matter and the resulting formation of humus. A dependency is clearly revealed. No matter what we grow, organic matter must be returned to the soil to maintain natural cycles of fertility. In a vegetable garden, cover crops of legumes, or suitable green crops such as mustard, may be grown for the purpose of working back into the topsoil while they are still green and soft. Always avoid bare, uncovered soil. If we defy the natural Law of Return, we are expecting Nature to operate efficiently outside a wholistic framework, and this is not possible. If you practise conscious gardening, you will find the natural Law of Return to be of great benefit in your everyday life.

Generally, Nature's response to a soil lacking in organic matter is a weed infestation. What we call weeds Nature calls salvation. Even weeds have a place as organic matter so long as you recycle them while green, well before they flower and seed. However, do not encourage weeds. Learn to discern between easily controlled weeds that can be used to your advantage, and those that make a serious takeover bid for the whole garden. On a hillside near where I live, some morning glories, *Ipomoea purpurea,* which undoubtedly began in a nearby garden, now cover tens of hectares, smothering and killing every plant in its path, including trees.

Not surprisingly, agriculture has a very definite basic need for organic matter in the soil. Below 1.5% organic matter, soil is considered as unstable, critical. In dry zone farming 2% organic matter is the lowest acceptable. In more equitable climates with a reasonably fertile soil, 4% organic matter should be the minimum. For high rainfall areas 6% organic matter should be the minimum for sustained production. When a consultant, I visited a few farms involved in cropping where the organic matter had receded to less than 1%. The soil was seriously compacted, badly eroded, chemically complexed and very unstable.

HUMUS

If organic matter is the raw material of the soil, then humus could be defined as the digested product. *Humus is the nutrient reservoir of the soil.* We can compare the living soil with a human stomach. When raw food is passed into our system it is the enzymatic and chemical processes in our stomach and small intestine which perform the digestion. In a similar manner in the topsoil, it is the microbial and enzymatic processes which feed on and convert organic matter into humus. While organic matter is in a raw state it is insoluble, the nutrients locked in the organic matter, thus it is unavailable as plant food.

Humus contains a percentage of its structure as soluble and neutral, while a percentage is composed of insoluble humic acids. Acid humus can occur in soils with a pH lower than 5.5. Although certain plants can thrive under these conditions, most garden vegetables require soil with a neutral humus formation. Neutral humus is stable, unless of course the soil is flooded, or experiences prolonged drought. Such humus is teeming with soil life, plus it has the ability to absorb its own weight in water, a most valuable asset.

Humus has the ability to absorb plant nutrients and hold them to be available for plant use. To make certain of forming a neutral humus we need only ensure an adequate pH and good aeration of the soil. Humus is a perfect medium for nitrogen fixing bacteria. Humus is the stability of the soil, counteracting erosion. Neutral humus is often referred to as colloidal humus. The word colloid comes from the Greek word "kola," meaning glue. Thus a humus colloid (particle) has a high absorption or holding power pertaining to certain mineral nutrients.

Humus truly is the pantry of the soil. When the pantry is empty the plants that feed on the humus become malnourished, and that is when plant disease and sickness sweep in. Organic gardening feeds the soil, forever restocking the pantry of humus goodies. Put simply, chemical gardening or farming invariably speeds up the breakdown of organic matter, thus speeding up the whole humus making process and the nutrient cycle. If organic matter is not added to the soil in copious amounts the humus formation dwindles, thus depleting the reserves in the pantry.

LIVING ORGANISMS OF THE SOIL

Earthworms: Not only does the soil contain a multitude of microscopic soil life, it also contains many larger soil animals. Among these, standing supreme as a soil conditioner, is our friend the earthworm.

According to climate and season, our friendly earthworm is constantly moving through the ground, literally eating its way through the soil. Following the adage of what goes in must come out, true to form the earthworm excretes what could be described as the perfect soil, enriched and revitalised by its journey through the earthworm's intestinal tract. Everyone must be familiar with earthworm castings on the lawn, yet for some people they are considered a nuisance. How incredible! These castings are the perfect medium for a host of pot plants and seed trays, or even to scatter over the vegetable garden as a true fertiliser.

I am aware that not everyone likes earthworms. How sad. When I was once in England I learned that if an earthworm had the temerity to cast its enriched goodies on a bowling green, then the grounds man would react with standard earthworm killer— sulphate of ammonia. While killing the earthworms, this product simultaneously stimulates the growth of grass, for it is a chemical fertiliser/stimulant. All chemical so-called fertilisers are really chemical stimulants. Surely this would appear to reveal a conflict of interests. Lethal to the earthworm, sulphate of ammonia is one of the chemicals that empties the pantry of the soil, while the earthworm is a major contributor to filling it.

I will list a few of the beneficial effects of a rich earthworm population in the garden:

- Earthworms break down the thick layers of mulch and are invaluable in recycling it.
- They improve the physical structure of the soil, thus promoting easier entry of water and a greater absorption capacity in the soil.
- Earthworms increase and promote availability of mineral nutrients to plants and soil life.
- Healthier plants. Earthworms promote an increase in the vital aerobic soil life, a vital contribution to healthier plants.
- Earthworms combat compaction. In fact, where earthworms are prolific, there can be no soil compaction.
- Earthworms go deep in the dry weather, creating flow tunnels for water and roots to penetrate the soil. They come closer to the surface with sufficient moisture and favourable climatic conditions.

The earthworms in the garden soil are not the same as those you find in a fast compost heap. These are smaller, a reddish colour, and are known as compost worms. Putting them in your garden soil will not increase the earthworm population. Create a good moisture retaining mulch and all the neighbourhood earthworms will come visiting.

Without a doubt, conscious gardening means that you cultivate an interest and awareness of the earthworm, for no garden can be healthy without them. As much as possible turn your garden into one that attracts earthworms. Once the message goes out on the earthworms' internet that you are providing free food and accommodation, they will be on their way!

AEROBIC SOIL LIFE

We will now turn our attention to the microscopic soil life, for to enrich the soil naturally requires some understanding of its function.

When describing soil life it becomes necessary to define two very different types of organisms. Most important to us is the aerobic soil life, the oxygen requiring proportion of microorganisms.

It is generally estimated that our planet is covered by a thin skin of fertile soil averaging no more than 20 centimetres (8 inches) in depth. Just imagine, all life on earth depends on this thin, fragile layer of soil. On this vital layer we grow our food crops. To maintain a healthy soil it must be able to absorb moisture and oxygen, and drain freely. It must be sustained and enriched with a constant supply of organic matter. Such a soil becomes rich in aerobic soil life.

The aerobic soil life seeks to decay and break down organic matter, constantly making it available to plant and other life forms. It becomes obvious that if we fail to replace the organic matter of the soil, the aerobic soil life will consume all available organic matter until it is literally digested, the pantry bare. At this stage—

common in agriculture—the physical structure of the soil will begin to deteriorate. Clay particles will bind and clod, like cement, and when shattered will become dust. The soil will become prone to wind and water erosion, becoming increasingly impoverished. This reveals the basic problem in modern agribusiness. Far too many chemical stimulants are used and nowhere near enough recycling/ replacing of organic matter. The focus is all above the soil, instead of what is happening within the soil. The role of natural, conscious organic growing is continually to replace the organic matter, thus maintaining a dynamic, healthy, active soil life.

All vegetables produce a certain amount of residue which can be, and should be, returned to the soil. It is calculated that corn (maize) can return as much weight to the soil in vegetable trash as the weight of the harvested cob, or grain.

Aerobic soil life lives in the oxygen rich topsoil. Below this aerobic level conditions change quite dramatically, yet there is no abrupt demarcation line between aerobic and anaerobic levels. Under natural influences the proportions of aerobic soil life vary according to the soil structure and climate, but under cultivated conditions those proportions may be drastically altered. I have visited impoverished gardens and farms (the chemical approach) with an aerobic layer reaching no deeper than 8 centimetres (3 inches) while, on the opposite extreme, I have seen a biodynamic system of nourished soil with the aerobic conditions penetrating well over 1 metre (1 yard) into the soil.

This indicates that by our management we can either seal the soil, preventing the essential oxygen penetration, or we can open it, promoting deeper oxygen/aerobic levels. If through tillage malpractice we cause compaction, bogging, or a powdery soil, then there is a gradual resistance to, and lowering of, air penetration. With less oxygen entering the deeper soil profile a greater percentage of carbon dioxide remains trapped. It is under these conditions that we find the anaerobic soil life.

ANAEROBIC SOIL LIFE

Anaerobic soil life prefers almost zero oxygen in the soil. They have a very different function to aerobic soil life. To emphasize the difference we need to remember that aerobic soil life causes organic matter to become *available* continually as plant food. This keeps the soil fertile, in movement.

Anaerobic soil life seeks to stabilise organic matter, thus rendering it *unavailable* as plant food. Peat is a good example of this. In ideal peat forming conditions, the acidic saturation allows for little more than superficial aerobic activity before the conditions defy oxygen entry into the soil profile. In this medium the anaerobic soil life locks the huge mass of organic matter into a stable acidic condition, defying decay.

Our coal is a gift from the anaerobic soil life which turns dense carbon-bearing plant tissue into a fossil fuel. As useful as peat and coal are for their specialised requirements, the conditions which bring this about make it impossible for growing crops. Speaking of coal reminds me of the Fens in Cambridgeshire, in the United Kingdom. The Fen soil is a rich black, and was once considered the most fertile soil in England. For many years when farmers ploughed the land, they would snag the remains of old tree trunks buried deep in the soil. Before the Fens were drained by dykes and ditches in the seventeenth century, this huge area was peat marsh and oozing, yielding bogs. Massive oak trees, which for millennia had flourished and fallen, were gradually submerged and sealed in the soft, wet anaerobic bogs.

When agriculture reached this land and the soil was opened by the plough, those long dead, sealed and preserved oaks were disturbed. The farmers believed that the oaks rose slowly to the surface of the soil, for each year new ones were snagged by the plough. These oaks were known as bog oaks. Time has now revealed that the oaks did not rise to the surface as supposed, but that the centuries of constant agricultural erosion relentlessly stripped the topsoil, layer by layer. With a soil that was easily abused, turning to dust, the erosion was caused not so much by water, as it was by wind.

For many years these bog oaks were pulled from the land and burned, but now, too late, the value of the wood has been realised. Imagine this timber, aged by untold years, black as coal, very dense and heavy, clean grained, quite unique. I still have a piece that I collected over thirty years ago. If those bog oaks had been preserved for furniture making, they would have been the richest harvest the Fens could yield. In many areas of the Fens this process is ending. As the topsoil erodes, a yellow, clay-like subsoil is being revealed. I have seen this, and handled it—a substance with the feel of cold, dead liver. It is speculated that this will terminate cropping in some areas of the Fens within a lifetime.

Nature has devised a soil medium which, on receiving organic matter, filters a certain proportion past the aerobic soil life down to the deeper anaerobic levels where it is rendered insoluble, and thus held in suspension as a type of reserve. Herein lies the value of our larger plants, such as the mighty tree. As the tree roots penetrate the soil profile, burrowing actively into the deeper soil, they allow a percolation of air to filter into the subsoil within the region of their root disturbance. Thus, as the twin activities of root disturbance and oxygen engage new deeper profiles of soil, an aerobic element moves with them, making soluble nutrients from the locked organic matter and releasing nutrients from the various mineral forms for the benefit of the tree. This is Nature's way of recycling the deep minerals of the earth, a natural system of mining designed to maintain and foster soil fertility.

Having read about the needs of both aerobic and anaerobic soil life, consider the gardener who insists on digging the garden with a spade each year. The spade is pushed into the soil and lifted with a spade full of soil, which is then turned over and replaced. Now, all the aerobic soil life in the top few centimetres is plunged deep into the soil, with insufficient oxygen to maintain it, so it literally dies of suffocation. Equally, the anaerobic soil life has been turned up to the surface, so, in a rich oxygen saturation, this also suffocates, starved of its needed carbon dioxide. Both aerobic and anaerobic soil life are forced into conditions that are unable to sustain their life. As with the spade, so too it is with the plough. By the time the soil life has fully recovered from this assault, a year has passed and it's time to go out and dig the garden again!

I confess, when I was a young man I was proud of the speed and perfection of my digging technique, able to turn the soil by spade for hour after hour without a break. But I was not truly conscious of what I was doing. Nor was I aware of the mayhem in the soil. I was lost in the pride of my endurance and ability. It takes the getting of wisdom to look further and deeper into life, rather than just 'more of the same'. Always attune to the task you are doing, *be with it.* Be aware of whether you are creating discord or harmony by your actions in the garden. This is also a very good rule of thumb for life!

SOIL AIR

Mention has been made throughout our discussion of soil life of the necessity of oxygen in the soil. The wisdom of Nature has ensured that the soil is able to breathe. Yes, breathe! With the rise and fall of barometric pressure and the fluctuation of midday heat with midnight cold, our soil system is in constant motion. This process is essential not only for air to enter the soil, but also for carbon dioxide to exit. In an open, friable, fertile soil approximately 20% of the volume should be oxygen. This is vital for the aerobic soil life. When the soil oxygen falls to about 10% by volume, then the aerobic activity is greatly curtailed. This whole process is similar to our own body. People do aerobic exercises to increase the oxygen levels in their body. This keeps the body more vital, maintains a higher, healthier pH, and keeps the muscles in good order. Inactive people suffer from sluggish systems, are more acidic and much less healthy and toned. As it is to the earth, so it is to our bodies.

So often the conditions in the soil can be aligned with our body. Compaction of the soil has the same deleterious effect on the earth as compaction of our bowels has on us. Compaction of the soil and dust bowls hinder the soils ability to breathe, hampering the natural exchange of gases, yet both conditions are commonplace on grazing land. To have garden soil compacted would require some seriously poor gardening techniques. While soil air is obviously affected by cultivation, it is also affected by rain. As moisture seeps and penetrates into the soil, it squeezes air outward and downward, forcing an exchange of the two major soil gases. Try placing a brick in a bucket of water. The bubbles indicate the old, stale air streaming out of the porosity. Remove the brick and the soft hissing sound is of new, fresh air being absorbed.

> *The era seems to have passed when farmers and gardeners alike were aware and conscious enough to walk the land and simply 'be with it' . . .*

In a prolonged drought, the soil becomes saturated in carbon dioxide, this in turn having a negative effect on the aerobic soil life. Both drought and floods are death to the aerobic soil life, causing a serious imbalance in the soil. A seldom recognised part of this imbalance is the loss of soil energy. When the soil energy has been eroded by harsh climatic conditions, no amount of chemical stimulants are going to make any difference. The era seems to have passed when farmers and gardeners alike were aware and conscious enough to walk the land and simply *be with it*, able to tune into the soils' level of energy. By varying degrees, that energy fluctuates daily.

As with the brick exchanging air, so too, as stale air leaves the soil it takes carbon dioxide with it. While only 0.25% of our atmosphere, in the soil it can be as high as 4%. Too high a percentage of carbon dioxide in the soil disadvantages the aerobic soil life. By our skill and management we should aim to keep the soil open enough for a natural exchange of these soil gases. In this way we are adding to the enrichment of the soil by making it life supportive for desired plant growth. As we add to the enrichment of the soil in our own small space, so we add to the enrichment of the whole planet.

Soil Water

When I was at school we were taught that water transpires through the leaves of a plant into the atmosphere. This is true, but not for all plants. In Chile there is a tree known as the Tamarugo. It grows in very dry areas where rain may fall only a few times each decade. Despite this, the tree is able to grow and produce seeds at all times. One could say that the Tamarugo reverses the normally expected movement of water, for instead of transpiring from the tree into the atmosphere, it takes moisture from the night air relocating it into the soil. Plants such as this are being investigated for the value they offer in increasing soil moisture in dry zones, thus helping to meet the needs of other plants in a close community.

I mention the Tamarugo to illustrate that the movement of water is not quite as obvious as we are given to expect. In Tasmania, it came as a surprise to me when hot, dry weather had sucked the moisture from our land, to find that high above us on the summit of Mt. Arthur lay a swamp, unaffected by the prevailing heat. It seemed incongruous to have water above us, while we were dry. Yet, again, high on our farm hills on the foothills of Mt. Arthur, water seeped from the ground into a waterhole. Permanent, apart from the longest, driest spells, it seemed strange that water could be found on the hills, while below, in one of the natural shallow valleys, it was dry. My education had suggested that water should trickle from the soil into the valley, not the hilltop.

Water is vital to a fertile soil and it should be managed with careful attention to detail. A sprinkler left running, with the assumption that it must be good, is sheer folly. When the soil is mulched, far less water is needed to maintain a moist—not saturated—soil condition. Mulch allows the water to percolate slowly into the soil; that slows the rate of evaporation. If the soil is bare, a different scenario is revealed.

When heavy rain is precipitated over bare soil, not only is the water inclined to run off, it carries with it the fertile top soil. Should the same damaging intensity of rain fall onto an open porous soil rich in organic matter, then the rain will easily penetrate to the subsoil, with a valuable percentage being absorbed by the humus.

By our management of the soil we determine whether we gain or lose the life-nourishing rain. When in my early days of farming, before I had dramatically increased the earthworm population, I estimated that in a heavy shower on our pasture I would be lucky if the soil gained a quarter of what fell. Most was lost in runoff. Years later, when the earthworms were well established and our pasture was growing in a porous, living soil, I have watched very heavy showers of rain fully absorbed on the same location. The difference was not in the intensity of rain, but in the soil structure. When each soil particle is coated in an absorbent layer of humus, the soil becomes sponge-like, capable of absorbing amazing quantities of water. As the humus swells and expands, the soils' porosity is increased, thus facilitating a freer movement of soil, water and air. The oxygen/carbon dioxide exchange is audible; lie down on the rich soil in a rain shower and listen to the music of a vital and alive earth.

∽

We have now defined the basic ingredients of a living soil. All exist in Nature, and are not artificial.

Having revealed the ingredients, indicating their function and place in the soil medium, we must now look at a few of the processes which determine the efficiency of those functions. My intention here is to present a wholistic picture, drawing in the factors which pertain to a living soil, while not getting lost in all the technical detail. In this way I hope to allow the 'whys and wherefores' of natural, organic gardening to emerge strong and clear for the conscious gardener.

THE CARBON/NITROGEN RATIO

We will begin by looking at the carbon/nitrogen (CN) ratio of the soil and its ingredients. All plant residue has a CN ratio. Before plant trash and organic matter can be converted into humus by the soil life, certain specialised bacteria, enzymes, and fungi must change it to a CN ratio equating with the surrounding soil.

Here are a few common examples:

Material	CN Ratio
Fertile soil	12:1
Compost	12:1
Green legumes	12:1
Legume hay	15:1
Mushroom compost	15:1
Grass hay	20:1
Rotted manure	20:1
Fresh manure	33:1
Soft plant trash	36:1
Corn straw	60:1
Wheat straw	80:1
Sugar cane straw	100:1
Pine bark	300:1
Sawdust/wood chips	400:1

Carbon/Nitrogen ratios of organic matter

This gives us some insight into the required conversion of organic matter into humus. It indicates, for example, the reason sawdust makes a good garden path in the vegetable garden, and why it takes several years to break down. Use any available sawdust as garden paths for a number of years, then, when it has turned blackish and is breaking down, spread it onto the garden as a mulch and replace it with fresh sawdust for your paths. This is an intelligent way to use sawdust.

The CN ratio also indicates that by mixing fresh poultry manure with the very high carbon content of sawdust, the result is a much more balanced CN ratio when breakdown has taken place, plus this dynamic combination assists and accelerates the process. Also indicated is the reason why green legumes and compost are so good for the soil, so rapidly assimilated. A glance at the CN ratio of legumes reveals why the legume is such a good companion plant for grains, corn, and other more fibrous plants.

By knowing that fertile soil has a CN ratio of approximately 12 parts carbon to 1 part nitrogen, we realise that all mulch and other organic matter must eventually be converted to this ratio before it can become humus, and therefore food for the plants and soil life. And remember, in a natural cycle of fertility and growth, it is the soil life that feeds the nutrients into the plants. Only in the commercial hydroponic system is this natural cycle discarded for direct chemical-nutrient stimulation. A glance at the CN scale indicates why straw mulch would benefit by the occasional application of a handful of blood and bone per square metre—more nitrogen to balance the carbon. This is most beneficial when the soil is warm and moist, the soil life active.

The greater the carbon content of your mulch, the more fibrous it is, the slower the breakdown. In the case of wood chips and pine bark, this is obviously the reason for their choice as a mulch. Unless a slow breakdown is your choice, I recommend mixing mulches, high carbon materials with mulches that are high in nitrogen. Of course, blood and bone is always available to do the required CN balancing act.

Even with only a basic understanding of the CN ratio, and it is simple, we can avoid some of the pitfalls of ignorance, gaining better results from our mulch.

THE pH OF THE SOIL

The next process to be considered is the pH of the soil. All pH tests measure the soils acidity, stating the soil as acid, neutral, or alkaline in varying degrees. Neutral is pH 7.0. Below this the soil is more acid, above is more alkaline.

Some people are a bit nervous about the soil pH, but it really is quite simple to understand. Although it truly is soil chemistry, the pH is not without a large range of flexibility regarding growing most garden plants. A pH preference is usual for most plants, but it is the comparative few that refuse to grow outside their preference. Certainly there are very few vegetables that need an absolute pH certainty.

I have designed the pH chart on the following page to show not only a graph of acidity and alkalinity, but to place emphasis on the real difference that such values indicate; pH 4.0 is one thousand times more acid than pH 7.0. With this in mind you will realise that the difference between pH 4.0 and pH 6.5 is vast. The perfect pH condition is pH 6.5, just on the acid side of neutral.

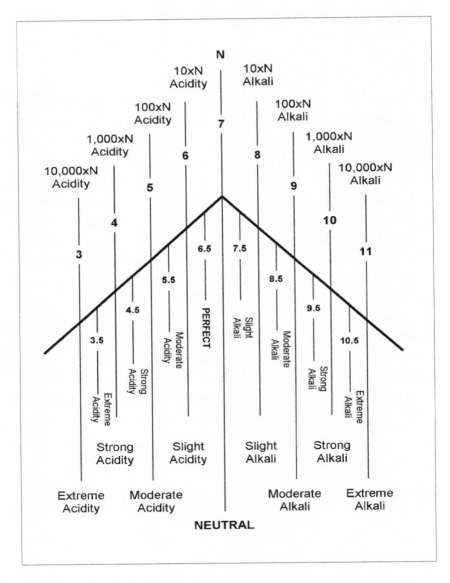

These are the commonly used materials which will change the pH of the soil in your garden:

- Limestone: a carbonate of lime
- Hydrated lime: a reacted calcium hydroxide
- Dolomite lime: a carbonate of calcium and magnesium

- Gypsum: a slightly acidic sulphate of lime

For general purposes, lime, dolomite and gypsum are all ideal. All are natural crushed rock, although hydrated lime goes through a further process making it far quicker acting. Hydrated lime is also known as builders' lime and used with moderation, is excellent in the garden.

We should approach the matter of soil acidity with caution. Soil acidity is one of the factors responsible for breaking down minerals from a stable, rock form. If dolomite is applied to an acid soil, it is the soil acidity that helps remove magnesium and calcium mineral nutrients from the crushed dolomite rock.

Generally speaking, a correctly pH adjusted soil is beneficial. However, this should not be done for the express purpose of changing the pH, but rather to adjust the cation exchange ratio existing in the soil. (We will look at this in the next chapter.) As you will have realised, no movement in Nature is an isolated act. All is connected in a complex inter-exchange and interaction of naturally occurring chemicals, mineral nutrients, and microorganisms, each affected by and affecting the soils environment.

My comments so far have applied to crushed rock designed to add calcium to the soil and to adjust the pH. Other types of powdered rock may be used for a different purpose. Basalt, volcanic larva, dolerite, rock phosphate, and other rock when crushed to a fine powder, have the ability to 'mineralise' the earth, and over a period of time can release many valuable mineral nutrients into the soil. There is huge evidence available now showing that our vast agricultural lands are becoming seriously deficient in natural minerals. And if our food producing land is deficient, so are the people who consume the food. Mineral deficiency is a rapidly growing problem in human health. I strongly support the re-mineralisation of the soil. The problem is, if we do not do it Nature will probably respond in her own way. This entails an ice age, with all its mobile glaciers grinding the mountains into powder. Effective . . . but very inconvenient!

Some of the soils which have become de-mineralised need the powdered rock not only for the nutrient value, but to restore a vital missing paramagnetic energy. Nature works on many subtle levels, but all involve energy. If there would be one trigger for an ice age, I believe it would be a lack of paramagnetic energy in the earth, rather than simply climate. The earth and its climate speak with but a single voice.

All life is pH dependent. Soil, plants, animals, humans, bacteria, fungi, moulds, each has its own pH range. Just as plants have various pH preferences, so does the soil life. Remember, pH 6.5 is an ideal. A pH around 6.0 is excellent for the majority of soil life and crops. While soil fungi are most active in a pH range from 5.5 to 8.5, the bacteria of the soil have a more refined need of pH 5.8 to 7.2. Obviously there is not an abrupt halt to fungi and bacteria beyond this range, but studies reveal that it is no longer so beneficial to plant health.

By using a simple, inexpensive soil test kit to determine the pH of our garden soil, and by gradually—not abruptly, drastically—gradually raising or lowering it to the desired pH 6.5, you will reap the reward of your efforts. Anywhere in the pH 6.0 to pH 7.0 range is good, and your plants will reflect it.

When purchasing specialist shrubs and plants, remember to ask if the plant has a definite pH preference. If it is not an acid or alkaline lover, then the above stated range will be perfect.

TOUCH THE EARTH

Having learned something of the properties of the soil, I suggest that you now become more familiar with it—if you are not already. Go out into the garden and pick up a handful of moist soil. That's Mother Earth you are holding in your hands. Smell the earthiness of it. You can learn to read the soil by its smell. If it smells fresh and slightly sweet, it means the soil is close to a neutral pH. If it is a really sour, acrid smell, then you may have an acidic soil, or a soil that is not adequately draining. Now feel the texture of it, become aware of it in your hand. You can learn a lot about the soil simply by the feel of its physical properties. If it is gritty in the soft tissue between your fingers, you know that it has a certain percentage of sand and coarse minerals in it. This indicates that it should drain freely and easily. However, if there are enough clay particles to prevent drainage, then this soil will probably respond to gypsum. Generally a gritty soil is dryish, so organic matter will feed new life into it and help to improve moisture retention.

If the moist soil in your hands holds together when squeezed, yet crumbles to a touch, you are probably holding a fairly trouble free soil. If your handful of soil squeezes into a dense clay ball, feeling slick between your fingers, then you have a wet heavy clay soil. In this case spreading a few centimetres (inches) of sharp sand over the surface of the soil would be of lasting value, but treating it with gypsum would work wonders. And remember, in all soil extremes, mulch is the modifier.

Learn to know the differences in your soil when wet and dry. Study its unique characteristics, even using a powerful magnifying glass. You may surprise yourself, for the more you learn about your soil from observation the more easily you will make correct gardening decisions.

Care for the soil with conscious attention. Be aware and conscious of the soil as a living medium. The soil is alive, and it is your responsibility as a conscious gardener to support and value that life. It is estimated that the weight of life in the soil far outweighs the weight of all humans, animals and creatures that live on the soil. That is a sobering thought. It is up to us, as conscious Beings, to support this natural balance, in however small a measure, by the care and intelligence of our actions in the garden.

CHAPTER 5

How and Why
of Natural Fertilisers

W E NOW APPROACH the rather controversial area of fertilisers for the soil. While I have no intention of debating artificial chemical stimulant so-called fertilisers in these pages, I feel obliged to point out the fundamental difference between natural and artificial fertilisers. Artificial fertilisers are designed to chemically stimulate the plant growth; natural fertilisers are intended to enrich the soil. *Enrich* is the key word. This is Nature's way of fertilisation. This is the principle to which we will address ourselves, to enrich the earth.

Apart from the living component of the soil and its food—the organic matter—for natural fertilisation we need to understand the mineral nutrients and their role in plant growth. Essentially, the lime, dolomite, and gypsum that are used to change the pH of the soil are fertilisers. Equally, tricalcium phosphate in its crushed rock form is a natural phosphate fertiliser. When it is treated almost weight for weight with sulphuric acid, it becomes a very acidic monocalcium phosphate, better known as superphosphate. In this form it is no longer natural, and it now has a pH around 2.3. It is interesting to note that for optimum health the human body prefers a slightly alkaline pH, while cancer thrives in an extremely low pH.

To understand the mineral nutrients of the soil, we need to take a brief look at what they are and how they exist in Nature.

The mineral nutrients which provide much of the plant's food are present in the soil as 'ions', meaning electrically charged particles of matter. They are almost equally represented in the soil as positively charged base elements called 'cations,' and negatively charged acid elements called 'anions'.

Cation base minerals are calcium (Ca), magnesium (Mg), potassium (K) and the base trace elements.

Anion acid minerals are nitrogen (N), phosphorus (P), sulphur (S) and the acid trace elements.

CATION EXCHANGE CAPACITY (CEC)

From our familiarity with batteries, we are aware that positive (+) and negative (-) poles must be aligned to the correct flow of current when charging a battery—or else we are in trouble! So it is we have a similar attraction and repulsion in the soil. Like iron filings to a magnet, the positively charged cation minerals are attracted to the negatively charged soil particles to become fixed to their surface. Here, the mineral nutrients are safely held against leaching.

As stated earlier, colloids are minute particles of clay or humus which hold a negative charge. The power of the soil's capacity to attract and hold positive mineral elements is known as colloidal energy. It is this which is a true measure of a soil's fertility. Conversely, the negative charge of the soil particles which attracts and absorbs positive cation nutrients 'repels' negative anion nutrients. Thus nitrate (NO_3), phosphate (P_2O_5) and sulphate (SO_4) exist in the pore space between soil particles and in humus.

It is worthy of note that humus has a three times greater attracting and holding capacity than clay particles. This obviously indicates that in a soil lacking humus, anion nutrients are very prone to leaching. The value of organic matter leading to the formation of humus becomes even more obvious.

Purely as an aside, it is interesting to realise that while the earth has a negative energy field, we humans have a positive field. Thus we polarise our energy by our contact with the earth. Connecting with the earth is essential to keep us energetically in balance. If this connection takes place on a conscious and aware level, the effect is undoubtedly magnified.

The cation exchange capacity, CEC, is the amount of cation nutrients the soil particles can absorb. When we realise that open sand, without humus, has a very low ability to hold nutrients, we can see why we have a problem when growing our plants in that medium. On the other extreme, dense clay soil has a very high attracting and holding capacity for cation nutrients, even though this soil is prone to serious compaction. We can get a soil fertility indication from the cation exchange capacity as indicated.

SOILS WITH LOW CEC	SOILS WITH HIGH CEC
Higher sand content	Higher clay content
Nutrients more prone to leaching	Greater capacity to hold nutrients
Less lime or dolomite to adjust pH	More lime or gypsum to adjust pH
Lower water retention	Higher water retention

Having outlined some of the major properties and functions of the soil, let us now consider the question of natural fertilisers. With this in mind we will explore the various natural products which can be used as a fertiliser, always remembering—to enrich. We will look first at the three major cation nutrients, all able to be absorbed onto the soil particles and which may be contained in humus.

THE CATION NUTRIENTS

CALCIUM

This is the most abundant mineral nutrient in the soil. It seems rather a paradox that whereas the soil requires as much as 65% to 75% calcium to perform an efficient exchange, only 4% of a plant is made up of calcium in the cell tissue. Most of the calcium is fixed permanently in the cell walls, particularly in the stems of older leaves. This indicates that calcium is a slow moving nutrient, not able to be drawn from old cells to new ones in the manner of more mobile nutrients. It is also slow moving from soil to plant.

Calcium is essential for the proper functioning of the growing root tip and bud points, plus it has an important role in metabolising nitrogen. I have already indicated that calcium is applied to the soil as either lime, dolomite or gypsum.

Under normal acidic conditions lime is applied to neutralise the acids in the soil. The amount should be calculated according to the cation exchange capacity of the soil. Normally however, the pH is measured and, according to the acidity, a guess is made as to how much lime to apply. In the garden this is perfectly adequate, but for agriculture it is definitely not accurate enough.

A safe general lime recommendation for garden soil is approximately 1 kg per sq metre (2 lb per sq yard). Personally, I favour hydrated lime at a bit less than half that quantity per application. It is more quickly absorbed onto the humus particles, faster acting, and much higher in calcium. Experience indicates that in an acid soil calcium needs adding to the soil each year, or until you reach the desired pH 6.5. At this point you only need add enough each year to maintain it. Use your pH test kit.

In an alkaline soil the calcium requirement is met with gypsum. These often have high levels of sodium which forces up the pH; even excess magnesium may raise the pH considerably. However, apart from certain areas, magnesium is commonly deficient in our soils. It seems to surprise the owners of some high pH soils that despite a high pH, it can be low in the essential calcium. All too often, in ratio to the cation exchange capacity, this is the case. The beneficial effects of gypsum on tight, cloddy, alkaline soil can be quite dramatic. This natural crushed rock is an excellent soil conditioner. You could safely say that all alkaline soils would benefit by regular applications of gypsum. Use the same application rate as for normal lime.

MAGNESIUM

Unlike calcium, magnesium is quite mobile in plants. When a deficiency occurs the plant is able to draw magnesium from the older leaves, relocating it into new, vigorous leaves. Because of this, a deficiency is more easily detected by observation of the older leaves.

One of the reasons magnesium deficiency is indicated by pale green or yellowish leaves is because it is the only mineral constituent of chlorophyll. Magnesium plays a key role in the transportation of phosphorus in the plant.

Magnesium is also needed in considerable quantities in the soil, although not as large a percentage as calcium. With 12% to 15% magnesium in the soil, our crops are assured of a permanent supply of this vital nutrient. The ratio of 70% calcium to 15% magnesium in the soil is important to maintain, for this ensures balance between two very important and major cation nutrients.

When required, magnesium is generally applied to the land as dolomite. This usually contains approximately 25% magnesium carbonate, along with the calcium percentage. An application of dolomite is often more beneficial than lime, unless you live in a magnesium rich area. You can always check this with your local department of horticulture.

If you apply dolomite, use it at the same rate as for lime.

Personally, I favour dolomite over lime because of that essential magnesium. In the world of naturopathic health, most Australians are regarded as being deficient in magnesium. Another method of supplying magnesium to plants is magnesium sulphate—Epsom salts. The effects are rapid. As in us, so too in the plants! Use at the rate suggested on the container for horticultural purposes. Epsom salts have the advantage of supplying sulphate, an element all too often lacking in the garden. Tomatoes and cabbage which are not thriving respond dramatically to a few applications of magnesium sulphate. However, I recommend this more as a short-term solution. Dolomite is more compatible with the soil life, and in the long run is superior as a natural nutrient.

POTASSIUM

This nutrient is not part of the cellular structure of plants, rather it is involved in a number of metabolic processes. It is an aid in the process of photosynthesis and essential in the formation of proteins. Potassium is the K in the common NPK formula of artificial fertilisers. As a rule of thumb, nitrogen, N, benefits the foliage of a plant, phosphate, P, benefits the roots, and potassium, K, benefits the flower and seed. This is why so many fertilisers combine these three nutrients.

Potassium helps in the plants' natural resistance to disease, plus it helps maintain internal pressure in the cells by its involvement in the plants' respiration. Potassium and nitrogen are taken up by plants in greater quantities than any other elements.

For organic growing we need a natural supply of this important nutrient, a supply which is compatible with the soil life. Under normal conditions of a fertile soil I have found little need to look for outside sources of this nutrient, owing to its presence in the soil.

Organic matter contains plentiful potassium, although it is not available to the plant until the material has been converted into humus. Hence the need of an active, thriving soil life. Within the minerals of the soil, such as basalt and granite, we find large deposits of potassium, although it is not available to the plants in this form. There are two main sources of supply in the soil, organic matter and mineral particles. Together they can amount to a huge reserve of potassium, which is largely unavailable to the plants. The problem is how to promote its release and avail ourselves of this supply. The organic grower should concentrate on organic matter to supply potassium, via humus. This can be a rich, abundant supply.

Before plants can utilise the potassium from minerals of the soil, a long, slow process is involved. The mineral potassium, reacting to soil acids and enzymes, slowly converts to a form of potassium which is available to plants through the acids exuded by their root hairs. This is now an available potassium to plants, but it is non-exchangeable on the soil particles. With further time and soil life activity, the mineral element continues slowly to convert into an exchangeable potassium cation, ready to load onto soil particles.

For the aware grower with an organically rich living soil, the non-exchangeable but available form of potassium offers a good reserve, a backup to potassium from humus. If potassium is brought in, I suggest granite or basalt rock dust, but remember it is subject to the above process before becoming available. The timing of this is determined by the abundance of soil life, and climatic conditions. We need enough moisture in the soil to keep this soil life active. In freezing cold or hot drought conditions it all comes to a standstill. All composted animal manures also offer an excellent supply of potassium to the soil.

However, because of the fickle nature of potassium, there are many gardeners who need, or want, a quick-acting supply of this vital nutrient. By far the best of the artificial supplies is Potassium Sulphate. This is readily available in all garden centres, most hardware stores, and in the garden section of many supermarkets.

An ideal approach to NPK in the garden is to use eight parts blood and bone—mainly N and P—to one part potassium sulphate. This is a tried and true formula that is compatible to the soil and the plants, while providing the required results.

THE ANION NUTRIENTS

It is now time to give some attention to the three basic anion nutrients, all unable to be held to soil particles, but which may be contained in humus.

NITROGEN

This is an essential element, not only in plants, but in all living organisms. Chlorophyll, the green pigmentation in plants, contains nitrogen. Hence our need for green food. A deficiency of nitrogen decreases the plant's ability to traps the sun's energy, and the plant becomes inefficient at converting nitrate nitrogen (NO3) into amino acids and proteins. Nitrogen is essential for reproduction and growth, and increases the yield and quality of vegetables, seeds and fruit.

There are several materials capable of supplying the soil with natural sources of nitrogen, and all are compatible with the soil life. Blood and bone, poultry manure pellets, compost, legumes, humus. All these forms of nitrogen share certain characteristics. They are not prone to leaching while in their organic form; they are available over a prolonged period of time; they help to increase the quality and content of soil life.

Spring is the ideal time to apply blood and bone in cooler climates, in tune with the increasing activity of the soil life. In fact, only apply blood and bone when the soil is moist, warm and active. Apply at approximately 240 g per 4 sq metres (8 ounces per 4 sq yards). In warm weather zones, application should be about six weeks ahead of the main growing time of the plants to be fertilised, and may be applied on a fairly constant basis throughout the growing season.

Even where you do not plan for a particular crop, a spring and autumn application of blood and bone is ideal as it will promote a great proliferation of soil life in your garden. Be aware that blood and bone will not produce overnight miracles, but it will be enriching the soil.

Treated pellets of poultry manure probably came about as a means of utilising the huge amounts of excreted wastes from battery hens and the chicken meat industry. Whereas I do not doubt necessity promoted this form of fertiliser, it is a windfall because of its benefit as a soil food. With a slightly higher nitrogen content than blood and bone, treated manure does not attract flies and has no offensive odour—until wet! It is a very viable fertiliser which improves conditions in the soil while supplying nitrogen.

Legumes are an easy and obvious source of organic nitrogen, devised and perfected by Nature. Nitrogen-fixing bacteria cause a root infection in legumes, which results in root nodulation. It is in these nodules that nitrogen is stored in a type of symbiosis, where each life form benefits from its association with the other. In a soil rich with organic matter and legumes, the nitrogen-fixing bacteria weave a miraculous synthesis. This is too valuable for the aware organic gardener to ignore, for it is a natural soil enrichment of Nature.

Finally, and most important of all as a supplier of all nutrients, there is humus. When a soil is depleted, degraded, it has been eroded of its humus. Blood and bone, treated manure, compost and legumes all help to improve the humus content of the soil, thus we come full circle, for really, humus is the beginning and the end of soil fertility.

PHOSPHORUS

This is a mobile nutrient in the plant. If a plant is limited in its supply of phosphorus, it will withdraw a supply from older cells to relocate in the growing root tips and leaf points. It seems that it is required throughout most stages of plant growth, but is of particular importance during its early development.

Plant species which fruit continuously over an extended period, such as tomato, capsicum and cucumber, need a more constant supply than plants that are picked as a single crop. Equally, lawns that are continuously cut have a great need for phosphate, as opposed to grass which is left uncut. Our main sources of natural phosphate are soft rock phosphate, the bone from blood and bone, and soil life.

Finely crushed soft rock phosphate is an ideal source of this essential nutrient. Unfortunately phosphate is a very unaccommodating nutrient, so there are a few things which must be observed. Phosphate is a very easily 'complexed' nutrient. This means that it easily combines with other minerals, becoming locked up, complexed. Below pH 5.5 it will combine with manganese, iron, zinc, and a few other trace elements, thus becoming complexed and unavailable to plants. This complex intensifies as the soil acidity increases.

However, if rock phosphate is applied to soil with a pH range from 5.8 to 6.8 then positive results can be expected. If the soil is very acidic I suggest you apply hydrated lime for quick results. Leave it for a week in a moist state to react with, and sweeten the soil, then apply the crushed rock phosphate. This may be applied at approximately 170g per 4 sq metres (6 ounces per 4 sq yards) annually for several years to obtain long lasting results.

Under highly alkaline soil conditions phosphate will complex with calcium. Quite an aggravating nutrient, isn't it? It may be possible to buy a mixture of crushed rock phosphate mixed with elemental sulphur. In an alkaline soil environment, the elemental acid sulphur compounds are enzymatically reacted with the mineral phosphate, thus phosphate slowly becomes available. This is an intelligent approach to mixing elemental sulphur and phosphate, with consideration to the soil life; superphosphate is the result of a purely commercial approach with no consideration to the soil life. If you cannot obtain this mix, you could try mixing it yourself, or seek help from your local horticulture department.

Blood and bone not only yield nitrogen, they are even more

rich in phosphorus from the crushed bone. There was a time when we could buy bone powder in Oz, but I believe this is no longer available. If this should prove to be available where you live, then it would be a supreme supply of phosphorus.

Over and over in this book is the constant reminder of the value and importance of organic matter in the soil. This is the very crux of organic gardening, to feed the soil. You could not be a conscious, aware gardener and not garden organically. Organic gardening is no passing fad; Nature has been recycling its organic waste and feeding the soil for millennia. Organic matter is the natural foodstuff of the soil, fodder for the soil life. Soil life has an important role as a supplier of phosphate, both from our beneficial earthworms and the vast abundance of microorganisms. This microbial life acts rather as a built-in organic reserve, a natural supply of phosphate. When you consider that a cupful of fertile organic soil contains many billions of microorganisms, or that the soil life may weigh several tonnes/tons per hectare/acre, they are a worthy and respected source of phosphate. Incidentally, it is the soil life which converts phosphorus to phosphate, sulphur to sulphate, and nitrogen to ammonia and nitrites to a required nitrate form. It is the soil life that converts unavailable elements into available nutrients. This . . . is a living soil.

Sulphur

Sulphur appears in the plant as part of the amino acids and proteins. It does not appear in chlorophyll, yet it is essential for its formation, thus sulphur deficiencies may show up as a yellowing in the new plant leaves. Sulphur in the plant strengthens it against climatic extremes, while playing a major role in the plants' resistance to disease and insect attack.

Sulphur is often overlooked as an essential nutrient, and at quite a cost to plant health. When sulphur deficiency occurs in pasture, the grass and accompanying legumes are compelled to compete for this vital nutrient, usually to the detriment of the legumes. The same is true in a grass and legume lawn. The trend today is for all grass, but a lawn without any legumes, such as white clover, is like a bird without a song.

The grass and legumes demand for sulphur is almost equal to their need of phosphorus. An even higher demand comes from the cabbage family.

Probably the most easily obtained and easily applied form of natural sulphur comes from gypsum—calcium sulphate. This is ideal for the alkaline soils owing to its pH neutralising influence.

For acid soils I recommend that first the pH is adjusted by the use of lime or dolomite, to be followed by an application of powdered elemental sulphur. The amount depends on the status of the soil, but 500g per 4 sq metres (1 lb per 4 sq yards) should be sufficient. It is worth noting that despite the acidity of powdered sulphur in an acid soil, it would take many years of quite extreme applications to have an adverse effect on the pH, for lime acts as a buffer.

The principle source of sulphur under natural conditions is humus. Sulphur is contained by humus at approximately one part sulphur to ten parts nitrogen by weight. I suggest that this is Nature's perfect ratio!

Over and over we come back to the fact that Nature has it all perfectly worked out. The proof is in any rain forest. Even when we grow crops intensively in our garden—and a rain forest is intensive—all we need to do is judiciously intensify Nature's already perfected technique.

CHELATE FERTILISERS

We have now dealt with all the major cation and anion nutrients concerned with plant growth, basically recommending fertilisers which are natural—existing in or by Nature—not artificial.

Other nutrients are required, particularly a whole range of

micronutrients, generally known as trace elements. Really, a living, fertile soil should have no trouble in supplying all these naturally. If a specific trace element is required, it can be bought in a chelated form. Chelate (pronounced kee-late) is a derivative from the Greek word 'chele', meaning claw. The function of a chelate (an organic complex) is chemically to surround the positively charged trace element to protect it from chemically complexing in the soil. Where there is a serious trace element deficiency, the chelated micronutrient can be very effective.

In Oz you can buy quite a number of the various chelate trace elements in Garden Centres and the garden department of many of the big hardware stores. I have noticed chelate of iron, chelate of manganese, chelate of copper, chelate of zinc and chelate of molybdenum on the shelves. Always follow the instructions carefully, and remember more is not better.

In our twenties, when Treenie and I emigrated from the UK, we bought a farm in Tasmania, the island state of Oz. The previous farmer told us that he had spread molybdate/superphosphate—which is super with the trace element added—on certain pastures that were deficient in the trace element molybdenum. Proudly, he told us that he had put it on at double strength. With the cattle in that pasture stripping and eating bark off the gum trees, showing symptoms of distress for the next four to five years, we knew exactly what the problem was.

FOLIAR FERTILISERS

For me, the most natural approach to provide trace elements is by regular foliar fertilising based in fish meal or seaweed, or a combination of both as a liquid spray. Over the years many reputable growers, in gardens, vineyards, orchards and farms have proved to their satisfaction that these foliar sprays have produced excellent results. Personally, I am a great believer in foliar spraying. The underside of a leaf is covered in stomata, Nature's way for a leaf to ingest the airborne nutrients that are available in the evening breeze, fog, mist, dew and rain.

Do your foliar fertilising in the early evening, making sure it is not about to rain. The evening moisture encourages the stomata of the leaves to open, taking in airborne nutrients from the atmosphere. A still evening is the ideal time, an almost magical quality in the air. You can feel Nature holding its breath, awaiting your cooperation.

Never underestimate the value and effectiveness of foliar fertilisers. A plant can absorb nutrients through its leaves, twigs, stem, bark, even through the buds and flowers. For trace elements in particular, the foliar method is easy and supreme. By following the prescribed strength in the mixture, you cannot overdose the plants. Research has indicated that a plant can absorb as much as 95% of its nutrients through its foliage. The first purposes of the root system are anchorage and water. Certainly an enormous amount of nutrition enters the plant through the feeder roots, especially in agriculture where the water intake is exploited to contain water soluble chemical stimulants. Only in more recent years has the foliar intake been recognised for its true potential and value.

Always bear in mind that any fertiliser we apply is only as effective as our intelligent use of it. For example, the timing of application. It is far better—essential—to fertilise, whether by foliar spray or materials onto the soil, when the soil is moist in the growing season. When the soil is dry, the weather hot, it is quiet and dormant in the soil. An application of fertiliser now would be a complete waste of money and effort. I have actually seen a gardener spreading fertiliser by hand onto frozen soil. God only knows what he was thinking, but he was certainly not conscious of the soil, of its inactivity, of its almost total shutdown.

We are very fortunate with the products that are now available to us as gardeners. There are more than enough to confuse the inexperienced gardener! Avoid the chemically-based products, and look for the plentiful organic types that are available. Almost certainly, the combination of fish and kelp spray would cover every trace element deficiency known, and there are many trade brands marketing these. Happily, in our present hi-tech times there are some very sophisticated hi-tech foliar sprays on the market. We have a very progressive local company combining hi-tech with organic nutrients, Nutri-Tech Solutions. They are reaching out to an international market with many excellent products.

I applaud this. I use selected Nutri-Tech products in my garden. When we are experiencing drought conditions—and that is all too often—I spray all the plants with a hi-tech organic solution that strengthens the walls of the cells of the plants, helping them to withstand adverse conditions. This is not done to stimulate growth, but simply to offer support to the plants when conditions are harsh and demanding. When the conditions for growth are good, I happily stand back and let a living soil provide all that is needed.

6

THE CONSCIOUS GARDENER

THIS IS A BOOK ABOUT the gardener and the garden. It is not a book devoted to gardening techniques on how to grow all the individual plants, but rather of how to connect with the consciousness of the plant kingdom by having a greater knowledge of the living soil, the nutrients, and how they all work together as a seamless whole. Equally, this is not a book of glossy pictures. The only picture that captures and holds my attention is the constantly changing picture of a living garden.

WATER STORAGE

I mentioned earlier about tank and town water—let me explain this further and what it means in my garden. People who live in many of the country areas of Oz—and I am one of them—for a variety of reasons are unable to have main water from the town. Often, the town water supply is insufficient. We depend on tank water. This means, in effect, that the only water we have is the rainwater that falls onto the roof of our house. This is directed from the gutters along underground water pipes and into water tanks to be stored.

This is not at all primitive. We have water with pressure at the turn of a tap the same as anyone else, along with a bonus of no added chemicals!

Twenty years ago one 20,000 litre (5,000 gallon) tank for a family was considered plenty of water storage, but then the climatic changes began and now 80,000 litres (20,000 gallons) is considered more appropriate. Of course, during that time family water consumption has also risen very considerably. The water off the roof really needs to be clean before it is stored; some people bother with this, others could not care less! I do care, and we have a good system. I have a fine steel mesh fixed in place between the edge of the roof and the outside edge of the gutter, so that all the rainwater has to flow through the mesh to get into the gutter. This cleans the water and keeps all the leaves, gum-nuts, twigs, insects and general bush debris out of the gutter.

Over the years the manufacturing of water tanks has progressed from mainly galvanised tanks to concrete, and now to polythene tanks, with a food grade liner inside. They still make all types, but polythene tanks are light, durable, and very popular. About ten years ago a few of our friends laughed to see me putting in more and more poly-tanks, bringing our storage capacity up to 160,000 litres (40,000 gallons). When, without any preamble, year after year of erratic rainfall and a cycle of droughts set in, I was very pleased with my foresight. One of the reasons I wanted a greater than normal water storage was so that I would have a plentiful supply to share with the garden.

DROUGHT

For quite a number of years I took our garden through a series of droughts, just managing to keep it all alive. Then one year the drought was prolonged, and I was buying a truckload of water every week for house and garden. And having water trucked in is comparatively expensive. Not only was I buying water by the truck, but the garden that I was watering looked sick and sad. A lot of expense for very poor results. If you use a sprinkler in the garden you really need to apply 25 mm (1 inch) every time. Because of my limited supply, I was not able to do this, putting less than half this amount on. Rather than positive, the result was definitely negative.

I remember the hot day in 1999, when I walked around the garden looking at the shrivelled and desiccating shrubs and plants. The plants were stressed from lack of water, and I was stressed because my garden was hurting. I sat down on a bench and thought about how I would like rain on our mountain top. I really focussed on this: please, rain, rain, rain . . . and more rain . . . please, and I was visualising rain.

Sitting there, relaxing, moving into a state of meditation, calm, my awareness expanded. Unfolding into my consciousness came a series of pictures. They were pictures of drought conditions. In one picture I saw hundreds of skeletal children, so weak they could hardly move. They were dying of malnutrition and dehydration. Third World drought, no crops, no food, no water to drink . . . death. I saw another village of black people almost fighting each other to get water from the single well that supplied them. It was obvious that the well was drying out, the fear and desperation on the people's faces reflecting this reality of despair. I saw a picture of sheep and cattle in outback Oz, falling over as they staggered along, trying to reach a water hole. I saw those that reached the water hole, now deep mud, and I saw dozens of them bogged, too weak to struggle, held like flies on sticky flypaper, dying in a slow and horrible torment.

One picture after another slowly appeared then faded from my inner vision, while I sat relaxed and calm.

Then I saw deserts of sand and sparse grey-green plants in which life was flourishing. All the plants and animals were specialised, all able to live and thrive in their harsh conditions. So specialised in fact, that for them, these were not harsh conditions. For them, the desert represented the abundance of life.

As I watched the pictures, their message came to me with great strength and clarity. I was so blessed, so fortunate, so very much living in abundance, yet I had allowed myself to see drought. I had slipped into seeing 'lack' when, in truth, my reality was one of abundance.

THE GARDENER'S ATTITUDE

When I opened my eyes, I looked around me knowing that I would never see my garden in the same way again. For years I had been looking at each dry day as another day of drought. Now, I would see each dry day as one day closer to the next rain, the next 'wet' day. And the difference is huge!

I walked around my garden after that, seeing it with new, opened eyes. I felt overwhelmed with gratitude with what I had, along with the deepest, most profound appreciation for the extravagant vegetation of where I live. I told the garden that I would never again water it, and that any plants that could not grow in the natural conditions of my garden, were welcome to withdraw. I told the plants that in dry times—we coastal gardeners do not know what drought is—they could draw energy from me to help sustain them, and when it was wet, they could give me some back.

I learned that it was not the garden that had a problem, it was me, the gardener. I was trying to keep alive plants that were entirely unsuited to the changing climate where I live. When I began the garden they fitted in well, growing and thriving, but as the weather became more unpredictable, more erratic, there were some plants that lacked the ability to adapt.

What causes me to smile is the fact that I had been looking for the perfect sprinkler for my tank-water pump for four years. I found it and bought six of them just two weeks before this happened. During the next year of intensifying drought I lost about half of the shrubs in my garden. If a plant succumbs to dry weather, I never replace it with the same species. I was surprised to learn just how many plants there are that can thrive in prolonged wet weather and do equally well in prolonged drought. While I have no intention of listing such plants, the bromeliads are an outstanding example. I have a bed of *Portea* in clumps which have flower spikes well over a metre (yard) tall, lasting for four to five months. Spectacular, rather than beautiful, they attract the admiration of most visitors.

I am reluctant to name the plants that thrive under very wet or very dry conditions simply because I would not deny you the fun of the chase that I so enjoy. If you simply follow a recommended list, you have lost the spirit of adventure that lurks in every true gardener. A conscious gardener enjoys the hunt for another ideal plant. I am forever looking for the next one! It's fun, it's conscious gardening.

GARDEN CLIMATE

I need to restate that I live in the subtropics. Where I live there is never a frost, and the rainfall is high—or should be! We can get a year with five months of drought and still get close to our annual rainfall. This is what I mean by erratic weather. In the early 1990s, in February, we had 750 ml (30 inches) of rain in 30 hours. This was both preceded and followed by drought, yet the annual rainfall would suggest a year of good rain. All it did was run off the land causing massive flooding, drowning thousands of cattle and sheep, and doing a huge amount of damage.

Vast areas of Oz are naturally dry, but only comparatively small areas have people living in them, apart from the farmers. South Oz is dry, yet with skill and knowledge you can have a magnificent garden without any need to water it. Some keen gardeners achieve this. You look for the plants that specialise in these conditions. However, if you took the plants that thrive in the dry of South Oz and planted them in a drought in our subtropics, they would die. The longest they would live would be until the first rain.

First and foremost, the humidity that accompanies rain in the subtropics is very high, and these dry-land plants cannot tolerate humidity. It is the same with West Oz plants, with cold, wet winters and hot, dry summers. We have cool, dry winters with hot, wet summers—or should have! Of course, this is a generalisation about dry-land plants. There are quite a few plant species that are extremely hardy, but generally, they are not native plants. Many of the succulent family would have no trouble in either region providing it was not too cold for them. Plants like the many types of Yuccas, Agaves and Aloes are very tough and versatile providing they have adequate drainage.

As a generalisation, Oz native plants are very indigenous to the area in which they have evolved and are living. After all, they have been there for a very long time! It usually requires extensive hybridisation of the plant for it to flourish in the varying conditions of other states of Oz. Even then, only a comparatively few species are suitable.

A ONE-OFF

Every garden has its own microclimate, every garden is unique, every garden is a one-off. By this I do mean a gardener's garden, rather than each garden in a street of basically neglected gardens. Although the plants in your garden will not affect the overall climate, they will affect the microclimate in your garden. To varying degrees, you can increase or lower the humidity around your plants, you can create a shaded or sun-filled garden, even a wetter or drier garden.

Over the years since I stopped watering our garden, I was never once aware of the plants drawing energy from me during a drought in the way that I had invited, but I am fairly certain that it happened. I have noticed that when the rains come, following a period of drought, there is the most powerful outpouring of energy I have ever felt in a garden. When I walk around the garden during or directly after a rain, I feel the garden and plant energy pouring into and over me. It is quite extraordinary. I have never felt anything like this in any other garden.

It is this sort of energy exchange that makes a garden unique. There is a huge storehouse of energy in a loved garden, but this is always energy in movement, not held static in the garden storehouse. That energy is being used to help heal the land. Equally, it is healing the aware and conscious gardener.

GARDEN ENERGY

I know that this may sound odd, but no garden ever suffers from low self-esteem. I have visited many gardens, good, terrible, and indifferent, yet in every garden there was positive energy. We humans mostly use our energy field rather poorly. Our energy field follows the direction of our thoughts, and human thoughts are notoriously negative, resulting in our present times of galloping depression, stress and suicide.

Nature does not operate in this way. The energy of a desert is very different than the energy of a rainforest, but it is every bit as powerful. The desert has no focus of what it cannot grow any more than a rainforest has on what it can grow. Yet both different conditions produce a field of energy that is unique in its conscious expression, and both are major contributors to the energy of the planet. So, too, are we.

If an off-world Being created a scale of awareness for life on earth, we would be near the bottom of the scale. I am not talking about self-awareness, but the awareness of *being conscious* in the moment. All Nature lives and expresses from the moment, and because we, too, are an expression of Nature, so also our consciousness is intended to operate this way. But while all Nature is aware of the *moment* of life, humanity is not. We are too busy thinking. And you cannot think your way into the moment!

So what am I getting at? I have visited gardens and genuinely complimented the gardener on creating a fine garden. Then I have had to listen to a litany of what is wrong with the garden; why this does not grow properly, how that could be a lot better, how this area is full of weeds, how that area is damp, why the gardenia is failing, how I don't have enough time to do it better . . . on . . . and . . . on!

None of this has anything to do with the garden; it is a statement about the gardener's relationship with life. This is a person who probably loves the garden but projects their—mostly false—self-image onto the garden. So for them, the garden is not good enough. Of course, all this happens subconsciously. This is the whole point and purpose of this book, Conscious Gardening. Conscious gardening is not subconscious gardening. It is about gardening from the moment, rather than gardening from the past. Gardening from the heart, rather than gardening from the head. With every moment you spend in the garden you are affecting and creating the energy of your garden—and all Nature. You can do this with awareness, creating a supportive healing energy in the garden, or you will do it subconsciously, creating an energy of indifference.

COOPERATION

The garden that is loved has a consciousness of cooperation. I have written quite a bit about drought, because when you live in an area that seldom ever had a drought, it has a far greater impact on the flora than a drought does in an area that has long had a pattern of droughts.

During the early nineties, we had a few continuous years of drought conditions. This means that we had rain, but never enough to reach the subsoil. When the subsoil dries out, then the large shrubs and trees suffer. A shower of rain, even a heavy shower never reaches the deep subsoil, this takes sustained rain. It was at this time of climatic stress that most of the messmate *Eucalyptus* gum trees on the hills in the district died. And many of these were mature, well-established trees. To my knowledge all gum *Eucalyptus* trees are evergreen, which basically means they are always dropping leaves—especially when dry—yet they are always in leaf. Just as well for the koalas!

When a drought is getting serious in our garden, I walk among the evergreen shrubs suggesting that they drop their leaves. I project a mind picture to them of having no leaves and going dormant, thus using and losing no energy. In cold climates deciduous shrubs are normal, but not in the subtropics. Despite this, many of my evergreen shrubs do drop their leaves, and live. A few keep their leaves, endure and live, while others that were unable to do either, become stressed by dryness and heat to the point of death.

You might say that the shrubs would drop their leaves without my suggestion, and maybe they would, but I have species that died with shrivelled leaves prior to my suggestion, and have dropped their leaves and lived after it. Usually they drop their leaves about a week after I walk among them with my conscious and visualised suggestion.

The beautiful jungle flame, *Ixora*, is one species that seems unable to drop its leaves, and in drought they get stressed to the point of insect infestation, disease and death. I removed all my plants, keeping my two favourites to grow in large pots. I dug the sick plants out of dry soil, cut them right back to the base, potted them—and watered them. A year later they were about a metre (yard) tall and covered in beautiful flowers. Talk about gratitude!

My subtropical garden in a drought is reminiscent of a garden in winter in the UK. No gardener fights the English winter, other than trying to grow spring crops before the frosts have finished! Just as the cold closes the expression of growth, causing leaf drop and dormant plants, so drought has similar results. Hot and dry can close down growth just as effectively as wet and frozen. Once the gardener accepts this, the stress leaves the gardener, relieving the garden of the gardener's stress.

Life in the garden is all about cooperation. Nature is a conscious expression of life, as we are. The gardener who develops a conscious awareness of the garden, respecting and treating the whole garden as a collective of conscious intelligence, is able to connect with an energy capable of cooperation. The problem of cooperation seldom ever lies with the garden. It is the isolating factor of human arrogance. The gardener who is open to learn and can humble him/herself before Nature, has the potential to open a door into greater realities.

OPPOSITION

Of course, some gardeners are not able to open themselves to their gardens, to Nature. Our education has suggested that we are a superior species, above and beyond Nature. While we retain this foolishness, we remain shut away in the room of smug ignorance.

Whether you find it unpalatable or not, your field of energy is either supportive of your garden, or it is in opposition. The gardener who hates cutting the lawn is throwing all their energy into opposition while they are actually cutting the lawn. If the act of cutting grass is no more than a necessary chore, then don't grow a lawn. Far better to have no lawn than sow the seeds of discord in the garden while cutting it.

Most people seem to have no idea that we are fields of energy. At death, the physical field of energy recedes until the physical body has returned to the earth as organic matter, while the metaphysical energy of self continues unabated. Interestingly, when your physical body has returned to the earth as organic matter, it once again begins to generate more energy. There is never a moment that matter is not energy.

Everything around you is affected by your field of energy. When you know this, and use it wisely, you can be of great benefit to people and life, but most people are entirely unaware. When you are in your garden this field of energy interacts with the energy of your garden. This is always happening, it does not need your permission, or even your awareness that it is happening. Again, this is the whole point of conscious gardening—to creatively work with, and use, the field of energy that is both you—the gardener—and your garden.

Always see the best in your garden. If you see the best in you, you will easily see it in your garden and in life all around you. If you have a problem seeing the best in you, you will be critical of your garden and life, and of course, critical of yourself.

As I mentioned earlier, growing unsuitable shrubs that make prodigious growth when conditions are suitable is both growing work and creating resentment. More opposition to the garden. Growing weeds is another classic example. I have heard many gardeners groan about how they hate weeding. Be aware that the garden cannot separate hate for weeding in the garden from hating the garden as a whole. You know the difference, but the difference is in your head. The only place from which you can have a pure connection with the consciousness of the garden is from your heart.

PHYSICAL IMPAIRMENT

There are some people who, being elderly or for reasons of a physical impairment, love being in the garden but are unable to do any actual work in their garden. Being unable to work in the garden is in no way detrimental to your conscious relationship with the garden. You can have a garden contractor look after the physical needs of the garden. Generally, the person who goes from one garden to another doing the work seldom develops any lasting relationship with a particular garden. For most garden contractors it is work, a way of making a living. And this is okay. For some, it is a joy, being paid to do what they most love doing. These gardeners connect with every garden they work in, giving far more than the physical work for which they are paid.

Although the person unable to work in their garden has lost the 'doing to' ability, they now have a wonderful opportunity to practice *being with*. Most people find the work of 'doing to' much easier than the steady focus required for 'being with'. I once met an elderly lady who had such a love for her garden that it shone through her every word when she spoke about the plants. When I described her as an advanced gardener, she went into a guilty and embarrassed denial.

"I don't do any actual gardening," she protested, "I simply cannot because of my ageing body. I'm not a gardener at all."

I spent long enough in conversation to assure her that she most definitely was and still is a gardener. *For as long as your heart is in the garden, no matter who does what, you are the gardener. You are the person with whom the consciousness of the garden is connected.*

Once she had grasped this, understanding its truth, she actually wept with relief. For some reason she carried an inner grief that she was no longer connected to her beloved garden simply because she could no longer work in it. Once she realised that her daily routine of sitting in her garden, consciously connected to it in her heart, was the very essence of the true art of gardening, she was both relieved and overjoyed.

7

MAKING YOUR
OWN COMPOST

COMPOST IS, OF COURSE, the perfect fertiliser. Although I am fairly casual about making compost, this does not in any way detract from the value of good compost. Let me explain my position on this. First and foremost, I am a mulching gardener. This is the way I give organic matter to the soil. However, I do have a compost bin in which I make compost. For this purpose we use all the kitchen scraps, with only a small amount of garden trash. All my garden trash is mulched onto the soil.

In many ways, compost is the ideal fertiliser mulch. Its most important place is on the soil of the vegetable garden. If you are a person who burns garden waste then you should be making compost. Although you cannot use woody materials in compost, they can be shredded and returned to the soil as mulch.

DO'S AND DON'TS

There are many ways of making compost. The proper (if there is such a thing) method, in a bin, makes a fast hot compost capable of cooking perennial weed roots and nuisance bulbs. This is ideal because if you put weeds in your compost bin, it ensures that you do not return weed seeds to the soil. If you are not interested in the art of composting, then all you need do is simply put all your vegetative material into a large heap, adding a bit of blood and bone now and then, and just leave it. In about a year it should be compost. Drought will slow it down, as will prolonged freezing conditions. This type of compost is known as cold compost. It often contains weed seeds that are still viable, so keep noxious weeds out of the cold compost heap.

One golden rule for compost heaps or compost bins is to always build them on soil, never concrete. For those who do not wish to make a compost bin, or are unable to, there are many excellent synthetic compost bins available at your local garden centre. Be aware of what you actually want, but most of them do a good job. Remember that compost making is reasonably rugged and that you get the quality of the bin that you pay for. If money is an issue, go for inexpensive rather than cheap. Cheap is almost always cheap and nasty. Inexpensive is looking for the quality you want at a fair and reasonable price.

For those who want to build a compost bin, or who have someone around the house who is prepared to give it a go, go and look at a few compost bins to give you a basic idea of what they look like. I made my compost bins out of treated wood. I have two squares, side by side, each one metre (yard) square by one metre high. This is a good size for the average garden/family. I recommend that you do not make them smaller. Two metres square (2 yards) and a metre and a half high is good if you have a lot of plant material to compost.

If you have access to a regular supply of animal manure, tailor the size of your bins appropriately. I have two side-by-side bins. The idea is that when one bin is full—about a year for me—I then throw all the material from the full bin into the empty one. In this way the raw top of the heap gets buried, while the almost compost bottom of the heap now comes to the top. Unlike within the soil, a good compost heap should be rich in aerobic microorganisms from top to bottom, and full of compost worms.

To this end I often plunge a crowbar into the compost heap, lifting and loosening the compost. In the early stages a garden fork does this well. Keep the compost moist, not saturated, and sprinkle blood and bone into it periodically, along with a handful of lime. Aim to keep the compost sweet and reasonably aerated. Consciously connect with it, tell it what you are aiming for. Believe me, your compost heap is definitely alive, and where there is life there is consciousness. If you are concerned about what people might think, talk to your compost when your neighbour is watching television!

Ingredients of Compost

You start by putting thick-stemmed plants, such as Brussels sprout stalks, corn, cabbage, hedge clippings, prunings, et cetera, at the bottom. Sprinkle with blood and bone. Next, pile on about 20 cm (8 inches) of weeds, lawn clippings and garden waste all mixed up. Now add another couple of handfuls of blood and bone, along with some animal manure, i.e. rabbit, guinea pig, poultry, any farm animals, whatever you can get. On this goes another layer of kitchen scraps and garden rubbish, along with whatever else organic is available. Dust lightly with hydrated lime on a fairly regular basis, and introduce compost worms early in the process.

If you build a compost heap slowly, like I do, the compost never gets really hot, just warm occasionally, and the compost worms will thrive. If, however, you have a lot of material waiting to build into a compost heap, and it heats up as it should do, the compost worms will only live around the edges and at the base where it is cooler. You know what your conditions are, so don't be bound down by the idea there is only one way to make compost. As a generalisation, if the heap smells really foul, it is not getting enough oxygen, and has gone anaerobic. Too many lawn clippings can do this. You will learn good compost making from the experience of doing it. In cold climates it will make faster in the summer, while in the subtropics it makes into compost all the year round. In drought conditions I periodically water my compost heap to keep it active.

By the time your compost has built up in one bin, been forked into the other, and had more time to continue decaying, all that vegetable junk will have turned into a beautiful crumbly, very high in organic matter, sweet smelling, soil-like mixture. Compost—it's nearly good enough to eat!

Obviously, certain materials should never go in the compost heap. Knives, forks and spoons are not good candidates for compost. Neither are plastic bags or bottles! Don't use newspapers in bulk, unless they are shredded and moist, and only then in proportion to other materials. Orange peel is very resistant to decay, as are onions, and keep out mango and avocado seeds. Whole cabbages take ages, so cut them up. Keep bones and meat out of your heap, including whole chicken carcasses. Anything that has meat or bones I feed to our local lace monitors, *Varanus*. Actually, these giant reptiles probably devour as much of our kitchen scraps as the compost worms.

OTHER METHODS OF COMPOSTING

If, like me, you are mad on mulching, you will never seem to have enough organic material to build into a decent compost heap. However, for kitchen scraps, compost is a must . . . but there are other ways of making compost.

In a suburban situation, there is an alternative solution to kitchen scraps that you want to feed to your soil. Putting them in a garbage bin if you have a vegetable garden is a definite no-no. Dig a shallow trench across the vegetable garden. It need be no more than a spade's depth and width. Accumulate your kitchen scraps and once a day put them in a heap starting at one end of the trench, then simply cover each day's offerings with the displaced soil. Pile it up—it will sink level as the organic matter quickly decays. Gradually you will fill the trench with a wonderful, quick rotting plant food. All the local earthworms will congregate in your garden, and you will be their friend. Next season this will be ideal for growing tomatoes and capsicum, while you continue to enrich the soil as you keep on creating more underground compost.

By placing the kitchen scraps underground, you keep them away from flies and the local gangs of cats and dogs. Plus there is no smell, so you remain friends with your neighbours. If you are the owner of a scrap disposal kitchen sink unit, and you own a garden, just think of how you can more intelligently utilise organic matter to enrich the earth, rather than be part of our pollution caused by the thoughtless and inadequate disposal of household waste.

Another method, which produces excellent results, makes use of black plastic garbage bags. Place your kitchen scraps into a bag, roll the top down a few turns, peg it securely with three or four strong clothes pegs or large paper clips, and put it out in the sun. Add your kitchen scraps to this bag for a few days, turning it over each time you add more waste. When the bag is half full, leave it pegged and lying in the sun, and start on another garbage bag. Turn each bag twice daily for best results.

In two or three weeks, depending on the temperature—not too hot or too cold—the material in the first bag will be broken down ready for garden mulch, and the bag is available for refilling. Generally, about six bags will keep the sequence going nicely.

Be careful to fold and peg the bags securely closed. Not only will this prevent the entry of flies—maggots in the scraps are a bit off-putting—but it should also stop smells attracting night-prowling animals. If you have a large boisterous dog, or even an inquisitive small one, it is better to place the bags out of their reach. Warmth and the air from constantly turning the bags over are essential for success. By using black plastic bags, you generate greater heat in the bag. All in all, it is a fast, very valid way of making compost with minimum fuss and bother. Try it—you will be surprised just how simple and easy it is. Making it this way is much easier than describing and explaining it!

Again, as you put vegetable scraps into the bags, you are actually creating the conditions for micro organic life to flourish and proliferate. When you do this consciously, you actually assist the process by your own conscious awareness. If you think not, then try making it with some bags totally ignored as you prepare them, while the other bags receive your attention and appreciation. You may get a big surprise.

8

GROWING VEGETABLES
ORGANICALLY

MOVING HOME A FEW TIMES and travelling around Oz has taught me that vegetable growing is not quite as straightforward as I once thought. In this country of climatic extremes it gets difficult to say exactly when the various vegetable seeds should be sown. In fact, it is impossible to be accurate except in one's own garden. A gardening magazine or book published nationwide which gives a calendar of sowing times can do no more than generalise. In fact, it can be rather misleading.

TIMING

I lived in a valley for ten years, sowing my seeds and planting my plants. Only a few kilometres (miles) away, yet nearly a thousand metres (yards) in elevation on the escarpment, other gardeners did their sowing and planting at least six weeks later than we did in the valley. According to the charts of climatic range, we were all in the same bag. Not so! The times of sowing can vary from one side of the hill to the other, from one suburb to another, from one side of a river to the other. Wind, sun times according to the lie of the land, shade intensity, north or south facing—all these factors play a role in determining when sowing conditions are ideal.

For me to say when you should sow your seeds is both misleading and unreliable. You must learn to consciously know your garden, its strengths and weaknesses, and its many moods. Find where the summer hot spots are, the winter cold, the spread of summer sun, the limits of winter sun, the likelihood of late, sharp frosts, the vagaries of your weather pattern; all these play their parts in the art of conscious gardening.

Feeling

Be conscious of your garden, its whims and ways, the movement of sun and shade, the idiosyncrasies of your soil. Be conscious of what vegetables you actually eat as a family, and grow just these. Be aware that growing twice the amount of vegetables that you can eat generally equates as twice the amount of work. Be conscious *of* the garden, be conscious *in* the garden, and your intuition will be stronger than you have ever experienced. Trust and follow your intuition in the garden. Sow your vegetable seeds when it *feels* right. Listen to older local gardeners who are more knowledgeable in local garden lore, but be open to your own insights. Be open and flexible in your approach to growing vegetables, and don't be afraid to go against tradition if your intuition guides you in a different direction. Trust in your abilities.

Conditions

Let me share the different climates I have experienced as a gardener, moving from a summer mild, winter very cold English climate to a summer temperate, winter cold in Tasmania, then to a summer hot, winter cool in coastal New South Wales, and finally to summer hot, winter mild in south east Queensland. It all adds up to a series of learning curves as you move from one climate to another. You see some odd things, like sun-bronzed Queenslanders going to Tasmania and getting badly sunburnt, and the same with deeply tanned Tasmanians getting burnt in the Queensland sun.

Just as the sun intensity in different states has a differing effect on human skin, so too it has a very different effect on the growth of plants. The conditions you live in are not the same as the conditions in any gardening magazine or book, including this one. Be conscious of your conditions, and be aware of the vigorous, or poor, growth of certain plants and the places in the garden where this occurs.

Before we get started, let me state very clearly that in my present garden I do not grow vegetables. I have no choice about this. If you look at the cover picture you will get an idea of the tree intensity in our garden. Our garden is literally a garden in the forest. Sunlight is totally essential for a vegetable garden; vegetables and fruit are sunlight made edible. The other essential is water. You must have water for a vegetable garden, there is no 'if, but, or maybe' about this. I do not have anywhere near enough water for a vegetable garden, and even if I did I do not have enough sunlight. Most vegetables need the sunlight all day.

Our garden is a moving mosaic of sunlight in the shade. Some places get a few hours of sun in midsummer, but not enough enduring sun to grow vegetables. Naturally, those trees also like water. When I used to water my garden, I often felt the trees got the most benefit. My surface watering brought the tree roots closer to the surface. Now, with no watering, they have returned to harvest the subsoil water. These are the things a gardener learns by being conscious of his or her actions and their consequences. If you are a gardener with similar conditions to mine, you may have to make a similar decision.

Personally, my passion in the garden is for ponds and exotics, for fun with slightly unusual plants, so it all works out. When you follow your passion you are more likely to embrace conscious gardening. Meanwhile, organic growers who outlet their produce through our excellent local Natural Food store are benefiting. I buy their organic produce, hopefully, some may buy my books!

APPROXIMATE SOWING/PLANTING TIMES

COOL/COLD CLIMATES

Spring – sow/plant:
Dwarf bean, runner bean, potato, cucumber, zucchini, pumpkin, all root crops, sweet corn, lettuce, onion, leek, tomato, capsicum, egg plant (aubergine), celery, silver beet, Asian greens.

Autumn – sow/plant:
Cabbage, Brussels sprout, kale, cauliflower, broccoli, broad bean, spinach, silver beet, Asian greens and Chinese cabbage.

WARM/HOT CLIMATES

Spring – sow/plant:
Tomato, capsicum, eggplant, okra, cucumber, zucchini, all melons, sweet corn, lettuce, sweet potato.

Autumn – sow/plant:
Dwarf bean, runner bean, potato, pumpkin, all root crops, sweet corn, lettuce, onion, leek, spinach, celery, silver beet, Asian greens and Chinese cabbage.

As I have stated, this is a rough guide, so use it as such. There are many variations in a climatic range and each particular location is unique. It is to this you must give your attention.

This is not a 'do as I say' follow me book; it is an *observe, learn, apply* book. Observe other proven local organic gardeners. Better still, join your local organic gardening club and talk about seed sowing times with them.

SITE

One very important decision to be made before you grow your vegetables is the site of the vegetable garden. It must be in a sunny position and well away from trees. If you are in a very windy area, it is a good idea to build or grow a windbreak—but not with trees. As I have said, trees and vegetables are not good companions. There are a few exceptions to this regarding some fruit trees and summer lettuce, but these are tricks you learn from experience.

I have mentioned sawdust a few times, and I said that it makes an excellent garden path, but it is the vegetable garden where it excels. Simply place 10–15 cm (4–6 inch) boards pegged down for the path container and fill it with fresh green sawdust. In many places this is very easily obtained by the truckload, and it is the only way I would use fresh green sawdust. It is soft and easy to walk on, drains freely, and has quite a few advantages over a concrete path. You can move your path easily—try that with concrete!—and a fit elderly person can easily build one. When the path is really black and decayed, it is a simple matter—when it is moist—to shovel it onto the vegetable garden for extra mulch, and refill the path with fresh sawdust. This could be anywhere from three to six years, depending on the speed of decay in your climate. Wetter and warmer means a quicker decay.

Having made sure that our vegetable garden is in the right place and that we have an adequate windbreak (if necessary, I suggest a slatted fence 2 metres (6 feet) high, with a 5 cm (2 inch) gap between slats to avoid wind resistance, while allowing a good air flow over the vegetable garden) and that the soil has been checked and treated for the right pH, we should have everything in our favour to grow some very tasty, nutritious vegetables. In fact, grown properly and eaten fresh, they taste almost unbelievably good compared with the commercial vegetables we are offered today.

PREPARATION

Prepare the soil carefully to make a seed bed. Remove all the mulch for fine seed sowing, and place it in a heap nearby. Fork over or heavy hoe the ground to loosen the surface, then rake until you have obtained about 2.5 cm (1 inch) of loose soil, or tilth. This is vitally necessary to get the best seed germination possible. If the weather is wet do not try to make a seed bed. The soil needs to be moist and friable, not saturated and clinging. Also, if the weather is extremely dry, water the soil well—the perfect inch—to obtain a friable moist soil that can be easily worked.

Here, then, are the vegetables which appear in most vegetable gardens, or should! A few are selective about climate, most are selective in their seasons of growth, and some deserve greater popularity. Also, there are now new hybrid/cross vegetables and many varieties of what are commonly referred to as Chinese cabbage (but they are not) that I have never grown, so I will not guess at their culture. By the time you get around to them, you will have your own skills.

∾

I am listing five categories: Perennial vegetables, Root vegetables, Green vegetables, Fruiting vegetables, and Seed, Pod and Bulbous vegetables.

PERENNIAL VEGETABLES

ASPARAGUS

These tasty, rewarding plants are well worth growing. I used the mulch method and it worked very well. If you are about to plant an asparagus bed, site it where it has room to develop, as the plants grow large and bushy. Dig or loosen the soil and spread a heavy application of dolomite or lime on the ground. Rake this in, then hollow out a shallow hole in which to place the plant. Plant it with its roots spread well out, not forced into a hole that is too small. Spread a good layer of soil back over the roots and cover with 30 cm (1 foot) of straw, sugar cane, hay, or any suitable mulch. With this method you must always keep the plants heavily mulched. This also means no weeds!

Do not pick any tips the first year. Let the plants grow and develop, then die down naturally for the winter.

The following year you may pick a few tips but for no longer than one month, then leave the plants to grow and mature. The year after this you can pick some tips for three to four months before allowing them to grow to maturity. Do not weaken the plants with continual picking. With a good deep mulch you can part it where the asparagus tops poke through and follow the long, clean, white stem to its base. Cut near the ground.

If at all possible, I suggest you buy 2–3-year-old male plants. They have a much thicker stem for eating, which is why you are growing them! The female plants have a thinner, more slender stem.

They are delicious steamed, even raw. Well-maintained—and mulch does this perfectly—asparagus beds can last for many years. On a chalky (lime!) soil in England, my favourite great aunt had a bed of asparagus that lasted for about thirty years. And seriously, asparagus responds very well to the potent fertiliser of appreciation.

Choko

This warm climate vegetable is the last of our true perennials. It is a climbing plant of rampant, vigorous growth, and I can think of no other plant that gets close to giving as much return from a single seed as the choko. From one seed, one vine, I picked three sacks of chokos!

It grows so fast under good conditions you can measure the growth daily. This indicates that the choko needs copious water and heavy mulching, with plenty of sun. It has no pH difficulties, but it does need a deep soil rich in organic matter for it to produce its abundance of vegetable fruit.

Do not grow it in the immediate vicinity of other vegetables. This is a hungry, greedy plant. It has large leaves which must transpire with water at a very rapid rate on a hot day. This vegetable thrives best in a warm, humid, wet climate. The choko's fruit is fist sized, green, and very tasty. The first one that I tasted left me pleasantly surprised. Because of its abundant energy, I have always felt that the choko is a superior food vegetable. Given enough water, there is so much energy in the plant that nothing seems to hurt it. Bugs, fungi, disease, a well-grown choko just shrugs them away.

Maybe because it is so packed with sunshine, the choko feels like a 'go' food. The fruit contains a large, fleshy seed which, when really young, can be eaten. When it matures, the seed is discarded.

To start a new plant all you need do is buy a good choko from the vegetable section in a supermarket and place it in a light place out of the sun. Very soon a strong shoot will emerge. This can now be planted near an old shed it can cover, or against a fence or trellis, even a dead tree. Be warned however, this plant is not content with just a little space, it needs plenty of room. It is a perennial in its favoured climate, although they can sometimes deteriorate. I have known them last several years and to die after a year—a frost would do this. I consider this plant as well worth the room. If you have a large family and are on any kind of budget, give the choko a try. The choko is best sliced and steamed.

COMFREY

This incredible herb has come from being an almost unknown plant to one of the more controversial plants in the garden. Part of the controversy is the allegation that comfrey has slight carcinogenic properties, thus the more traditional nutritionists have condemned it. I am puzzled by this hypocrisy. Peanuts—which are not nuts but are nodules on the roots of a legume—also contain varying levels of carcinogens. They even require laboratory testing to ensure the level does not exceed an acceptable limit. Despite this, the peanut— which I detest—is widely promoted as a food and consumed as such. Hence my confusion. Many people have died violently from a reaction to the peanut. Have you ever heard of anyone dying from a comfrey-induced death?

Another perennial plant, comfrey can be grown from crown offsets or root clippings and should be spaced about 60 cm (2 feet) apart. It should be left undisturbed the first year, apart from removing flowering stems. When established this plant can grow 1–1.5 metres (3–5 feet) high. It has large furry leaves which should be cut or pulled continuously for salads and coleslaw. My preferred way was lightly steamed and served with a squeeze of lemon.

If you cannot keep up with the prolific production of leaves, or have a few plants but are wary of eating them, use the leaves to add to your mulch. They are high in potassium and excellent for the soil. They can also be used for the compost heap. If you keep hens, tie a bundle of fresh young leaves and hang them up for the hens to peck. Rabbits, guinea pigs and hamsters will all thrive on these high quality food leaves.

Herbalists recommend the fresh young leaves for external use as a poultice for bruises, sprains, fresh wounds and moist ulcers.

GLOBE ARTICHOKE

Similar name, but don't confuse this with the Jerusalem artichoke as it is a very different plant. This is a member of the thistle family, and instead of eating tuberous roots we eat the flower buds.

Globe artichokes like an open, sunny position in moist, well-drained soil. Keep them very well mulched. It is best to buy a couple of plants from the garden centre, making sure of a named and proven variety. This is another tall, perennial plant, very handsome, and can be grown in the flower bed or among the shrubs. Plant about 1 metre (1 yard) apart. When the established plants seem a bit past it, or need replacing, simply remove a few rooted shoots from the base of the plant and begin again.

They are frost tender, so if you are in an area of late frosts, be sure to place plenty of extra mulch over the dormant crown of the plant in the early spring.

It is essential to pick the buds while young and tight. Steam until tender and serve with butter. Pick, steam, eat. Yum!

RHUBARB

This plant is a lover of organic food, moisture, and full sun. This makes it the perfect subject for a good mulch.

Set the roots of good proven stock in a fertile piece of ground and mulch it. Do not pull any sticks the first year, and go easy the second year. Let it get well established and it will reward you in the following years. Always pull the leaf stems firmly holding the base, never cut. Space plants about 1 metre (1 yard) apart. Do not force the plants in winter as it drastically weakens the plant. Water well in summer and keep mulched. You can grow these perennial plants anywhere suitable in the garden. It does not have to be part of the vegetable garden.

Never eat the leaves, use them as a mulch on the garden. This is a plant where you cook and eat the stems. A sweet (sour!) dessert.

ROOT VEGETABLES

BEETROOT

In the U.S. these are known as red beet. Beetroot like an open, sunny, well-drained soil. Make sure the soil is well limed, but do this several months before sowing. Beetroots like a rich soil, but no fresh manure.

The method for growing beetroot is to clean the required ground completely of mulch and put in a handful of blood and bone. Sow thinly into drills about 2.5 cm (1 inch) deep. Allow 30 cm (1 foot) between rows. When the plants are up, thin them to 10 cm (4 inches) apart and when they are growing strongly again, sprinkle the original mulch back between the rows to stop weed seeds growing and retain moisture.

Sow in mid-spring. If you sow the seeds too early, they are inclined to 'bolt', run up to seed. When harvesting beetroot, wring, don't cut the tops off before boiling. The tops are equally useful if steamed in the manner of spinach. Grated raw beetroot mixed with grated raw ginger is a surprising and interestingly different flavour for a salad.

CARROT

Many people think that if you are an organic no-dig gardener your carrots will not grow with a long tapering root. This is not true, however, show growers quite often plunge a crowbar deeply into the soil, fill the hole with old compost, then sow a couple of seeds per hole, removing one if they both grow. This ensures that super-tapering root.

Years ago, there used to be a major pitfall in growing carrots. Fresh manure was once the order of the day, and the application of fresh manure in any form causes the carrot roots to fork and split. These days, fresh manure is not so readily available, and seldom used.

Carrots like well-drained, deep soil, in a sunny position. When buying your seed make sure that you have a variety for summer eating, and another for winter storage. Do not sow too early. I used to grow Amsterdam Forcing for summer, Royal Red for winter. Clear the ground over the whole area of your carrot bed and put the mulch in a heap aside for later use. Sow the seeds in drills (the shallow mark in the soil) 1.25 cm (½ inch) deep with 30 cm (1 foot) between the rows.

When they are in visible rows, thin out the winter variety to about 7.5 cm (3 inches) apart, making sure the soil is moist and not too hard. Allow to grow to about 7.5 cm (3 inches) high, then hoe any weeds between the rows, gently loosening the soil. Follow this by replacing some of the heaped mulch between the rows. Generally, about 5 cm (2 inches) is enough. The plants will now grow vigorously. You can add more mulch as the carrots grow.

Sow the summer carrots quite thickly and do not thin out. As soon as they reach that sweet, succulent, fingerling size pull them from along the row to eat raw in salads. This thins the carrots allowing the smaller ones to develop for another day. Make sure you label the rows so that the winter variety is thinned out and grow on for winter use.

Carrots will keep in the soil in a reasonable winter if the soil is well drained and the variety is a winter one.

Again, they're delicious baked or steamed, or even raw.

JERUSALEM ARTICHOKE

Having discussed the globe artichoke, we will now consider the vegetable which I think is one of the most tasty of all the root vegetables. They seem, now, to be seldom grown, and this is a shame, for they are as nutritious as they are tasty. They are members of the sunflower family, with similar, though smaller, yellow flowers.

The very flavoursome root tubers—considerably smaller than the average potato—are super low in calories. An excellent dieters' food. They grow strongly, offering their tall growth as a windbreak, if needed. Because of this tall growth, do not site them alongside sweet corn, forcing them to compete for the sun. They need a moist, well-drained soil in a sunny, open position. Set the tubers 7.5 cm (3 inches) into the soil, allowing 30 cm (1 foot) between plants. Keep them well mulched.

Dig the tubers carefully in the winter and enjoy a rest from the usual unvarying diet of potatoes. This plant is not a perennial, but if you leave a scattering of tubers in the ground and keep plenty of mulch over them, you will have a crop year after year. This plant deserves a place in any vegetable garden. Steamed or baked, they are delicious.

Parsnip

This is a very deep rooting type of plant. Location should be, as with carrots, open and sunny, in a well-drained soil with plenty of old rotted mulch or compost. Parsnips are not fond of too acidic a soil, so use lime or dolomite well beforehand.

Prepare the site in the same way as for carrots. Sow in early spring. I found it best to sow the seed quite thickly, 1.25 cm (½ inch) deep along the drills. Space the rows 30 cm (1 foot) apart. When the seedlings emerge, thin them out to approximately 20 cm (8 inches) between plants.

When the plants have regained vigour after being thinned out carefully surround them with crumbly mulch, compost, or old sawdust between the rows. Parsnip seeds sometimes have poor germination. This is why it is advisable to sow seeds quite thickly and then thin out.

There is no need to dig parsnips to store as they keep very well in the ground. If your ground is likely to be frozen, dig and store, but frosts will not harm them; if anything a frost improves their flavour. When watering parsnips, or any root crops, fewer deeper soaking is far better than a little and often.

Potato: The Mulch Method

The organic method of growing the real 'spud' has proven itself to be superior whenever and wherever used.

Prepare the ground by hoeing out any weeds and letting them lie where they fall. Next, choose the variety of potato you prefer. There are potatoes that are more suited for steaming, others for baking, some are better for chips; some are red, some yellow, while most are white. Obtain your seed from your garden centre and try to get potatoes about the size of a small egg. Do not cut them for this method. It is a good idea to allow them to start a few sprouts before planting, not long, weak yellow shoots, but short, strong green ones from plenty of light.

Place them on—not in—the ground in rows 30 cm (1 foot) between potatoes and the same spacing between rows. This will take nearly double your normal seed potato requirements for the same space.

Now spread straw, any old hay, pea straw, sugar cane, grass hay, or any similar type of mulch over the seed potatoes to a depth of 15 cm (6 inches). It does not matter too much if you inadvertently step on a few potatoes during this process. Shake the mulch so that any weed seeds are buried with the hoed up weeds beneath the mulch. Water well. Potatoes like plenty of water so long as the drainage is good.

When the potato shoots appear through the mulch, spread another 30 cm (1 foot) layer of mulch material over the entire potato patch and water again. If using a dense mulch add only enough to ensure that the growing tubers are always covered. This is essential. It is very important that this extra layer is applied. If, as the mulch breaks down, the potatoes are exposed to sunlight, they will go green. A green potato is poisonous and must be discarded. Remember, the potato is a member of the deadly nightshade family, along with the tomato. Respect this. Keep them well mulched, the tubers covered, and all is well. This applies to any method of growing potatoes.

This is the end of your work. No digging, no hoeing, no ridging up along the rows of potatoes; just watch them grow.

There is a reason for putting on the mulch in two applications. Too much mulch in one go retains the deep soil cold after winter, causing the seed potatoes to grow more slowly. A thinner layer allows the sun to warm the mulch and soil, so the potatoes grow quicker and stronger. You will not need to water the mulched potato bed as often as with the normal method, but check regularly by feeling under the mulch. Do not allow it to dry out. Keep moist, rather than wet.

At harvest time, start at one end of the potato patch, pull the dead and dying potato tops off and remove the mulch by placing it behind you. The potatoes will all be on top of the ground, clean, large and tasty. Work your way across the patch and when all the potatoes have been picked up, it should be mulched by the action of putting it all behind you. To be clear, you take the mulch off a potato plant putting it behind you, then pick up the potatoes and move to the next plant, all the way down a row—then the next row. In this way you replace the mulch as you go. After doing this once, you will get the idea. Spread the potato tops as mulch, then add a few bales of old hay or straw over the top of the old mulch and it is ready, weed free and self-fertilising, for next year's crop.

One of the great advantages of this method is that you can grow potatoes year after year on the same piece of ground, and the potatoes get bigger and better each year. Let me explain this.

Although the potatoes all grow on the ground, not in it, the feeder roots of the seed tuber grow into the soil. Each year the humus in the soil increases, thus the soil fertility is constantly escalating. This results in bigger and better potatoes. After twenty years the results are astonishing! If anyone tells you that you must grow potatoes on fresh ground each year, that applies only to the traditional method. Once I learned about this method, it was the only way I grew potatoes—and always on the same patch.

If you like new potatoes then you can copy Treenie. She used to move a bit of mulch aside, carefully take a few of the biggest potatoes, and then move the hay back so the little ones could continue growing. In Oz, this is called 'Bandicooting!' Potatoes grown by this method are far tastier than any commercial potato, and when cut in half and allowed to dry, shows a far better colour.

For the conscious gardener, the mulch method is a must. It is innovative, engaging your attention, rather than simply following the old traditional way without a thought.

To cook, baked is best!

RADISH

This root is mostly grown as a salad crop for summer use. Radishes like well-drained soil in an open sunny position. Sow in drills 1.25 cm (½ inch) deep in rows 30 cm (1 foot) apart. Either sow very thinly and space them as you use them, or thin out to 5 cm (2 inches) between plants. Radishes can be grown in succession from early spring to late autumn. They must be grown fast with adequate water to obtain a good flavour and crispness.

SWEET POTATO

Purely as a matter of interest, the sweet potato is a member of the *Ipomea* family of climbers, of which the morning glory is probably the best known. It is not a yam, *Dioscorea*, not even related, and, of course, is a totally different species from the ordinary potato, *Solanum*. Personally, I prefer sweet potatoes. I recommend that you buy a few of the different varieties, and let your taste buds select the type you prefer. For me, it is the orange variety, Sweet Gold.

The critical factor here is climate. Sweet potatoes like a long, hot, dryish summer season in full sun. They cannot tolerate frost or cold soil. So, if you don't qualify as a grower, buy some anyway from your local organic shop—and bake them. Very tasty!

For the fortunate people, put six tubers in a tray of shallow water and place in a light position in your house. Now wait for the tubers to sprout. If your climate is marginal, you need not do this until late spring, because one frost will kill them.

Sweet potatoes like a warm, free draining soil. Don't even attempt them in a waterlogged soil. They do not like or need a lot of watering. Just enough. Remove all mulch from the sunny, open area where you intend to grow them and allow the soil to warm up. When all frosts have finished and the soil is warm, take the sprouted tubers from the tray and with a knife carefully remove each sprouting piece complete with a small section of the tuber. Plant the sections of sprouted tubers with the green shoots above the soil, at about 45 cm (18 inches) apart. Now spread all that mulch back around and over them, adding more if necessary. Do not bury the green shoots under dense mulch, but be sure that adequate mulch is applied. Add more mulch as they grow.

Remember, regulate the water, they like it hot and dryish. Harvest the tubers carefully. Don't carelessly stab them with a fork. It is wise to harvest them before frost destroys the abundant vines, or makes the soil too cold. I repeat, sweet potatoes are very vulnerable to the cold.

TURNIP, WHITE AND SWEDE

Prepare soil as with all other root crops. The soil needs to be rich, well drained, and all turnips should be grown in an open sunny position.

Sow in late spring in drills 2.5 cm (1 inch) deep and allow 37 cm (15 inches) between rows. When seedlings emerge, thin out to 15 cm (6 inches.) Mulch as with other root crops.

You can thin white turnips to 10 cm (4 inches) between plants, for they are not as big as swede turnips. The space between rows should always be plentiful, allowing for your feet to move without crushing plants.

Turnips seem to have lost their popularity as a root vegetable, but they are easy to grow and reliable in the winter, especially the swede.

White turnips can be pulled and eaten while young. Any root crops to be eaten young taste better if they grow rapidly with plenty of water.

❧

GREEN VEGETABLES

THE CABBAGE FAMILY

Every member of the cabbage family likes plenty of lime. In other words, they like the pH around neutral, and they like calcium. If your soil is acidic, bring the pH up to 6.5 for all of these lime lovers.

I include here, cabbage, broccoli, Brussels sprouts, cauliflower and kale. I have never grown Chinese cabbage—wong bok—nor have I grown Asian greens—bok choy, pak choy, tatsoi—so I will not write about them.

Everything I have written in this book is from my experience. However, if you treat them as with the smaller cabbages, you should be okay! All these plants need plenty of open space, sunlight, and a well-drained soil.

Most people today buy the cabbage family as young plants in a garden centre. Be wary of cheap supermarket plants. The growers often hurry them along with chemical stimulants for a quick turnover. Although they look all right to an inexperienced eye, when planted out in the full sun they may quickly collapse. This is where conscious gardening comes into its own, for if you *feel into* the energy of the young plants you can *feel* if they have the vitality necessary to survive.

Have the ground well limed (or dolomite) and mulched a few months before you are ready to set your plants. In this way the lime is activating the soil, and the mulch is feeding the soil life well before the plants go in. Once you are into the swing of it, you will have your vegetable garden mulched almost the whole time, with a few heaps next to their seed beds awaiting their moment to return.

Make your row of young plants by parting a space of about 30 cm (1 foot) in the mulch where you want each plant to go. Allow 45 cm (18 inches) between both rows and plants for cabbages, and 60 cm (2 feet) between rows and plants for broccoli, cauliflower, Brussels sprouts and kale. Some gardeners advocate closer planting, but this robust family like room to breathe and grow!

So, we have set our plants directly into the mulched soil by creating a space for the young plant. Into this space, sprinkle a handful of green sawdust around the plant. This is to deter slugs and snails. If you wish, you can set the plants directly into the mulched soil without making a space, but this very much depends on the type and state of your mulch, and the amount of slugs and snails in your garden. Personally, I never had a problem with them, but for some gardeners they are a real pest.

As soon as the plants are growing strongly, you can pull the mulch right up to them, keeping the soil cool and moist, and stopping any weed competition.

I am not going to tell you when to sow or set your cabbage family plants because you will set them when you buy them in the garden centre. They usually have them at the appropriate times, and they are the people to give you advice about local conditions. I can tell you that there are spring, summer, autumn and winter cabbages, so they can be both planted and harvested for much of the year in the right climatic conditions. When planting winter eating greens don't try to be first to get them in. There is no rush. Gardening is not a competition to see who is first, biggest, or most colourful; gardening is a conscious exchange of energy between you and the earth. Don't be first in the Garden Centre; wait a week or so and the young plants will be stronger. Greens planted too early will often be of poorer quality in the winter.

The ideal way is to create as much of a succession as possible. You can do this by choosing early, mid-season and late varieties. And make sure you get the strongest, healthiest, sturdiest plants possible. In fact, don't settle for less, even if you have to go further to look for them. Some garden centres make sure all their plants are top quality, others are not so diligent and sell them cheaper. Avoid forced plants, tall, weak and sappy looking. Slugs and snails love them!

I knew one person who always allowed his container of young

plants to dry out to the point of wilting. He would then set them, watering them well, and they always thrived. His theory was that drier plants offered no attraction to slugs and snails the first few nights, and it worked for him, but the timing would be critical. There is only a small margin between a dried out plant and a very dead plant.

All members of the cabbage family like the same basic treatment. Plants like kale and green or white sprouting broccoli—if you can still get them—all like even more room, for they are large plants. Personally, I am not keen on the modern tight, drumhead type of cabbage. The leaf is all yellow/white inside the tight head, whereas the loose-heading cabbage were green almost right through. And it is the green with its chlorophyll that is so good for you. Nor do I like the large modern hybrid broccoli. To gain such size, the price was loss of flavour. The old green sprouting broccoli were far superior in flavour, if not in yield. Whoever decided that more is better?

To give all these plants a good start it is a good idea to sprinkle a handful of blood and bone to every three plants, before you set them. Keep the plants well watered, but not saturated. This family appreciates moist soil, but does not do well in wet, poorly drained soil.

As I said, you can grow cabbages for eating all the year round, but be sure to get the right variety at the right time. Brussels sprouts are for winter eating only, and are only for cool districts. A frost on the young sprout buttons definitely improves the flavour. Cauliflower can be grown for most of the year, but again, choose the right varieties.

CELERY

Growing celery organically is very different from the traditional method, and much easier. Celery likes a very rich and fertile soil, a sunny site and *plenty* of water. Few people realise that celery is a *marsh* plant.

Young plants can be bought in containers, or the seed can be grown. Clear the ground of mulch and put it in a heap for later use. Sow the seed in drills 1.5 cm (½ inch) deep in rows 37 cm (15 inches) apart. When the seedlings are up, thin out to 20 cm (8 inches) apart. When they are growing strongly, use that mulch to put back between the rows.

In late summer, when the plants are large and reaching toward an edible size, they are ready for blanching. You can use a newspaper wrapped around each plant and secured with string, or old carpet can be cut to size and shape, or clay pipes can be used. My way was to fill in between the rows with masses of mulch right up to the top of the stem, with only the leaves showing.

The leaves can be eaten green, and while it is true that blanched celery loses much of its vitamin C, which is in the green parts of a plant, the green stems of celery have nothing like the flavour, texture and crispness the stalks acquire when blanched.

CHICORY

This is a very different vegetable. It grows as a root vegetable, offers green leaves for pulling, yet ends up eaten as a crisp, white heart vegetable. It is another of those vegetables that lacks the popularity it deserves, although it is much more widely grown and used in Europe than in Oz. To be fair, it is a vegetable that is best grown in a cooler/cold climate.

Prepare the soil as with other root crops, sow in mid-spring in drills 1.25 cm (½ inch) deep, in rows 30 cm (1 foot) apart. Thin seedlings out to 15 cm (6 inches) apart and mulch when plants are growing strong and sturdy. In winter dig a few roots at a time and lightly trim them, then cut the leaves back to within 5 cm (2 inches) of the crown.

Place these upright in a box (a tea chest is ideal) and cover with 30 cm (1 foot) of straw, hay, or any light mulch. The warmer the storage area the better, within reason. The chicory will now grow a new heart. This is cut and is very tasty either in salad or as a cooked vegetable. The roots are discarded. The leaves can also be eaten, steamed like silver beet. Use in summer, pulling a few from each plant. The flavour of the chicory heart is a very different flavour from all other vegetables. Push back your boundaries and give it a try.

KOHLRABI

This is a member of the cabbage family, but with a difference. The soil should be rich from rotted mulch, in a sunny open position. The soil requirements are the same as for cabbage, with lime or dolomite added to the soil well before growing time.

Clear the area to be sown, and pile the mulch in a heap to continue rotting. Sow the seed in mid-spring in drills 1.25 cm (½ inch) deep, spaced 37 cm (15 inches) between rows. Thin the seedlings out to 15 cm (6 inches) apart. Give kohlrabi plenty of water, and when big enough bring back that heap of mulch. They need to grow fast. This is the secret of good flavour.

The plant has a turnip-like appearance and you eat the purplish swelling globe which grows just above the ground. Eat this when it is about tennis ball to fist sized. Too big and old and they get tougher. This is yet another plant that deserves to be more widely grown. The flavour is very cabbage, but with a difference. Steamed is best. I like it.

LETTUCE

Lettuce comes in a huge variety, with textures, colours, shapes, sizes and flavours that are all different. Some specialise in mild/warm climates, others in cool/cold, so the varieties you choose are going to be a major contributor to your success or failure in growing them.

It would be difficult to say whether the average gardener prefers seeds to sow or plants to buy, so we will cover both. Without any doubt, seed is by far the most economical. I used to buy cabbage plants and lettuce seed.

Lettuce needs a rich, moist, cool, open soil. Basically, the lettuce is a cool climate plant, and although it has been developed to tolerate heat, it is best grown in winter in subtropical and tropical climates. Generally, if you have lettuces growing in conditions that are too warm, they quickly go to seed without developing that typical lettuce heart.

Lettuce are shallow rooted plants, so any compost you can provide is well rewarded. Clear the lettuce bed of any mulch and heap it up to rot and decay. Sow the seed thinly 1.5 cm (½ inch) deep in drills 30 cm (1 foot) apart. Thin the seedlings out 15–35 cm (6–14 inches) depending on the size of the variety you are growing. Some gardeners mix the seed with a little fine, dry sand to get a better spacing between plants. This works very effectively.

When the seedlings are strong and sturdy, mulch with old sawdust or a well-rotted, crumbly, mulching material. If plants have been purchased, make sure that they are strong and sturdy, sun hardened, not leggy and weak. Look at the soil in the container; if it is all sand you can be sure these plants have been boosted along with chemical stimulants, and they will quickly collapse in the garden. Be sure that they are growing in a good potting mix, not one that is mostly sawdust.

Set the plants out in the evening, preferably one that is not about to rain. That makes it a bit too easy for the slugs and snails! If setting in a mulched bed clear a row about 30 cm (1 foot) wide and set the seedlings at an average of 22 cm (9 inches) apart in a moist soil. Next, sprinkle green or dressed timber sawdust 5 mm (1/8 inch) deep all around the plants, covering the soil in the whole row to keep slugs and snails away. Almost always, slugs and snails are attracted to transplanted seedlings far more than they are to plants grown from seed and thinned out. This applies to any type of plant.

I used a method that was rather popular. Simply sow, as thin as possible, a band of lettuce seed onto the soil about 30 cm (1 foot) wide and lightly rake over. This provides a lot of delicious green lettuce leaves and almost no heart.

Enjoy your organically grown salad, filled with your own good vibes.

SILVER BEET

This plant is always good value, providing both stalk and leaf in autumn and early winter. It likes rich, moist, well-drained soil. Sow the seeds just as for spinach. When the plants are growing strongly, thin out to 22 cm (9 inches) between plants. They are usually bigger and more robust than spinach. When they are again growing strongly, put that heap of mulch back up each row, right up to the plants. Silver beet grown this way will reward you with plenty of tender stems.

The white stalks should be held at the base of the stem and pulled firmly away from the plant. Never cut. The white stems are best steamed separately. The green leaves need very little time steaming, and if cooked with the stems, they tend to end up rather soggy.

Silver beet has been bred to grow and produce all the year round, but in my humble opinion, the autumn/winter version is best.

SPINACH

Popeye's 'strength' food! Spinach is another vegetable that has a preference for a cool/cold climate, so that makes it a winter grown plant in most regions. Spinach requires a very rich soil and an abundance of plant food. If you can, position it in a cool part of the garden, because spinach does not like heat. As it is a winter crop, sow in autumn.

If using mulch—and you should be!—clear the area to be sown and put the mulch in a heap to decay ready for use. Sow the seed in drills 2.5 cm (1 inch) deep and 15 cm (6 inches) between rows. When the plants are growing strongly, thin out to 10 cm (4 inches) between plants, and when they are again growing strongly, replace the mulch back between the rows.

Spinach likes a cool soil, so the mulch not only feeds the soil, but it also keeps the soil cool. The reason you allow time before putting mulch back is because when plants are thinned from a thick row they are white and weakened, making them more vulnerable to slug and snail attack. Left exposed for a week or two they quickly harden off.

Be sure to get a winter variety of the true spinach. With all the hybridizing taking place, spinach and its silver beet cousin will quite likely be turned into something that loses the qualities of both. Hopefully I was not too influenced by Popeye, but for me, of all green vegetables, spinach stands out above the rest. I eat my share! Steam it lightly, and remember, although you fill a huge saucepan, you only get a cupful to eat!

WATERCRESS

This is a rarely grown cool/cold climate plant that is probably one of the most nutritious of all green plants. Like spinach, the leaves are rich in natural organic iron, making it a valuable addition to our diet.

If you live in the country and have a stream or a water hole on your property, then you can grow an abundance of it. Otherwise it is easy to grow in a watertight container. These days you can get polystyrene boxes from your local Fruit and Vegetable shop. They seem to have heaps of them. If it's the type with slits in, you only need lay a piece of polythene sheet over it. Put about 10 cm (4 inches) of a good rich soil into the box, then fill with water to about 2.5 cm (1 inch) over the soil. Maintain it at this depth always.

Now buy some watercress at your fruit and vegetable shop and set the stems into the soil. In wet weather place a sheet of glass over the box to prevent it filling, or even better, make a few large holes so that the water overflows at the required depth.

Pick the leaves when they are young and tender. In cold climates this is a good summer crop, while in the subtropics it is ideal for winter. I sometimes grew watercress for Treenie. She loved it.

FRUITING VEGETABLES

AUBERGINE

Often known as eggplant—for obvious reasons—I wish I could make a bit more razzmatazz about this very tasty fruiting plant, but the culture is exactly the same as for capsicums. It may grow a bit taller, and it needs a rich, organic soil, but all the conditions are similar. It's very tasty when stuffed and baked.

CAPSICUM

The pepper family is both widely known and grown offering great value in salads and when cooked. This plant is very frost tender and should be set out at the same time as tomatoes.

Clean the area of mulch and put it in a heap ready for further use. Grow in an open sunny, well-drained position. Set plants 45 cm (18 inches) apart in rows spaced at 60 cm (2 feet) apart. When the plants are growing strongly, bring back the mulch, spreading it thickly around the plants. Capsicums do not like strong wind and benefit from some shelter. When the fruit is colouring, yet still firm to the touch, they can be picked. Depending on the variety, the fruit can be yellow, red or green.

Interestingly, cayenne pepper (a capsicum), which is one of the hot chilli peppers is the best heart protection that you can ingest. I have been taking tincture of cayenne in a glass of water first thing in the morning for many years. I recognise how positively my heart and body responds to it. Cayenne opens the arteries, veins and capillaries, while coffee restricts them, yet both appear to give that energy surge. Cayenne is a positive surge, while unfortunately, coffee is negative. Despite that, I still enjoy a cappuccino! For those who want to grow any of the many chilli peppers, the culture is the same as described for capsicum. Same family!

CUCUMBER

I will assume that we are growing this family of plants from seed, although a lot of young plants are sold in the garden centres. The first thing to remember is not to be hasty. Clean the mulch away from the soil where you plan to grow them, and allow the sun to warm the soil. Be sure to wait until all frosts have finished. This will be at different times in the spring according to your area. When the soil has been warmed by the sun, we are ready to begin.

We need a moist, well-drained soil in an open area. Cucumbers love rich organic matter in the soil and will thrive in a heap of compost. Also make sure the soil is enriched with some blood and bone. As a conscious gardener, you can feel the plants getting excited over rich, fertile soil! Cucumbers do not like acid soil, although they can tolerate some acidity. So add lime or dolomite well ahead of your planting time.

The best method for organic culture that I found was to lay a strip of compost across the vegetable garden, or to place a series of heaps of compost across the garden. Make the strip or heaps about 45 cm (18 inches) wide, or square, and about 10 cm (4 inches) deep. Press the seeds into this 1.5 cm (½ inch) deep, and about 30 cm (1 foot) apart in the rows, or about 3 seeds to a heap.

When they are growing strongly, make sure they are not too close together, and then put all that delicious mulch back piling it up really close. Allow the runners out only about 30 cm (1 foot) or so on either side of the plant. This seems to force a lot more flowering, hence more of the fruit. Of course, you can also grow them up a lattice fence, or make your own support. Cucumbers are very effective climbers.

It is best to let them reach a good size before picking, but not mature enough to start going yellow, when they become rather bitter. Grown quickly in good conditions, they are sweet and tasty. There are quite a few hybrids available now, so try a few different types.

PUMPKIN

All gardeners are aware of how easy these are to grow and of their value as both a summer and winter food. In an open, sunny position, make a 'hill' 1 m sq (3 feet sq) and about 30 cm (1 foot) high of any old rotted animal manure and rotted mulch. Prepare this in early to mid-winter, ready for late spring. Preparation is literally the name of the game for successfully growing vegetables. If manure is unobtainable—and you can buy it in plastic bags at your garden centre—then use rotted mulch with a fair bit of blood and bone mixed in. The hills will be matured and settled by late spring, and warmed by the sun.

Sow three pairs of seeds to each hill, and take away the weak one from each pair when they are growing. Pumpkins run over a lot of ground, so I consider a couple of hills is enough for the average family. It is possible to grow different varieties of pumpkin on the same hill, providing they have the same pattern of growth. To put a vigorous runner with a smaller, clumping type would spell its demise. It is easy to keep your own seed if you get a variety you really like, but pumpkins cross-pollinate with each other, so the seed will not grow true to type unless you grow only one variety.

When harvesting summer pumpkins—and there are many varieties— pick as often as possible to keep them flowering and new pumpkins coming along. For the winter varieties, allow them to grow to full size and mature. Make sure you leave 5 cm (2 inches) of stalk attached to the pumpkin and store in a cool, dry place.

Winter pumpkins have a huge range of flavours from the dry, tart, Queensland Blue to the strange curved shape of the sweet Gramma. My choice is the trusty Butternut. They keep an amazingly long time if harvested carefully without bruising the flesh.

We leave this whole family with the reminder that these plants require a lot of water, plenty of sunlight and, if possible, a good flow of air. In my experience they are all best watered in the early morning so that the leaves are dry at night. This helps to control mildew, as many of these plants grow such a dense mass of leaves the air can become stagnant within the plant. This encourages fungal diseases. In spells of wet weather it can help to judiciously remove some of the older, yellowing leaves to assist air flow around the plants.

Tomato

We will begin with the best known and probably most popular of all the fruiting vegetables. Today, most growers buy their tomato plants from their local garden centre, where there is a wide selection of varieties. It is of the utmost importance that you choose strong, green healthy plants. Reject any spindly, leggy, yellowish forced plants. They would be costly if they were given to you and you had to grow them! Pay more for good plants. This is better than replacing cheap ones.

Remember that tomato plants are frost tender. They are a warm climate plant. It is advisable in cool/cold climates to give the young plants protection when you first set them out; chilling wind or frost can delay their growth, stunt them, or even kill them. They can be protected in a number of ways. One of the simplest is by purchasing a few metres of clear polythene tubing, cutting it into 60 to 90 cm (2 to 3 foot) lengths—depending on the size of the plants—and slipping this over 3 strong stakes in the ground.

The tomato needs and loves a rich, moist soil filled with organic matter and humus. Aware gardeners prepare the tomato soil many months ahead, making sure the soil is as good as possible. In the winter dig a trench 30 cm (1 foot) deep and in rows 25 cm (10 inches) apart. Fill in the trenches with any old manure and rotted mulch, adding blood and bone. Then cover them with the displaced soil, heaped along the rows. This should ensure that your tomatoes will be top quality and abundant. Be sure the site is sunny and open.

By late spring the rows will have settled, filled now with rich, fertile compost. Set the young tomato plants 45 to 60 cm (18 to 24 inches) apart in rows 75 cm (2 ½ feet) wide. The spacing depends entirely on the size and vigour of the variety you are growing. I suggest that you experiment with a wide variety as they can be very different in flavour.

If growing tall varieties, like tree tomatoes, be sure to set the tomato plant in its hole with the stake already in position. Driving a stake in afterwards cuts and damages the roots, often leading to a plant wilting and dying later when a fungal disease attacks the damaged roots. Bush tomatoes generally need no support, but be sure of the requirements of your varieties before you plant them. Tie the tree tomato carefully to the stake as it grows. Keep them regularly watered. When the plants are fruiting, irregular water often causes distorted and split tomatoes.

Mulch right up to the base of the plants when they are growing strongly at about 45 cm (18 inches) high, and the ground is thoroughly warmed. Tucking the mulch in tight to the base of the plant as it grows encourages the development of base feeder roots up the first 15 cm (6 inches) of the main stem. These secondary roots can be valuable in feeding the developing fruit.

Pinch out shoots that grow from the base of leaf stalks in the tree varieties only, and pinch out the top of the plant when it reaches to the top of the tomato stake, or when the plant has five to six trusses of fruit on it. Pick fruit when it begins to ripen, do not wait until over ripe before picking.

Do not remove the leaves to allow the sun on the fruit. The plant breathes through its leaves. This is a common practice that offers nothing except a depleted plant. The fruit does not need sun to ripen it; it needs warmth. Pick the fruit when it is turning red, or yellow, depending on the variety, and allow it to ripen in a warm place in the house.

Tomatoes respond magnificently to organic culture, rewarding the gardener with a fruit tasting far beyond anything grown commercially. They are also worth the extra trouble of winter preparation of the soil, for the nutritional value of the tomato rates highly. Choose the varieties that are best for your locality, and grow early, mid-season and late varieties to extend the season for as long as possible.

One last thing: An organically grown tomato has a superior flavour all its own. Never, never, never refrigerate tomatoes while they are being kept. It drastically impairs and reduces their unique flavour.

ZUCCHINI, COURGETTE AND MARROW

In Oz we call them zucchini, while in Europe they are courgettes. But they are the same plant, with the same tasty fruit. Every gardener should grow these. They are easy to grow, and highly nutritious.

Sow them in exactly the same way that I have described for cucumbers, but allow about 60 cm (2 feet) between plants. If you buy them as seedlings, again make sure they are sturdy, green, and strong. Set them at the same spacings as if you were thinning seeds. Zucchini do not climb like cucumbers, but grow into sturdy clumps. Generally, six plants would be enough for the average family. I always found them much easier to grow than cucumbers, which is really a warm climate plant. Zucchini have large, rough, dark green leaves and fruit prolifically.

Herein lies the secret; they must be picked constantly to continue cropping. Unpicked, they get bigger and bigger, and fewer of them. Cut the fruit from the plant when they are about 15 cm (6 inches) long. The more you pick them the more they crop. If you allow them to reach full size, as much as 60 to 90 cm (2 to 3 feet) they will not taste as good and gradually stop production.

My favourite way to eat them is to slice thinly with the skin on and fry in butter. They have a definite mushroom flavour and are very yummy.

They're one of my favourite vegetables.

A zucchini is actually a type of marrow that you eat while young and undeveloped. A marrow is grown the same way, but you leave the fruit to fully ripen and mature. No longer common, yet they are very good stuffed and baked. If you grow this plant, make sure you get true marrow seed. You do not want an overgrown zucchini.

POD, SEED & BULBOUS VEGETABLES

BROAD BEAN

These like open, unshaded ground, very rich in mulch or compost. Sow the seed in drills 15 cm (6 inches) between plants and about 60 cm (2 feet) between rows. Press the bean into the soil approximately 2.5 cm (1 inch) deep. If you are using mulched ground it depends on the condition of the mulch. If it is well rotted and crumbly, the beans can be pushed directly into it, and that is all that is needed. If it is fresh mulch, pull it all away and put in a heap ready to mulch back around the beans when they are growing strongly. This is at around 15 cm (6 inches) high.

Broad beans can be sown in the early winter in mild districts, but wherever you are, it is desirable to have plants growing strongly by the end of winter.

Grown in mulch, broad beans are more resistant to aphids. When the flowers have set, pinch out the growing points to force the plants' energy and growth into the pods. Keep them well watered, in a well-drained soil. Pick the beans while young and tender. Older is tougher.

DWARF BEAN

Also known as French beans. They like a rich, moist, well-drained soil, in an open sunny position. You may prepare the soil for these in the same way as for broad beans. Dwarf beans are not quite so frost tender as runners, but be careful. Sow at 2.5 cm (1 inch) deep in a strip of cleaned ground in a double staggered row about 22 cm

(9 inches) apart. When the plants are growing strongly, replace all the mulch.

Sometimes the heavily cropping plants can get top-heavy. If this happens tuck wedges of straw or old hay, or any bulky mulch, all around them for support. This also helps to prevent wind from twisting and whipping heavily bearing plants around. These crop earlier than runners, therefore making a succession of beans for you to enjoy.

Pick while young and stringless. Tie in little bundles with cotton and steam them. Serve a bundle or two per person.

RUNNER BEAN

These excellent vegetables like a rich, moist soil and an open, sheltered position. Because these are climbing beans, they are going to need a support on which to climb. Two metre (6 feet) high, three-legged tripods work well, with two plants to each leg. Or they can be grown up a simple frame. I grew them on a permanent frame with great success. I put a 2 metre high post at each end of the row, with a long piece of wood fixed atop of each post. You could use strong wire stretched across the top. Into the overhead beam I hammered a row of staples at about 15 cm (6 inches) apart. Using wire, I stretched it from one post to the other about 15 cm off the ground. Then I tied a piece of strong baling string from each staple down to the wire at the base, securing both ends. Equally, if you have a supply of bamboo, you could make a row with a couple of plants to each bamboo stake.

Having decided on your method of support, the next step is sowing the seed. If you are an early type, make sure that the young shoots do not come through the ground while the nights are frosty. Runners are very prone to late frosts in the spring.

Sow the beans just buried at 7.5 cm (3 inches) apart. When they are growing strongly remove alternate plants—you will have no gaps this way—and then mulch the plants with plenty of rotted mulch.

If you want to grow runner beans but have no way of supporting them, you can constantly pinch out the growing tips forcing them to grow into a bush form. I have had great success doing this, but they are more prone to slugs and snails on the pods.

Keep the plants watered using the sprinkler regularly. This also has the effect of helping the flowers to more reliably set pods, especially in very hot weather. Pick your runner beans constantly, and pick them young and tender. The bigger they get, the tougher they are.

Cool/cold climates have runner beans that are best suited to those conditions, i.e., Scarlet Runner, while mild/warm climates also have runners more suited to the warmth, i.e. Blue Lakes.

CHIVE

This small onion plant has value in every garden, but it does have a preference for a cooler climate. It need not be grown in the vegetable garden as, owing to its appearance and pretty flowers, it looks good in the flower bed.

There are two types of the easily obtainable plants, dwarf and large. Both are equally good, but with different flavours. Set bulbs of young plants about 15 cm (6 inches) apart for dwarf, and double that for the large.

Cut the young green stems and eat in salads, coleslaw and sandwiches. Have enough plants so that as you harvest them they can easily recover and regrow.

GARLIC

This very popular bulb likes a rich soil that is well drained. Grown as a border plant around your vegetable garden, garlic is a very good pest deterrent. It is said that rabbits will not go through a row of garlic owing to its very pungent odour. The strong odour is also good at masking the scents of other vegetables, helping deter pest insects.

The bulbs can be bought in any supermarket, but be sure to get the common variety. The variety Russian Giant is too mild to benefit the palate. Break the large bulb down into the small cloves, and plant at about 15 cm (6 inches) apart in a staggered row at 2.5 cm (1 inch) deep.

Harvest and store as for onions. I have read respectable research which indicates that garlic has the effect of confusing left and right hemisphere brain coordination. People who meditate will find it far easier without garlic in their system. Equally, for intense concentration, do not eat garlic. Psychics also will find that garlic has a detrimental effect on their focus. For me, garlic is an excellent medicine, not a food.

Leek

Still in the onion family, but with the leek we eat the stem, which is a bit like an elongated bulb! This popular plant is grown mainly for use in the winter. However, they are sold as both plant and seed in the summer months, so we will address the culture of both.

They like a well-drained soil in a sunny, open position. Rake aside some mulch to prepare a small area for sowing. I used to clear about 1 metre square (3 feet sq), and broadcast the seed quite thickly over this area, and then rake the soil. The seedlings grow into good sturdy plants using this method. When they are about 15 to 22 cm (6 to 9 inches) tall, select the required amount of the strongest plants for transplanting.

Prepare the well-mulched leek bed for planting by making 15 cm (6 inches) wide rows through the mulch, spaced 30 cm (1 foot) apart. Next, using a sharp pointed dibber, make a row of holes 15 cm (6 inches) deep and 15 cm apart. Drop one seedling into each hole, and then fill the holes with water. When the seedlings are growing strongly, close the mulch up to the plants, add more if necessary, and keep moist.

When the plants have reached a good size in early winter,

it is time to blanch them. The stem of a leek needs to be white to make it both tender and tasty. Some people use a whole newspaper wrapped around the stem and tied in place, other people use a clay pipe by pushing the leaves through it. You could also use old carpet cut to fit. My method is virtually the same as for celery. When the plants are strong in early winter, fill the space between the rows at least 30 cm (1 foot) deep with mulch. Straw, hay, old sawdust, leaves, or any combination can be used. It blanches the stems and feeds the soil at the same time.

Leeks are most useful in mid-to-late winter when other vegetables are getting a bit scarce. They are delicious in casseroles, coleslaw or soup. My choice of variety is Musselburgh.

ONION

So, having dealt with the pods and seeds, we come now to the bulbous plants. Of these, the grand champion is undoubtedly the onion. Luckily, this valuable vegetable family is easily grown.

Onions like a rich moist soil with exceptionally good drainage. If the ground puddles, don't bother to grow them for they will quickly rot. Clear the area of mulch and heap it up, but this time you will not be putting it back on the onion bed so you can use it elsewhere.

Sow the seed in drills 1.25 cm (½ inch) deep in rows 30 cm (1 foot) apart. If using plants, take them from their containers and set them a fraction deeper than their original depth. For onions, seed is best.

Thin out the young seedlings, allowing 15 cm (6 inches) between the plants. It is important *not to mulch* the onion bed. If you should have a supply of wood ash from winter fires, it is good to spread thinly over the soil around the onions. Keep the plants watered, moist, not saturated.

Although onions require plenty of nitrogen, make sure that you apply it to the soil well before sowing time. This is all part of preparing any bed well before sowing or planting time.

As the onions grow it is important that any hoeing or cultivation does not hill up around the bulbs, as this causes a thick stem at the expense of the bulb. When the onions are mature, the stems should be bent over so they can quickly dry off. Any thick-stemmed plants should be discarded, as they will not keep.

Always choose a suitable variety for winter storage. There are many varieties and types of onions, and summer onions will not keep for the winter. Personally, I liked Brown Spanish for storage. An easy way of storing onions once they are thoroughly dry is to fill an old stocking with them and hang it up. The free flow of air keeps them very well. Make a small hole in the toe of the stocking to remove the onions as you use them, sealing it with a clothes peg.

Of the summer onions I always grew, White Lisbon, sowing them thickly in a band and pulling for spring onions and for use with salads. Now, we buy the milder red onions for salads and omelettes. Onions are reputedly good for warding off winter colds. Happily, they are also very tasty.

PEA

They tell me that the pea is a tasty, succulent vegetable, but I have a strong reaction to all legumes. However, this rewarding vegetable is easy to grow and should be in all vegetable gardens. Peas need a rich, moist, well-drained soil, and will grow well in partial shade; they enjoy cool conditions.

Prepare the ground by clearing 30 cm (1 foot) rows in the mulch, spacing the rows 60 cm (2 feet) apart. Sow peas 2.5 cm (1 inch) deep, allowing 5 cm (2 inches) between plants. There are many varieties for early and late crops, so you choose according to your locality.

When the peas are growing they should always be given some support of which to clamber, i.e., brushwood, any open netting, sticks, whatever is easiest and available. When they are growing strongly, put back the mulch and keep well watered.

While it is normal to wait for the pods to swell with young peas, the sugar pea is best eaten as a sweet, flat pod. Peas should always be picked when young and sweet—according to Treenie, who ate them! Apparently, organically grown peas have a flavour all of their own.

SHALLOT AND ESCHALLOT

Shallots do not seem to be grown as much now, which is a pity for they are milder than onions and good for older people who find it more difficult to digest the onion.

The position of the site and soil preparation is the same as with onions. Set the shallot bulbs—you can buy them at a supermarket in the food section—spaced at 10 cm (4 inches) in rows 30 cm (1 foot) apart. Harvest as for onions and store in a similar way. The shallot has a very delicate flavour, and is well worth growing. If you can only get seed, sow some in a block, and when they are good-sized seedlings, pull and transplant as described.

The eschallot is actually rather different. Again, sow and/or plant as with the other onions. Eschallot develop into a whole cluster of stems and are eaten as a young growing onion rather than for storing. This makes them a useful plant, especially for salads. Again, a more delicate flavour than young onions, and well worthy of growing.

SWEET CORN

Sweet corn needs to be grown quickly, and is a demanding plant. It requires a very rich soil, able to hold moisture, but well drained, and in a sunny, open position. It needs all the sun it can get. Sweet corn should be grown in a block for pollination reasons. A single row will mostly lead to a disappointing lack of cobs.

Sow the seed when all frosts have finished at 2.5 cm (1 inch) deep in drills 15 cm (6 inches) apart for about four to six rows. The shorter the rows and wider the block, the better, within reason. Allow about 60 cm (2 feet) as a walkway between blocks and sow another block, if required. The other advantage of a block is that they create their own wind support. Space the young plants to about 15 cm (6 inches) in the rows. When the young plants are about 15 cm (6 inches) high, hoe and clean the block, sprinkle blood and bone and potash at the ratio of 8 parts blood and bone to one part potash at one handful per sq metre (sq yard). Finally, mulch between the rows with a thick crumbly, well-rotted mulch.

Sweet corn likes plenty of water and sun. Water and warmth are the essentials to a good crop. Do not sow too early. It is best to grow a succession of three or four blocks, allowing two to three weeks between each sowing.

The way to tell when the cobs are ripe is to expose some corn and press it with your thumb nail. If the liquid pressed out is milky, then it is perfect for picking. If it is clear, wait a few more days. Remember to harvest it as you eat it. Once cut the sugars quickly turn to starches and lose nutritional value, as well as that incredible sweetness of fresh corn.

From plant to plate, that's the method. While most people like their corn steamed, believe me, it is far tastier if you eat it raw. Fresh and raw sweet corn straight from the garden would have to be the finest flavour of any vegetable. Honey sweet, my mouth waters just thinking about it!

Vegetables for Flat & Unit Dwellers

Before I finish this section on organic vegetables, I would like to consider the people with no garden, but who would like to grow just a few of their own vegetables. This is very important for some people, and I would like to encourage them.

This is definitely possible. Just as you can grow pot plants, so you can grow some pot vegetables. If you have a verandah or a very light position near a large window, quite a number of salad and/or sandwich vegetables can be grown to the benefit of your health and well-being. I say 'well-being' because psychologically, just being involved with growing plants, especially for food, induces a feeling of well-being. By being involved with plants, getting soil on your hands, watching the plants grow and interacting with living plants is beneficial for you emotionally, mentally and spiritually, not to mention the physical benefits of the activity.

With the use of a few large pots, small tubs and plant troughs, you can be involved with Nature and grow some of your own food. Purchase a few bags of *top quality* potting soil at your garden centre, and take it home ready to fill your pots. Before you do this, make sure that your pots have good drainage, that they are standing on something suitable—a tough rubberised door mat is good—and that you have a base container of enough depth to catch minor drainage. Actually, large water-well pots are ideal. You have no drainage problems, and with the water-well topped up your plants have a constant supply of water. You can also add a teaspoon of liquid organic fertiliser to this occasionally. Water-well troughs are also obtainable. It is worth adding that you can now get inexpensive plant pot stands that have little wheels, so you can move your pots about as you need. This is very good, especially when the sun is too hot and harsh through a window, or the wind too fierce on the verandah. If you are elderly, or have difficulty with heavier than usual items, or find it difficult to get this set up, I am sure you have a relative, neighbour or friend who will assist you. Just ask!

Okay, with all that in place, now you can put the potting mixture into the pots, leaving a good 5–7 cm (2–3 inches) of rim visible. You are now ready for planting. As a start, I suggest several chives—for a perennial supply of that tasty onion flavour—in a pot, along with a couple of plants of parsley; Champion Moss Curled is ideal. Or, you can have a pot of just chives, as they are a long-lasting perennial, and a pot of parsley and basil.

If you like mint, this is easy to grow in a pot; you could have Spearmint, Peppermint and Apple-mint all in one trough. Mint tea, very nice!

In a trough or pot, you can have some baby carrots and baby

lettuce together, all to be eaten young and tender. You can grow dwarf bush tomatoes and radish, and a smaller pot of thyme just for flavouring salads and soups. As you grow these, so you can experiment further. Generally, all these would be best on a verandah, but that big light window is also possible. If grown in front of a window, I suggest you have pots on wheels, and turn the pots around daily.

All these plants can be grown snug and close, and can be bought as young plants in a punnet. They will grow easily and provide you with both fresh, homegrown nourishment, and some exercise and activity. Plus you reap the benefit of being consciously involved with Nature.

The growing plants will need sun, but they will not want, or need, to be exposed to it all day. If you are growing them on an exposed sunny or windy verandah, rig up some shade or shelter with an old sheet or shade cloth for the mid-summer afternoons. In very shady locations, try to give your plants as much sun and light as possible. In the summer, morning sun is always preferable to afternoon sun.

When your vegetables have been harvested, cut the remaining part of the plant away just below the surface with a knife. Add a bit of potting soil if necessary, and you are ready to plant again. And you will have no problems with slugs and snails! The plant root left in the pot will decay into organic matter. Make sure to rotate the growing sequence as best you can, i.e., lettuce and carrots change over with tomatoes and radish, rather than lettuce, lettuce, lettuce all the time. This will discourage any disease.

Keep the soil moist, *not saturated,* and make sure drainage is good. Never let the container under your pot be full of water all the time, it means you are over-watering. More often than not, pot plants are ruined by too much water rather than not enough. This is where the water-well pots are supreme. If in doubt, always let common sense prevail.

Get inspired! This is a simple healthy hobby that can consciously and enjoyably connect you with Nature.

So there you have it . . . high-rise veggies! Enjoy.

GARDEN MAGIC!

Did you notice that with every type of vegetable, no matter how different, a good well-drained soil rich in organic matter is essential? Over and over you realise that water, drainage, fertility and sunshine are the magical ingredients of growth. Magical . . . why magical?

When freely draining water is combined with a rich fertile soil, an alchemy is involved. Add sunshine to the mix, stir in a little warmth, and you would have a difficult job stopping Nature from producing life with such a magical mixture. Please, don't tell me you don't believe in magic! If you are one of those unfortunate people, and you own a garden, I suggest you spend a lot more time *being with* the garden, instead of just the usual working in the garden.

Time spent doing what you love is not work; it is both a great privilege and an honour to own or rent a piece of land in which you can participate in the grand art of gardening. We are the magic of life, you and I, but it is passion that ignites the magic, releasing it into the world.

Vegetables grown organically and eaten fresh are incomparable to commercial vegetables. It is not that commercial growers do it badly, but their main focus is growing money, while the home organic growers' focus is growing food. When we eat fresh organic food, we are eating the very energy of life, a life force, something that cannot be measured in any way other than in the health of the grower/consumer.

If only food was all we need for good health. It is said we are what we eat, but I dispute this. We are what we think, and our thinking will affect our choice of food. An angry person is a person with angry thoughts, even if unspoken. This will affect the choice of what they eat, mostly tending toward sweet and fat. It's called emotional eating. Fresh and organic food is not attractive to people with anger, anxiety, or negative thinking. And unfortunately, negative junk thinking is all too common—hence, the attraction to junk food.

Grow top quality organic vegetables, but practice 'being with' the garden and the work as you are sowing your seeds or setting the plants. Cultivate a feeling of being One with the garden, One with the earth, One with all Nature. As much as possible, quiet your thoughts and simply focus on what you are doing; you are involved in the miracle of growth.

Let a fair measure of that growth be yours!

SCRUMPTIOUS SOFT FRUIT

As a gardener who now lives in the subtropics, I am rather miffed that the berry fruits are basically cool/cold climate fruits. Of course, with hybridisation, we now have subtropical strawberries, and even a seldom grown raspberry, but they are winter fruiting and—sorry about this as I am—they are inferior in flavour to their counterparts grown in a cold climate.

Overall, the berry and currant fruits are small plants—compared to a fruit tree—and collectively are generally categorised as 'soft fruit'.

At least some of the family of soft fruits should have, and deserve, a place in the garden, even at the expense of some flowering shrubs. After all, soft fruits give us flowers and fruit. There is a large range of soft fruits, all easily grown and high in nutrition. Most of them can be quickly frozen and preserved, and they are fun to grow, fun to pick, and even more fun to eat. And fun should be the very essence of gardening, especially conscious gardening.

When I lived in Tasmania, I grew every one of these soft fruits, with the exception of blueberries and red currants. In those days blueberry plants were still comparatively scarce, and I did not like red currants! But picking the cold, dew-wet raspberries early in the morning, popping them into my mouth and biting into that explosion of sweet tartness still remains as a fond memory.

The advantage of all these soft fruits is that they do not take up a lot of room. They copiously reward you with their fruit, they offer their bounty year after year, and they are easy to grow. And remember, if or when you freeze any of the berry fruit, do not thaw them at room temperature. Put them into a pie, or however you are using them, while frozen so they thaw with the cooking. This way they have the texture and taste of fresh berries. Berries thawed in the room go mushy, losing flavour.

I have also included a soft fruit that is ideal for the mild areas right up to the tropics. Really, what more could you ask for?

This, then, is their organic culture.

BLACKBERRY

Although this is really a cool/cold climate plant, it is tolerant. When we lived in a warm/temperate zone, temporarily living in a rented house, I was given a thornless blackberry plant in a pot. The accompanying label said it was perfect for growing in a hanging basket. Knowing the blackberry from way back, I ignored this and planted it out along a suitable garden fence. A year later, as I admired the thick, strong vines reaching over 6 m (19 feet), I speculated on how ridiculous the label's recommendation was. Be warned!

The delicious juicy fruit of a blackberry is more than worthy of any garden, and certainly worth the effort to put the support system in place. Generous with its fruit, uniquely flavoured, I really like the blackberry.

Dig a couple of holes in the ground 9 m (30 feet) apart. Secure two strong posts 1.5 m (5 feet) high with concrete. Don't worry, this is a once only! The distance can be somewhat varied according to the space you have. Stretch and secure a wire, fencing wire, along the top between the posts, with another wire 30 cm (1 foot) below it and yet another the same spacing below that. You now have three stretched wires between the posts in the upper section. From the base of the posts, stretch and secure one more wire 45 cm (18 inches) above ground. You are now ready for the plant.

I recommend you buy a thornless variety for ease of handling.

Set the plant in a well-drained soil rich in organic matter. It has no pH fussiness. Set the blackberry plant—one is enough—in the centre, right between the posts. As the first year's vines grow, train them up and secure them along the top three wires, sending no more than six vines in each direction. Remove any excess vines as soon as they emerge.

In the second year, while these vines are flowering and fruiting, tie the new season's vines in a bunch along the bottom wire, again allowing no more than six vines in either direction. Remove excess shoots. When the fruiting has finished, so are the fruiting vines, so cut out these old vines and discard them. Now, bring the waiting vines from the lower wire to the top three wires, and secure. And so you proceed each year, all neat and tidy, plus an abundance of delicious fruit.

Never allow more than twelve vines to a plant. This ensures large, plump, juicy fruit. As I said, cut away all excess vines as they appear. Keep moist, mulched, and well fed with 8:1 blood/bone and potash. Do not allow the lower vines in waiting to lie on the ground. They will grow roots at the tips and dig in. This is, of course, how you get new vines. When the top vines reach the full length of the wire support, tip them to encourage side shoots. These are the fruiting laterals.

Again, I recommend a thornless variety; they are a treat to work with and the flavour of the fruit is 'full on' blackberry. It takes one morning to set up the support system, and you get fruit, literally, every year after. I recommend picking the fruit before the sun reaches them in the morning. Oh, and birds like them, too. Out with the soft netting.

Loganberries and Boysenberries are both very similar to the blackberry, with some variation in the flavour and colour and size of the fruit. If either of these are to your liking, you grow them in exactly the same way as for the blackberry.

BLUEBERRY

Now here is a berry with a flavour of distinction. Unfortunately it is a plant with specialised needs—and dislikes. There are several varieties, so it can be grown in cold and temperate climates, and with some skill the taller rabbit-eye variety will grow in a warm climate. I remember walking across a wild field in New Hampshire, USA, in the mid-1990s, on my way to a river. The field was covered in ankle high, coarse-leafed little plants, which seemed to be sprinkled with deep blue freckles. I crouched down to have a look, and to my total surprise the whole field was a mass of wild fruiting blueberries. I sat and 'pigged out' for the next hour! The flavour was simply scrumptious. I have never eaten better ones.

My advice is if you have the soil and climate in your favour, go for it. If not, forget it. Unless their requirements are in your favour, they are really difficult to grow. However, this is what you need to know.

Blueberries need an acidic, well-drained, but moisture retaining soil, *very rich in organic matter.* They like calcium, but need an acidic range pH 4.0 to 5.5. Remember, pH 4.0 is 1000 times more acid than neutral, pH 7.0. This is very acidic soil. You can make your soil this acidic, but you cannot change the overall character or properties of your soil, so it will always be reverting back to its natural state. If that natural state is not suitable for blueberries, sooner or later they are going to be in trouble.

To lower the pH and add calcium, simply use gypsum. Depending on the pH, you may need up to a bucket per plant. If this does not lower the pH enough, I suggest you then add 25 g (1 ounce) per plant of elemental sulphur. Also dig a bucket of peat—this is acidic—into the soil for each plant, and/or old sawdust. You must aim for a soil that is able to be continually moist, not wet, high in organic matter, with a very low pH.

Get advice from your garden centre where you buy your blueberry plants on the best variety for your locality. Depending on the varieties, set them at approximately 60 cm to 1.2 m (2–4 feet) apart. Make absolutely certain that the plants are not in a potentially boggy or very dry situation. When planted, cut the bush back to about 15 cm (6 inches) above ground.

During the first year's growth it is advisable to remove any flowers to encourage more new growth. Just think of next year's crop! Heavily mulch with old sawdust, peat, pine needles, bracken, straw or hay, and apply a handful of blood and bone—8 to 1 with potash—to each plant a few times during the growing season. You will need to check the pH each year. Aim to keep the pH around 4.5 to 5.0. Add another 25 g (1 ounce) of elemental sulphur each year, if required.

Pick the fruit by gently rolling between finger and thumb, rather than by giving a direct tug. You can easily keep the birds away with netting.

Eaten fresh, or in a pie, blueberries are superb.

Current, Black and Red

Black currants are an easy-to-grow, bush type plant growing about 1.5 m (5 feet) high with a similar spread. This is a soft fruit you can grow—three in a group—in a sunny part of the shrubbery. They are ideal for the cool climate garden, and are not fussy about the soil, but they do like it well drained. Set them in their permanent positions in the winter. Prune them back to about 30 cm (1 foot) high at planting time. In the following years keep older wood removed to encourage new growth from the base of the plant.

Water well at fruiting time and keep the plants permanently mulched to about 20 cm (8 inches) deep to avoid any weeds and to ensure strong vigorous plants. The fruit is a rich source of vitamin C and is excellent in jams.

Red currants are more vigorous than black currants, with a height and spread of about 2 m (6 feet). Grow as for black currants, but their pruning requirements are slightly different. Red currants bear their fruit on spurs, so it is best to keep the leader to a reasonable height which promotes the development of fruiting spurs.

Water well when fruiting and keep well mulched. The fruit is a bright red and is best used in jams.

FEIJOA

This is a hardy fruiting shrub for mild/warm regions, even disliking hotter tropical areas. It seems that the feijoa is often overlooked as a small fruit. Ideal for the small garden, this can also be grown in a sunny position among the shrubs. They seldom exceed 3 m (9 feet) and are planted with about 2 m (6 feet) between plants.

Easily grown, it prefers a well-drained, slightly acid soil rich in organic matter. Buy a named variety suitable for your locality. I found that they like to grow in groups of three, maybe for them three is not a crowd! Mulch generously, add any suitable animal manure, and keep well watered, especially at fruiting time.

The flavour of the small egg-sized fruit is reminiscent of pineapple and strawberry mixed, with an exquisite aroma. The aroma would be worth a fortune if you could extract and bottle it as a perfume! The fruit is so good to eat, and the plant so easy to grow, it is more than worthy of a place in the garden.

It is worth mentioning that the flowers are very beautiful in their own right. Taking care not to damage the pollination process, you can discreetly pick the petals from the flower and eat them. They are honey sweet.

GOOSEBERRY

Why a berry should be called a gooseberry I can only imagine! These plants are not too fussy about the soil, but the richer in organic matter the bigger the berries. These are strictly cool/cold climate berries, and personally I think a couple of bushes is enough. They grow to about 1 m (3 feet) in height, with a similar spread. Allow 1.2 m (4 feet) between bushes. Set the young bushes in the winter, and cut out all low and downward growing branches. Position them so they get plenty of sun, it really helps sweeten the berries.

Keep the bushes well mulched to control weeds and conserve moisture. Although basically a tough plant, they reward good care. Each winter prune them to keep the bush fairly open so you can pick the berries without getting too pricked. Prune to upward growing buds to keep them away from the ground. When the bushes are fruiting, keep well watered to ensure a good-sized plump fruit. Allow to fully ripen on the bushes to sweeten. Not vaguely scrumptious, yet Treenie enjoyed their tart flavour, eating them before fully ripe.

Gooseberries are very good mixed in pies and stews with other fruit, and make excellent jams. Although not a fruit to rave over, they are easily grown and pest free.

KIWI FRUIT

The name kiwi fruit is the result of a brilliant marketing strategy by the New Zealand growers. It is, in fact, a climbing plant native to the lower mountain slopes of China, and for years was known as the Chinese gooseberry. And of course, just to add to the confusion, it is no relation to the common gooseberry! The fruit is rather like a hairy brown egg, but the flesh is a green delight, of delicate flavour.

The kiwi fruit is quite a rampant grower and only suitable for gardens where there is plenty of room. Compare it more with a choko than a passion fruit for its growth potential. Be warned, this climber needs a lot of space. A good strong pergola or very strong lattice is required to carry the weight of the vine. It climbs like a runner bean, by twisting around its support.

This plant has sexual needs, so you must buy a male and female plant for cross-pollination. If you plan to grow a lot you can have seven females to one male. I think—I'm not sure—you can now buy a plant with both male and female grafts on the one plant. Seems like a good idea.

Kiwi fruit like a sunny open position, but strong or gale winds can damage the blossoms in spring. The vine is deciduous, and is both cool climate hardy or warm climate tolerant according to the variety. It is a shallow rooting plant and likes a rich, well-drained soil, high in organic matter. It will not tolerate stagnant water around its roots in winter.

Always keep mulched, as much as 2–3 m (6–9 feet) all around the base of the plant. They thrive in mulch, needing a cool moist root run with an abundance of organic matter in the summer. The fruit is generally picked from autumn to mid-winter depending on variety and location. Allow them to become soft to gentle finger pressure for full flavour.

Keep the vine pruned each winter so that it does not become a mass of tangled smothering growth producing only a few poor fruit. Providing you can support this vine it is worth the trouble and is a valuable addition to the variety of soft fruit that can be grown. It likes plenty of summer water and will reward you with a good crop of sweet, juicy fruit.

If you want to build a proper support system, this is the procedure. Dig two strong posts into the ground placed 5m (15 feet) apart. At the top of each post bolt on a crossbeam 150 cm (5 feet) long. From the crossbeams secure and stretch three fencing wires, one on each outer side and one in the centre. This gives you three stretched parallel wires between the two crossbeams. You can repeat this for as many vines as you want.

Set the vine of your choice in the centre, between posts, secured to a strong stake. As it grows, train the vine up and onto the wires. You now have access for picking fruit and pruning. This vine needs its laterals—side growths along the main stems—pruned quite hard each winter.

The kiwi fruit has a voracious appetite for nitrogen when growing and fruiting. Feed it with a handful of 8:1 blood/bone and potash, or fish and kelp meal biweekly. The nitrogen producing white clover is an excellent companion cover crop, or any other low growing legume favourable to your climate. Grass is an unsuitable plant to grow under or around kiwi fruit and will lower your cropping.

PASSION FRUIT

We come now to a very different type of fruit. Apart from the cool climate preference of the banana passion fruit, these are mostly frost tender when young, with some warm climate varieties permanently frost tender. The passion fruit is a climbing plant, liking a sunny sheltered position where they can grow up a lattice, fence, shed, or any suitable support. The soil needs to be rich in organic matter. Sprinkle a handful of blood and bone to each plant when you set them. On no account cultivate around the passion fruit when established. They like a lot of nitrogen, so keep them well supplied with blood/bone 8 to 1 with potash during the growing and fruiting season.

As mentioned, there are varieties available which will grow equally well from cool to hot climates. In hot areas a bit of light dappled shade can be appreciated. Obtain your plants at the time suitable for your climate, and set them in place very carefully. Make sure the climbing support is adequate, mulch around the plant for a least 1m (3 feet) around the base of the plant, and keep it well watered.

Generally, when the plant has been growing for a couple of years it will flower and commence fruiting. Pick the fruit when it has a good colour, but is still firm. It will ripen and crinkle indoors and is then ready for use.

Make sure that no wild growths come from below the graft. This is easily seen as it almost always has different foliage. Cut off carefully as soon as noticed. Passion fruit plants are generally good for around eight years, then they begin to deteriorate. They need practically no pruning. Choose your plant variety only after you have eaten and enjoyed one of their fruit. Passion fruit flavours can range from sharp to sweet, so be sure of your preference.

PINEAPPLE

Another plant for the warm climates, the pineapple requires very little space in the garden, and is so easy it is ridiculous not to grow it. And grown organically, the flavour is excellent. Several of the plants can be tucked, at about 30–40 cm (12–18 inches) apart in a convenient sunny, open position. One imperative, they *must grow in full all-day sunshine.*

Pineapples have a preference for acid soil. Around pH 4.5–5.5 would be ideal. If your soil is not acidic enough, this can be achieved by the addition of 25 g (1 ounce) of elemental sulphur per plant, possibly each year. If your soil is pH neutral or higher, don't even bother!

They prefer a fairly sandy, open soil, but can grow in a wide range of soils providing drainage and pH requirements are met. Under organic conditions, with the soil well mulched, the fruit takes on a far greater sweetness. Mulching also alleviates the need for constant watering, for while a pineapple likes moisture, it can more easily tolerate dry conditions than wet. If you live in a wet zone, then good drainage is of paramount importance. Hillside conditions are required.

Young plants can be obtained in two ways, suckers from a mature plant base or the crown of stiff leaves from the top of a pineapple fruit. By far the easiest method is from the top of a fruit. This also means that you can choose the variety that you consider most tasty. And there are new hybrids coming out that do taste better than the fruit basically grown for commercial canning.

When the fruit is *fully* ripe, remove the top by holding it firmly and twisting it off. Easy! Do not cut it. Next, peel the lower leaves away until you have exposed approximately 4 cm (1½ inches) at the base of the cluster of leaves. Mostly, with a ripe, mature fruit, you can see tiny, immature white roots under each leaf section you peel away. Allow the top to dry for twenty-four hours way from the sun, then plant it in the garden, or in a pot, or a bed of sandy soil.

If you grow a bed of tops from fruit bought over a period of many months, they will fruit in a natural progression. This takes from eighteen months to two and a half years, depending on climatic conditions and when the tops are planted. A fruit is considered ripe when the smell goes sweet, it is colouring slightly, and the flesh yields a fraction to gentle pressure. Commercially grown, they are picked just before fully ripe to allow for travel, yet a pineapple does not ripen any more after picking. Some people think they do, but they are simply decaying, and this can turn starches to sugar.

For the best of the best, make sure there is plenty of organic matter in the soil, and keep those little beauties mulched.

RASPBERRY

Choose a sunny open position, but it needs to be sheltered from strong winds. Raspberries are wind haters and a draughty place will stunt them and spoil their performance. They like a rich well-manured soil high in organic matter. The manure that is always easily available is chicken manure processed into pellets.

You normally buy raspberries as bare roots, which are set in rows 45 cm (18 inches) apart. Space the rows 1.2 m (4 feet) apart. At the ends of each row it is sensible to have hefty wooden posts. Strain a pair of wires between them near the top and about 30 cm (1 foot) from the bottom. The idea is that the canes will grow up between the wires, receiving lower and upper support, while offering easy access for mulching, removing old canes, and for picking.

Mulch with any feeder mulch you wish between the rows at least 20 cm (8 inches) deep. Let the raspberries grow to about 1.5 m (5 feet) high and then prune out growing tips. This forces the plant to throw out fruiting laterals from the cane instead of needlessly growing taller.

Raspberries fruit on the second year cane, i.e., they grow for one year then fruit the next. When the cane has fruited and ended its season it will die. Cut these dead canes out and leave four to six new canes for the following year's fruit. Four to six canes is enough. Carefully remove any further suckering with a sharp knife or narrow sharp spade, being careful not to damage the roots.

The fruit is borne early summer or late, according to the variety. Obviously it is a good idea to extend the season with early, mid-season and late varieties. It is also possible to cut the canes down to the ground in the winter and the new canes that grow will bear fruit in the autumn. If you have four or five rows, try one row using this method.

Raspberries are easy to grow. Do not cultivate between the rows because of their shallow root system. Keep them deeply mulched always and well watered when fruiting. Any suckers that run out of the rows are easily pulled out of the mulch as they run in the mulch rather than the soil.

This sumptuous fruit should be eaten raw to benefit from both flavour and nutritional value. But it is also very good cooked and used for jam. Raspberries can also be frozen or bottled for storage.

RED DRAGON FRUIT

Now for the *coup de grâce* of soft fruit—the delightful, beautiful and totally scrumptious 'new kid on the block'. And it is so easy to grow for the gardeners in mild, warm and hot climatic zones. The rest of you—enjoy your raspberries!

This spectacular fruit is from the tropical climbing epiphyllum species of cacti; *Hylocerus*, so named because, with a bit of imagination, its outer sepals, or tendrils, look like the flames from a fire-breathing dragon. Even though it is named a Red Dragon fruit, there are two varieties, both with identical appearing fruit. However, when cut open, *Hylocerus occamponis* is the deep-red-fleshed variety, while *H, undatus* has white flesh. And for me, the red-fleshed variety is far superior in its flavour.

I grow both. However, I had *H, undatus* long before I knew what it was, and I set it at the base of a tall gum tree. Now, the plant is hanging from the top, 20 m (60 feet) above my head, so the fruit bats and possums enjoy the fruit. I grow the red-fleshed variety on a weld-mesh frame where all is in reach of my hands. If it helps with identifying them, the plant often referred to as the American Orchid is a large-flowering epiphyllum, often seen in hanging baskets; the *Hylocerus* is a climbing variety of these, with equally huge and spectacular creamy white flowers that open at night. This gives it the common name Queen of the Night.

This plant likes to grow in a *very free-draining* soil that is rich in organic matter. Basically, you can grow it in any poor well-drained soil, but the quality of fruit can only be in proportion to the quality of the soil. Plant it in a sunny position, although dappled shade during the afternoon in a hot climate is beneficial. Give this sprawling/climbing plant a frame, or small dead tree, or shed, or fence, even a steep bank, whatever, but you need to be able to keep it under reasonable control. As with most cacti, it likes an acidic soil, and although mulch is equally good for this plant, keep it away from the main stem. Although in the cacti family, this is not a very spiny or thorny plant, having no more than a few short prickles at the nodes along the flat stems.

You can buy these plants in many garden centres now, or get a couple of cuttings from a friend, or a friend of a friend. You take a cutting by removing a mature piece around 30–60 cm (1–2 feet) long. Leave the cuttings in a dry shady place for a couple of weeks, letting the cut dry over and heal. Pot into a good quality free-draining potting soil, and be very careful with the watering until the cuttings have rooted. Keep the plants in the shade until rooted, then move them into dappled sun, gradually hardening them off.

Finally, plant them out at your chosen place. They can grow big with a lot of sprawl, so give them plenty of space. This is a cacti, so you need hardly ever water them. Mine only get water when it rains, and they have recently managed five months of drought without a trace of discomfort. In fact, they seem to favour wet and dry seasons, so leave it to Nature.

The fruit can weigh half a kilo (over a pound). When cut open, whether red or white fleshed, it is dotted with hundreds of tiny black seeds that are undetectable in the totally delectable experience of eating the fruit.

Unfortunately, flying foxes, possums, and even rats like them, so the fruit needs some protection. Generally it takes about a month from flower opening to picking the fruit. Surprisingly, they can be kept in a refrigerator for a few weeks; its subtle sweetness is superb when eaten chilled.

I have to offer here a word of caution. If left uncontrolled the red dragon fruit becomes a very powerful opponent to the gardener. The white variety that I foolishly allowed to climb a gum tree all but killed the tree, and took a lot of effort on my son Russell's part to clear the tree of its unwelcome invader. Keep it on a strong support, trellis, or climbing frame and ensure that you can keep it on that frame . . . then enjoy.

STRAWBERRY

This is a plant that thrives best in acidic soil. With a pH preference 5.0–6.5, you must avoid all freshly limed soil where you intend to grow strawberries. They like a rich fertile soil that has plenty of organic matter in it, as in decayed mulch. Remember that they will be in the bed for three years, so they will need adequate nourishment. Strawberries should be set as soon as good-sized runners are available for the next season's crop. You can get runner after runner in a long string of them. Never use more than the first two young plants from a string, and take the runners from a wide selection of your best cropping plants.

Young strawberries need to have had a good season's growth to crop well, so strong plants set in early spring will fruit later that year. For best results, strawberries need a lot of water, but they hate to sit in a saturated soil, especially in the winter. The following method will ensure success.

Clear the strawberry bed of mulch and any deep-rooted weeds that may be lingering. With a broad bladed hoe make a ridge as if ridging up potatoes in the traditional way. Set the strawberries on top of the ridge at

30 cm (1 foot) apart, allowing 60 cm (2 feet) between the ridges. This is one time you can mulch with *old* sawdust, not fresh, or use any mulch that you have between the rows. It is perfectly possible to grow strawberries without the ridges providing the soil has excellent drainage. In very high rainfall areas, ridging is a safe method.

The highest yield comes from the second year crop, after which the commercial growers cultivate the ground and start again with new plants. In the organic garden the third year is also very good, and it is third-year plants from which you take your runners. Try to replace one or two rows of strawberries each year. This way you will always have an abundance of fruit, rather than year 1 . . . not enough; 2 . . . too many; 3 . . . just enough!

Unfortunately, you will need to protect the fruit from birds. This can be done with nets, a permanent wire netting frame, or by placing each truss of fruit in a jam jar lying in the mulch.

Water well and regularly, particularly when they are fruiting. Keep the runners cut off them, except for when you need some. Never feed with too much nitrogen, even blood and bone, as this causes excessive leaf growth at the expense of fruit. Apply fertiliser when the plants are dormant, so that the plants have it when in early growth. In this way they get fertilised and you get fruit.

There are many varieties, so choose according to the dictates of your climate, along with your palate. Strawberries can tolerate most Oz extremes, but as I said, the cold areas produce a flavour of unparalleled excellence. Warm climate strawberries lose something in a plant which originated in cold alpine country.

When it comes to eating strawberries, fresh and raw is best.

A FINAL COMMENT . . .

So, there we have it, a whole scrumptious array of soft fruit that can be grown, albeit with a little preparation, in most gardens. Certainly some gardens are too small, and some gardeners may be a bit fainthearted when it comes to building a blackberry or kiwi fruit frame, but honestly, it really is simple. Half-a-day's work, help from a friend, a few cups of tea from the wife, and the thing is done. Then you get to enjoy many years of eating the fruit. When you do build such a frame and you do it properly, you also get a great feeling of achievement. Not because it is particularly clever, but because you are growing them in a way that other people will quietly envy.

As my Dad used to say, "Anything worth doing is worth doing well." And when you do it well, you increase your own self-worth! This is the way of conscious gardening!

THE GARDEN
AS A METAPHOR FOR LIFE

To grow your garden plants while being conscious of organic principles involves studying the actual requirements of the plants, the soil, and the climate. This is, or should be, a fully conscious process, not the usual automatic non-thinking act.

When gardeners think they know a lot about gardening, they generally move into one of two categories; the aware conscious gardener who develops a greater respect and love for Nature and the act of gardening, realising how much deeper the relationship can develop, or the subconscious gardener who slips into a fully automatic, 'I know how to do this' mode, thereby completely missing the deeper insights that are revealed to the more conscious gardener. Let me stress here that there is no right or wrong to this, no good or bad. All I am talking about is the potential of an aware, receptive gardener compared to a gardener who is satisfied with believing that a garden is just a place to grow plants.

In many ways, *the garden is a great teacher of life*. This is my speciality. I know a fair bit about a lot in the garden, most of it practical, but my great fascination is with the metaphysical aspect— that forever-unfolding energy of life expressing in the garden. For me, a garden is a place to connect with Nature, life, and living—this is my speciality.

Take pruning roses as a good example of life and living. The gardener knows that we have to prune modern roses. We mainly prune them in the winter when flowering is finished growth is at a standstill, the leaves have dropped; this is Nature's perfect timing.

PRUNING ROSES

I remember in the early 1990s, Treenie and I were in Western Oz. We were taking an afternoon stroll along a country road when we came to a house with a fairly big, unkempt front garden. An elderly woman was sitting on a step near some huge hybrid tea roses, looking very pale and distressed. We walked over to her, learning that she had just recently come out of the hospital after suffering a heart attack. Now, she was attempting to prune her large unkempt roses!

A single glance told me that they had not been pruned for several years. They were a tangled, thorny, overgrown mess, with long, spindly branches poking out all over the place. I asked her if I could help.

"Oh dear, no," she replied, "They have to be carefully pruned."

I pretended to look offended. "It's not fair," I said. "One of my great joys is to prune roses, and I'm very good at it. Now, here I am with all these roses that need pruning, and you won't let me help."

The frail lady smiled in surprise. "Well, when you put it like that, I'll be very grateful for your help."

There were about fifteen very overgrown roses, so I got straight into them. "You can throw all the cuttings in a heap. My son will clear them away," she said. Keeping my thoughts to myself, I reflected that he had certainly not put himself out to help her in the garden.

With just a pair of old hand secateurs, it took me quite a while. I needed a pair of the large-jawed long-handled ones. Meanwhile

Treenie got the trembling woman to sit comfortably and relax. She was exhausted just looking at the roses. I wondered at one stage if the secateurs would manage the job, but I persisted, and the roses got their pruning.

None of those roses resisted their pruning. When the many straggly growths are removed, it makes way for fewer, stronger growth spurs. As old, weakened branches are cut away, new strong ones will take their place. As light and air gets into the centre of the plant, it will be more able to resist fungal diseases. On an energetic level, you could feel the roses taking a deep, grateful breath of fresh air. You could feel the relief in the roses, the metaphysical knowing that new growth was now possible, no longer more of the same.

PRUNING PEOPLE

We are like this. Over a period of years we develop concepts and beliefs that are negative to our growth, and they need to be regularly pruned away. Unlike the rose bush, we resist. My life is now much more about pruning people than roses, but over and over I see the parallel. People resist strenuously when you attempt to relieve them of the weight of old, non-productive growth. People cling to their outmoded beliefs with all the tenacity of an addict.

Just as the roses need pruning in the stillness of winter, so people need to release old concepts and stagnant beliefs when the weight of these burdens brings their inner growth to a standstill. Just as a rose bush will become compressed and distorted with the weight of gnarled old branches, so people become depressed with the unproductive weight of negative thinking, and their life becomes stressed with anxiety. Just as the weakened rose becomes susceptible to disease, so, too, do people.

If you watch a tree in a strong wind or storm, you will see the branches bending, whipping back and forth, while leaves are blown away. The tree does not resist the storm. The tree does not say, "Sorry, I can't deal with a storm today. I'm too busy." But we do.

When the winds of change blow in our lives, we hang onto the old; we do not easily release the old leaves of habit. And when a fierce storm hits our lives, we become deeply stressed, simply because we fail to see that life is saying "Let go." We are much more attached to 'more of the same' than a tree is attached to its branches. Just as weather-based storms prune the tree of growth that is beyond its ability to support and maintain, so stress-based storms attempt to relieve us of our burdens, offering us a chance to release some of our fixations and attachments.

A hundred years ago, fruit trees such as apricots, apples and pears, even lemons and some of the citrus, grew into large, deep-rooted trees with a strong trunk and sturdy limbs. They bore a lot of fruit and had no trouble carrying them. Now, those trees have been hybridised to bear far more fruit on smaller, weaker trees, reduced to a caricature of their natural form. The result is branches that tear off with the weight of fruit on trees too immature to carry such weight. Why? So we can pick them more easily. So we do not have to go up a ladder and waste our valuable time!

PRINCIPLES OF GROWTH

You can see the same pattern in people. People who hold to the long-term values and principles that develop and grow a person of high self-worth, are easily able to carry the weight of burdens that each year brings. These people of uncommon sense are now uncommon people.

Too many people want more for less. The young adult wants and expects to have all the material goodies their parents have acquired after many years. But before you can reap the harvest of the fruits of life, you have to face the pressures and challenges. You cannot have the harvest without the necessary growth. Nature knows this, demonstrating it in all natural trees and plants. You can see this in your own garden.

Every plant, every animal, all Nature's creatures grow to a

certain maturity before they can reap the harvest of their growth; this is always in accordance with the life span of the plant or animal. The oak tree takes many years before it bears a harvest, while the tomato has its whole life and harvest in a single year. So short is the life span of a mayfly that it does not need to eat in the hours of its life, yet in its mating flight it finds the fulfilment and the purpose of its life cycle.

We, as human Beings, have reached our full physical growth within twenty years, but our mental and emotional growth can, or should, continue throughout our lives. Then there is our soul growth! We are a lot more complex than a tree or a mayfly, yet we are governed by the same forces and principles: growth = experience = wisdom = fulfilment.

Every living thing in Nature seems to abide by this; it is natural to all creatures—except us. Rather than us being shaped by our environment, we shape our environment according to us. Clinging to their 'more of the same' complex, many early wealthy British migrants tried to reshape the Oz countryside to reflect their English estates, thus denying the potential for newness in a very different and exciting new country.

SEEDS OF NEWNESS

Every fertile seed holds the potential of newness. No plant grown from seed grows into an exact duplicate of its prototype, any more than a child grows as a duplicate of its parents. As parents, we are inclined to point and push our children in the direction of our beliefs and conditioning—even if it has not worked for us, even if it has led us to depression and sickness.

This is not natural in Nature. In Nature, if a direction is not capable of the full potential of a life form, it closes it down. We fight to deal capably with life, while so often it is our actions causing the problems.

Back to the garden. If we sow seeds in a bed of soil, we have the seeds we want to grow, along with the seeds of many plants that favour the same conditions. We call them weeds. When our seeds come up they are going to be competing with a lot of other, very capable plants. So we hoe out the weeds to make growth more favourable for the plants we want.

The weeds in our lives are the negative thoughts that overcrowd the positive ones. We need to cultivate positive thoughts, for they create strong productive growth in us. In the garden we remove the weeds, but in our lives we seem to let them grow unchecked. Only after the weeds are removed does the gardener fertilise the garden, yet we fertilise our negative thoughts daily by watching negative news on television, or reading a negative newspaper. Amazingly, positive-news newspapers all go bankrupt, while the worst of the most negative-news newspapers are the biggest selling. This says something about us!

The reality is that our hospitals and medical systems are choked up with the sickest life forms on the planet—us. We cultivate so much that is against Nature, and offer so little that is supportive of Nature. The garden shows us so clearly that we are the Nature that we oppose. The garden can teach us how to reverse this if only we are able to become conscious enough to 'be with' and 'be aware' of the lessons from a living garden. Just as Nature is the teacher of life to all of 'nature,' so Nature is also our greatest teacher.

ENRICHMENT

For a conscious gardener, and most true gardeners, the garden enriches their lives. We may work hard—or play hard—in the garden, but the whole gardening experience is deeply rewarding. We all need to experience the magic of enrichment in our lives. I repeat, to fertilise means to enrich. Just as the garden needs to be fertilised, so we need to fertilise our consciousness with the alchemy of enrichment.

Enrichment—is this overlooked in your life? Do the years of life offer you ever greater enrichment? This is the way of Nature. This is the way it should be, can be. Your soul grows through enrichment. I like to see a good film, but it is rarely an enriching experience. It can certainly be enjoyable, emotionally rewarding and entertaining, but it is soon forgotten. However, 'making' a film could indeed be very enriching. Enriching experiences stay with us. Enriching experiences reach into the heart, not into the emotions, even though emotions may be involved. The heart is the soul centre, the solar plexus is the centre of emotions. Remember that 'gut feeling'? That's emotions.

Growing my first tomatoes as a six-year-old boy was an enriching experience, it is still with me—the wonder of those incredible big red fruits all coming from the tiny plants I had set. And of course, 'wonder' is part of enrichment. It takes wonder, even a little awe, to open the heart to be enriched. And a garden can do this so easily for a conscious gardener.

If you go into the garden in an open manner—even childlike, in as much as a child is in the moment, while unfortunately, growing *up* is mostly growing *away*—you are open to newness. This is not easy. Watch a flower unfold, and open. Only when it has opened to the sun and light can the bees and pollinating insects come visiting.

POLLINATION

Just as the flowers open to be pollinated, so we have to do the same. When we are open to life, receptive to the wonder of life, open to the unseen, then an inner pollination takes place. This spiritual pollination is true alchemy, the alchemy of the soul.

Sadly, so many gardeners miss this. A garden is not just about growing flowers, vegetables, trees and lawns. A garden represents the garden of the soul. Loving your garden is good for you, for the garden, and you are not separate. Some of that love spills its way into your life. When this happens, the garden is growing the gardener!

It is the love in a garden that opens us to the pollination of Nature, a fully natural process that too many pragmatic men shrug off as nonsense. A woman in the garden usually creates a very different garden energy than the male gardener. Why? Because far more women garden from the heart than men. Most men garden from the head, not all, but most. It is the nature of the beast! Actually, that is untrue. It is not the nature of a man to be more in his head, it is his inherent conditioning.

I am a heart gardener. This is the whole purpose of our garden, to create a heart experience of Nature, something I am still learning. In many ways, I am involved in the pollination of people—this is what I do. I consider myself a cosmic bee with a be-loved wife, and together we fly around the world pollinating open human hearts with Truth. Many would testify to this, for their lives have been enriched by the Truth of life and living. It is Truth that pollinates the soul.

I consider I am good at what I do, basically because I love doing it. I am certain that if I was not a gardener, I could not do what I do in the way I do it. In the garden I see the lives of people in the plants, and in people I see the lives of different types of plants. I see the people who are like fruit trees, wanting only to reap material rewards from life, convinced that this is their due, while others are like small, shade-loving violets, hiding in the shadows of their friends, never aware of their own more fragile gift of inner beauty.

COMPETITION

I have used the word 'competition' in this chapter, regarding weeds competing with the seeds we sow. In reality there is no competition in Nature, because in Truth, Nature as we know it is the expression and experience of life, not death. This is too big a subject for me to explore in this book, and not the book for it, but although I used 'competition' to convey the meaning in our language, I cannot let it pass without some clarification.

A casual observer of the garden, or Nature, would soon be convinced that Nature is all about competition, but to someone who has studied it in depth, the reverse becomes apparent. When I say in depth, I do not mean with the microscope, I mean studying the flow and movement of life on the deeper, metaphysical levels of energy.

Let me share a very abbreviated little story. George Washington Carver, the son of a black slave, was born around 1855 in America. Grown up and educated, he proved to be a genius. Dr. Carver was a scientist, an agricultural lecturer and teacher, spending most his life in the study of plants. In the laboratory he discovered one hundred and fifty uses for the sweet potato, and three hundred uses for the peanut. In his later years when he was retired, it was considered an honour by his students to spend some time in caring for this great man. One afternoon he had been sitting on a chair in the garden for a number of hours, when the evening chill crept in. The student caring for him came to him. "Sir, it is getting cold. You should come in now."

Dr. Carver nodded. A half hour passed. The student came again. "Sir, I must insist that you come in now. You could get chilled." He then asked a question. "Sir, how can you sit staring at that single flower for so many hours?"

George Washington Carver looked up at the student and smiled. "Ah, you see a flower," he replied, "I see the universe."

What a poignant moment for that student, a pollination of Truth.

George Washington Carver made a deep impact on my life when I discovered a small book, *The Man Who Talked to Flowers*. I resonated to his story, his words, as though, heart open, he stood before me.

To the humble gardener prepared to scratch beneath the surface, you find that Nature is not an expression of competition, but cooperation.

COOPERATION

Nature does not measure life in terms of winning, losing, beginning or ending. Nature knows only the endless continuity of life. This is a Truth that consensus humanity has yet to embrace. We see life as one lifetime, not endless continuity, so we think short term: winning or losing, beginnings and endings. This illusion gives birth to competition.

If you spend time in your garden seeing beyond the obvious physical expression, you will see the most incredible level of cooperation. I say 'see' the cooperation, but really you 'experience' it. If it is to be truly seen, it will be seen only by the eyes of the open heart.

As mentioned, we have some huge gum trees in our garden, all with large, widespread branches tapering off to the thin twigs. I love our trees, and they know it. When we get a storm, or very severe wind, branches are sometimes torn from the trees and crash to the ground. Our garden is under the trees, yet when the branches fall they always manage to land on our paths, or on an area which does not crush and smash one of our valued shrubs or plants— or us. The chances of this so repeatedly happening is laughable, but it continues this way. Not chance at all, but cooperation. You may scoff, but our trees manage to drop almost all their branches in places that avoid damage.

I remember a number of years ago a family who had about four hectares (10 acres) of land, most of it gum trees. They had an alchemy laboratory and made various health potions, tinctures, and fragrances. They needed to extend the laboratory, and so surveyed all their beloved trees on the property. Only one tree would give the exact requirement of timber, but emotionally, they could not cut down the tree. They considered buying the timber, but realised this also came from a tree and, not wishing to cause a tree to be cut down, were unsure of how to proceed.

You guessed it. One day while they were out, a storm lashed its way through their property, lightning blasting a tree and causing it to fall. When they arrived home, the tree that exactly met their requirements was the fallen tree, snapped at the base like a carrot. When it fell, it fell in the only space that it could fall without doing damage to any other tree or building. They knew then that this tree had willingly given itself to them to be used in extending their laboratory. For them, it was cooperation with Nature, the storm and the tree combining to meet their needs.

Intent

When you work in your garden, or have jobs to do, there is always an energy radiating from you—your intent. You can mask your words, deceive yourself with thoughts, but your intent remains naked. Nature—your garden—can read your intent with the ease that you read these words.

If your intent as a gardener is to compete with your neighbour, with or without their knowing, then your gardening experience will be limited to the field of competition. If your intent is to grow the biggest vegetables and flowers, you may do just that, but that is all you will grow. If you accept that your garden is your meeting place with Nature, and that you are the student meeting with and learning from the master, Nature, then your intent will take you into the metaphysical gardens of marvel and magic.

We humans are easily able to mask our intentions. Many politicians have it down to an art form. Our intent is our deeper agenda, our often hidden purpose in doing what it is that we do. This is not the intent of the soul, for that is simple and basic—Self-Realisation.

If a person were to walk into the bush with a can of poison, with the intention of poisoning a tree that is in the way of their most perfect view, Nature would know. There is no judgement in this knowing, no retribution for this selfish act. But the intent is known by Nature. We have all learned about the 'Web of Life' meaning that in consciousness, everything is connected, even though we seldom ever realise the full implications of just what this web of life actually means.

It means that nothing is separate from us. The thoughts, words, and actions we put out for, and/or against, other people directly affect our own life. Equally, the person intent on poisoning a tree because it spoils their view, will be unwittingly adding poison to their own life. In whatever form it takes, the intent to poison will manifest as deep discord in the life of the poisoner. A few disturbed people will poison a dog that barks all night, night after night. Lack of sleep and anger often create some heartless choices. Yet the same equation applies. No matter what the cause, when our intent is to cause harm to another life-form, that harm will visit our life. Even holding the intent, but not carrying it into action, will bring discord and suffering into the life of the person holding it.

The garden can teach us of this 'all life is one' connection if we are conscious enough and present enough to learn.

HEALTH BENEFITS

I was recently reading an article about mental disease and the gardener. It seems completely obvious to me, but research has now discovered that elderly people who enjoy working in their gardens have far better mental health than their counterparts who do not work in the garden. The experts advise: If you can, work in the garden!

Sorry, but that conclusion is ridiculous. The real gardener is out working in the garden because it is not work, it is sheer pleasure. Sure, physical activity is involved, but when 'work is love made visible' then, and then only, you reap the benefits of activity in the garden. To work in the garden disliking what you are doing would more likely instigate mental decline than prevent it.

A loved garden expresses an energy of love; a disliked put-up-with-because-it-is-there garden expresses discontent. A garden carries the energy of the people in the house, because it is a garden that makes a house into a home. Many years ago when I did organic gardening talk-back radio show in Tasmania, a man phoned in saying that the twelve-year-old tree in front of the house had never flowered. He wanted to know why. I asked a few questions about the soil and the position of the tree, what species of tree, and sunlight, but he was very vague. He just kept saying, "It won't flower but"

I tried every suggestion I could come up with, all to be met with the blank statement "It won't flower but." Finally, on a flash of inspiration, I asked him if anyone in the family liked the tree. Nobody did. I asked him why they kept it. "The wife's mother gave it to us but." Then I asked him if he, or any of the family, could find any redeeming features in the tree, any reason to like it. "No, it won't flower but."

I decided to give him something to think about. "If nobody in your family liked you, then you would not flower. You would feel disapproved of, not liked, and you would go into a long sulk. Your tree is suffering from bad energy from you and the family. I suggest you look for what you could like about the tree, talk to it nicely, and change your attitude to the tree. Then it may flower."

There was a long silence. "Is that bloody it?"

"Yes, that's it," I said. "Try it, you may get a surprise."

About six months later, the phone rang in a talk-back session. "I don't know if you remember me but . . ." (Oh yes, I did!) "I'm the bloke who had the tree that wouldn't flower but. Well, I thought you was bloody mad, but the wife was listening and she thought you made sense, so we all tried to see the tree in a better way. I found it had nice leaves, and the wife enjoyed its shade, and the nipper climbed in it. Anyhow, the tree is on flower right now and it's bloody beautiful. Just thought I'd let you know. The tree's a bloody ripper! Thanks mate."

I laughed, and thanked him for phoning to tell us. He was so proud of the tree; but, in his voice, I could tell that he was proud of himself. He wanted that tree to flower, otherwise he would never have phoned. But, unbeknown to him, changing his attitude to the tree in his garden promoted a change in his attitude to life. *Life and the garden are one, the garden 'is' life.* Knowingly or not, that man became conscious of the tree, creating and maintaining a far more healthy focus. The tree flowered, but by the change in the quality of his voice—not his words—he also was finding life a more vibrant, uplifting experience.

This is the way to get health benefits from the garden, activity plus attitude. For a person who does not like gardening—and they outnumber us gardeners—go for a brisk walk while reflecting on your good fortune that you can walk. Take up cycling, or go to the local fitness centre. All activity is good, but it is the mental and emotional relationship you have with that activity that will determine your mental and emotional health.

Make it a Fruit Tree

I F YOU HAVE ROOM for only one tree in your garden, make it a fruit tree. I always find it odd that flowering trees generally take preference over flowering and 'fruiting' trees in a garden where there is room for only one tree. I agree, a flowering tree is very beautiful, but so are the flowers of so many fruiting trees. Even more beautiful is to see a tree laden with its red, golden, yellow, purple or whatever coloured fruit. This is a beauty that has not only the fragrance of a flower, but you can eat it!

This book is designed to cover a range of climatic zones. It will be read by people all over Europe, possibly some Asian countries, and most certainly in America. But wherever the reader lives, there is at least one fruit tree included here that is suitable for your climate, and, hopefully, your garden!

To grow a fruit tree organically involves studying the actual needs and requirements of the tree instead of just putting it anywhere in the garden you have a space, or as is often the case, in the middle of the lawn. Indeed, it is worth making the fruit tree, or trees, the pivotal point in the garden so the design is around the trees, rather than the trees a hopeful addition. Fruit trees put any old where will mostly live, but seldom thrive, meaning they will not produce well.

Natural Fruit Trees

Our main requirement for fruit trees is that they produce an abundance of good quality, natural, unpolluted, non-poisoned fruit. This is becoming rare. The vast multinational chemical companies are producing more and more poisonous chemicals to spray onto our vegetables and fruit trees to kill the bugs. Apart from a few specialist firms in biological control, little regard is paid to encouraging the natural cycle of the predator bugs which eat the pest bugs. In this book we will focus on how to grow fruit on trees that are so healthy the bugs will pass them by, instead looking for the distressed trees they prefer to attack.

Most fruit trees need an open position, not one under or close to other large trees. Some fruit trees can be grown as espaliers in front of a wall, benefiting from the trapped heat, but in this book we are looking at the normal, organic way of growing regular fruit trees.

No matter what fruit tree you are growing, only grow it if you want it. Just as a tree malingers if unwanted, so a tree will get a boost of energy if it receives regular appreciation. Receiving the thought energy of being admired is a fertiliser in its own right, but it does have to be genuine!

In this book I am skipping over pruning. This is a skill to learn either from a specialist book, an appropriate DVD, or from a horticulture class. And I do recommend that you learn to know how, when, and why to prune your fruit tree. I will mention, however, that pruning should be done with awareness. You need to be aware that by your pruning you are shaping the fruit tree and determining the next year's fruit. You are opening the tree to an air flow, removing older non-productive wood and sucker wood, and creating fruiting spurs—in short, you are working with the tree to improve its cropping capacity, its shape and its overall health. You need to be conscious of what you are doing and conscious of the tree as you do it. By being focussed and conscious of the act of pruning a tree, you will create a greater harmony and balance within the tree.

I consider it a shame that most modern varieties of fruit trees have been dwarfed through hybridisation to cater to commercial purposes. They may be easier for picking, but they are more prone to disease on weaker, dwarfed, more vulnerable rootstock. They are more at risk in floods and drought, too shallow rooted, and too dependent on irrigation and chemical stimulants. Obviously, because of these (deliberate?) built-in weaknesses, the trees need more chemicals, both as sprays and growth stimulants, to keep them alive and functioning for commercial purposes.

I am not saying that these dwarfed trees cannot be successfully grown organically, they can. If your garden space only allows for one or two of these dwarfed hybrid trees, then go for it. Just make sure that deep mulch in the manner I describe is a permanent feature for them.

My advice is to ignore these types of trees if you have the room to grow an old-fashioned variety of fruit tree. With a little effort they can be found. The quality and flavour of some of these old-stock fruit trees is a nostalgic visit to the past. Some mail-order plant nurseries specialise in such plants.

Incidentally, just to be sure of the difference, plant nurseries are places that specialise in growing plants, mostly sold wholesale to the garden centres. Some are wholesale only, but many others also sell directly to the public. Close to towns or cities with high rent, only a few garden centres can afford, or have room, to grow their own stock plants.

EARLY FRUIT TREES

Another factor to be wary of is the hybridisation of trees for fruiting out of season. Peach trees have been produced which fruit exceptionally early in spring in temperate and warm zones, but the flavour is literally non-existent. Flavourless, a real letdown. I knew several growers who pulled their trees out because they were embarrassed by the awful quality of the fruit. They felt they were cheating the buyers. I agree. This is tricky, because the later peaches are invariably attacked by the great scourge of fruit in warmer climates—the fruit fly. However, the baiting of this fly is reasonably effective, and areas do vary. Generally, a fruit tree with optimum health and vitality is the greatest deterrent to all bugs, and believe me, very seldom is a fruit tree in total vibrant health.

Avoid the earliest variety of any modern hybridised fruit trees, but the older, proven, early varieties are all reliable. They have survived the test of time. If possible, eat a fruit of the variety that you are thinking of growing to be sure you really like it. The time to decide is before you plant the tree.

CONSIDER CAREFULLY

Think about what you want before you rush out to buy your fruit trees. Think carefully. Think about the space that you have, how many fully grown trees you can accommodate, the height they will reach and how best you can utilise that space. Garden space is valuable, precious. Consider the keeping qualities of the fruit. Organically grown old varieties mostly keep exceptionally well, but the same cannot be said for the all new commercial hybrids. The aim was, first and foremost, quantity. I doubt that qualities for home storage were even considered.

Let us assume that you have the space to grow two fruit trees. Of course, climate will mainly dictate what they will be. In a cold/cool climate, if you choose the apple as one of your trees, then with care at picking and careful storage without any bruising, you can eat apples for a long time if they stored in a cool room in the house.

When I was a young man in England, Treenie and I used to pick and store apples from an old orchard. In an unused bedroom, we stored them on untreated wooden racks, one above the other like a set of drawers. No two apples touched. We would be eating the last of the previous season's apples when the new season apples began. They would shrivel a bit, but the taste remained good. Any apple with a touch of mould was immediately removed. By comparison, today's apples have trouble lasting a couple of weeks after they come out of cold storage.

A mid-to-late-season apple tree with a peach tree would give you peaches to eat immediately, and apples for long-term storage, if you can supply a cold cellar or space in a cool room. Equally, in a warmer climate, by growing a banana and a pawpaw, you can produce a truly incredible amount of fruit from a reasonably small space, far more than you could keep up with eating. You simply dry the surplus fruit in a dehydrator, and keep it for real taste treats. Nothing is wasted.

Whatever the fruit tree, the ideal to aim for is optimum health. This requires no more than attention to detail. The difference between mediocrity and excellence is huge. Far too many organic growers think that if it is 'organic' then it is okay to produce mediocre fruit. I disagree. The pursuit of excellence is not to grow the biggest, or the most; it is the pursuit of energy in, and quality of, the fruit.

Obviously there are many hundreds of fruit trees that can be grown, especially in the tropical zones. I am including just a few of the popular fruit trees that can and should be grown in most gardens, along with one nut tree for each climatic zone. These are all covered in enough detail that you can literally go ahead . . . and when the time is right, start planting.

∾

I am dividing the home orchard into three distinct climatic zones:

COLD/COOL
Regular heavy frost

TEMPERATE/MILD
Occasional light frost

WARM/HOT
No frost, no chill

COLD/COOL CLIMATES
Regular heavy winter and spring frosts

APPLE:

Apple trees have been bred to produce a wide variety of fruit for all seasons, from the first early apples to the late, mostly long-keeping ones. You will choose the variety you like, and be sure that it is suitable for your district. It is a good idea to choose an early or mid-season and late variety, and to make sure from where you buy it that the chosen varieties are right for cross-pollination.

Apples like an open sunny position, and while not fussy about the soil, they do not like sitting in cold, wet, poorly-drained winter soil. Most of the pests and problems in apple trees come from a lack of understanding of the needs of the tree. We will attempt to correct this!

We have established that within rich organic soil, well supplied with organic matter and humus, there is an abundance of soil life. Amongst these squillions of life forms is a particular fungus—the important family of mycorhiza—that has a close symbiotic relationship with the apple tree. In fact, without mycorhiza in the soil where there are apple trees, you cannot have a healthy tree.

The tiny threadlike filaments of this fungus actually invade the root cells of the apple tree, and the exchange of nutrients, minerals and other probably unknown factors are beneficial to both the mycorhiza and the apple tree. To obtain soil rich in mycorhiza is quite easy and will ensure a healthy tree. Unfortunately, in many of our commercial apple orchards this relationship is non-existent. This means the orchard growers rely on chemicals to attempt some sort of control over the unhealthy trees. What is the answer? Mulch! Rotted mulch creates organic matter rich in mycorhiza and will provide for the needs of the tree for this natural relationship.

Apply a 30–60 cm (1–2 feet) layer of any mulching material you can get, preferably of a feeder type, and/or of as many different materials as possible. Starting from 60 cm (2 feet) from the base of the tree, lay the mulch so that it spreads out 60 cm (2 feet) further than the furthermost reach of the branches. The outside edge of the tips of the branches is known as the drip line. It is here that the tree roots are most active in collecting water and nutrients for the tree. With all species of fruit trees, from the coldest climate to the hottest, do not mulch directly at the base of any tree trunk. Leave at least 30 cm (1 foot) clear around the trunk to discourage disease or undesirable fungi in the bark or stem of the tree. A flow of air around the tree trunk right to the ground is natural and desirable.

Compost contains mycorhiza fungus and can be mixed with the mulch to inoculate it. If you have access to a forest where a thick layer of damp leaf mould and rotted debris has accumulated, this is excellent for spreading in the mulch to start the culture going. I am only talking about one barrow-full here, not stripping the forest floor!

Another item for your consideration; it is important to realise that the peripheral tips (growing points) of apple tree roots actively dislike grass roots. It is possible that the grass roots emit various gases that are incompatible to the apple tree roots. This means that where apple trees grow in grass, they are handicapped, unable to achieve maximum health and vitality. However, if they are grown in white clover, or any other similar legume, the roots find this beneficial. A common mix is grass and white clover. Encourage the clover, eradicate the grass. And if you have an apple tree in the lawn—make your choice! However, if you have an apple tree in a lawn, and want both, simply mulch out to that point beyond the drip line of the apple tree, maybe edge around it with some logs or small rocks, and you can have both.

Apple trees like a moist soil, but the prime time for watering is from fruit set, when the tree is flowering, to the time of picking the fruit. This is always the critical time for adequate water.

For the home gardener, the answer to apple tree health is simple; mulch the trees for mycorhiza, mulch to stop weeds growing, mulch to provide the soil life and tree with food, mulch to keep the soil moist, mulch to even out the soil temperature, and mulch so you can lay in it looking up through the branches of the tree while you sing it a lullaby!

Pear

This tree is not grown anywhere near as much as the apple in the average garden. The pear is a delicious fruit and it can bear prolifically if a few simple requirements are met. Basically, it likes a warmer, perhaps more sheltered position than the apple, and is even less tolerant of a heavy, wet clay soil. The pear will not produce quality fruit on poor soil, but it is very responsive to organic growing.

Do not grow it close to other large trees. It likes their shelter, but if grown too close it seems to get an inferiority complex! Really it is all about root range. Pears do not like mixing their roots with other trees. Try to have pear trees of different varieties on flower at the same time. Your local garden centre should be able to advise you on this. If you have only a single pear tree, and there are no pear trees in other gardens around you, then cut a branch in full flower from a friend's tree and stand it in a bucket of water beneath your tree. The bees will do the rest. This will ensure the necessary cross-pollination and a good setting of fruit. Of course, having two varieties for this purpose is the most certain way.

A deep mulch will retain the moisture that is so vital in summer for good quality fruit. You will learn to prune pear trees only lightly, cutting out branches that rub on others, are growing across the tree, or will cause splitting from the main trunk. Aim for openness and shape.

Water from the time of fruit setting to picking the fruit. This is when a steady supply of moisture is essential.

When eating a pear it is possible to eat the whole fruit as the seeds lie within the flesh, unprotected by a tough outer husk in the manner of apples. Tasting the juiciness and flavour of organically grown pears is an enriching experience, a wonderful reward for all your efforts. Just be a bit cautious about how much you eat in one go, because they are the most delicious laxative you will ever consume.

A VITAL ELEMENT FOR ALL STONE FRUIT

We are now about to deal with stone fruit. One element that leads to a lot of failure in *all* stone fruit is a lack of calcium in the soil. A high pH does not always mean an abundance of calcium; usually, but not always. When any stone fruit tree is flowering and setting the tiny immature fruit in a soil lacking in calcium, the tree will drop a large percentage of its tiny unformed fruit along with the flowers. A lot of gardeners put this down to frost, and it can be, but so often it is lack of calcium.

To ensure an abundance of quality stone fruit, add lime, dolomite or gypsum (depending on your soil type and pH) at approximately 2–3 buckets around the tree right out to a metre (yard) beyond the drip line of an established tree. For a new or young tree scatter the lime, dolomite or gypsum to a bit beyond your guess of where the drip line will eventually reach. In this way its roots will grow into soil that has plenty of calcium in readiness. Do this each winter to be sure that the tree will always have an adequate supply of calcium, and thus set its fruit. Within reason, it is actually quite difficult to give the soil too much calcium.

Just to explain the relationship between stone fruit and calcium a bit further, you need to realise that the tree is intent on setting fruit for seed. The tree is not trying to please you with fruit to simply eat; to the tree you are a seed sower. The tree is ensuring the survival of its species. If there is inadequate calcium to produce viable seed (the stone), then the tree will drop fruit until what is left will have enough calcium to fully develop the seed. It is the seed of the fruit that needs the calcium, not the flesh of the fruit. Remember, this is about calcium, not the pH. Before you add the mulch each year, first apply the vital calcium.

APRICOT

I am never quite sure whether it is the delicious apricot or the sweet cherry that is my favourite cold climate fruit. Commercial sweet cherries still taste the way they should, but some of the commercial apricots, ugh! The apricot grows into a big strong tree, preferring a sunny open position in a deep soil rich in organic matter. The apricot definitely favours the cool hills to hot valleys, but given the opportunity, it is 'the' stone fruit I would grow. The normal, non-hybridised apricot tree is a large, open, spreading tree and it does need some space. Again, this is a stone fruit, so the calcium factor is of great importance. You can now buy plumcots, a hybrid of plum/apricot. Personally, I have never eaten one, let alone grown it, but I would suggest the culture is similar to apricots.

Do not prune the apricot at all, unless it is essential surgery. If you have to do this, be very careful that the branch does not tear or split the bark of the tree when it is removed. The apricot tree bleeds rather easily, and is susceptible to disease if this happens. If strong winds tear a few branches from the tree, this is when surgical pruning should be done, leaving a clean cut.

Apart from the susceptibility to bleed, the apricot tree is remarkably resistant to bugs and pests of all sorts. Keep the apricot well mulched, spreading out to about 2 m (6 feet) beyond the drip line. The roots love a cool, moist, rich root run, and will fruit abundantly in return for such a favour. They love a moist soil, but not waterlogged in winter. An apricot tree in America was discovered to have sent a single root well over a kilometre (half a mile) to a constantly dripping tap. Smart tree!

The way in which a tree can reach out its roots to harvest its needed moisture and minerals is quite remarkable. They can hone in on minerals or moisture a great distance from the tree, sending out a root not one fraction bigger than is required to ensure a constant supply.

As with all fruiting trees, water is essential from fruit set to the time of picking. You may not have a dripping tap in the vicinity!

With a far wider root run than the peach tree, keep this tree well away from your vegetable garden. Quite a few gardeners can put poor vegetable crops down to the apricot tree that seemed so far away when it was small. Plenty of mulch, a smile or two and a whispered word, and you will have the most delectable reward. Believe me, all fruit trees respond to your conscious energy.

Cherry

Cherries come in two distinct varieties; sweet eating cherries, and cooking or morello cherries. Although their culture is identical, we will concern ourselves with the delicious, sweet eating cherries. They are so scrumptious my mouth is watering at the thought of them!

These are quite big trees and need an open sunny position in a soil rich in organic matter. Cherries are stone fruit, so everything I have said about calcium applies to cherries.

Keep the cherry tree deeply mulched as for other fruit trees. And remember this tree needs space. Be very sure that you have the space in your garden that it needs. As far as I know, there are no dwarfed versions of the cherry tree—thank . . . ! Deep mulch will ensure that moisture is retained during the spring rains for the developing fruit on the tree, while also feeding and enriching the soil.

If you do everything right, the humble bird is the only real problem with cherry trees. They like the fruit as much as you do. They get up earlier in the morning, they can hop on the branches, and they have wings. However, there are various ways to keep them away. Pitch a tent and live under the tree for a few weeks; attach a bell to the tree with a cord leading to the house, and ring it loudly every few minutes (your neighbour will love this!), or catch a barking dog and tie it under the tree.

Seriously, bright flashing objects are very effective, and hanging CDs from the branches are reputed to work well. The more in the sun the CDs or flashing objects are, the better. Some novelty shops sell what I call twisters that twirl endlessly in the breeze. A few bright coloured ones could do the trick. Old mirrors flashing in the sun also deter birds, so long as they are hanging, twisting in the breeze. If all else fails, cobweb netting (bird netting) designed and shaped for a tree should be effective. The hawk kites which are made for scaring birds are also very effective. Attached to a tall flexible rod standing through the tree, the hawks must look scary for fruit-eating birds.

However, there is another consideration to all this. Creating fear in your garden, even for the birds, is creating discord in consciousness. A method I have used successfully many times is to simply make an agreement with the birds. Just talk to them. Agree to share with them, along the lines of 75% for you, 25% for them. That seems fair—you did all the work, but they lived here first. If you do this with a true conscious commitment, it is very reliable, so long as you do not 'go to pieces' while they are taking their share.

It will also teach you how to trust, and that is a very worthwhile lesson. As far as balance and harmony in the garden is concerned, this is the only way for a conscious gardener. And when it works, as it will, it gives you a sense of really connecting with Nature.

With their deep roots cherries can reach quite deep water, but the occasional deep watering from fruit set to picking is also needed in dry weather.

Cherry trees need no pruning at all. They are best left to develop into the large and beautiful trees that they are. Just imagine, cherry blossoms and fruit. But you will need an extension ladder.

MULBERRY

Walking down a country lane with Treenie on a visit to Italy, we were delighted to see white mulberry trees in full fruit alongside the road. Yes, we ate plenty of the sweet juicy fruit! This is a comparatively little known tree, and while it is not practical for the small garden, for those with plenty of space it is a very rewarding tree to grow.

The mulberry can make a marvellous specimen tree. It likes a deep soil, rich in organic matter with a cool root run. The mulberry is suited to both cold and warm climates, and the whole range between, so it is a tough, versatile tree. I have seen fine specimens growing in England, Italy, and locally in the subtropics. It is very long-lived tree, becoming both huge and spectacular when it is fully mature.

There are two types, the black fruiting and the white fruiting. Some people feel the black mulberry makes a mess in the middle of the lawn, and it will certainly make a mess staining your hands as you gobble them up . . . but who cares! The white fruit is free of these sins. The fruit is like a huge, longish blackberry and should be eaten ripe when it falls to the ground. It has numerous uses in pies and culinary items, but for me it is best eaten raw. I think they are delicious.

If you decide to grow a mulberry, choose which type you want, and while the tree is young keep it mulched. They grow quite quickly, so as the tree gets larger, with a widening spread, a lot of leaves and debris will gradually accumulate under the tree. Allow all the low branches to develop so that in time they will almost touch the soil. As this happens, so you reduce the mulch, for the tree will provide its own deep biomass.

Deep water occasionally from fruit set to fruit falling. The better you treat the young tree, the more it will fruit and the quicker it will grow, ever becoming more self-sufficient. In drought however, give it deep water.

Grown well the mulberry is generous with both the size and the amount of fruit it will yield.

NECTARINE

Nectarines are easier to grow than peaches. Because they have a good deal more vigour they are more resistant to disease, and that is always a plus. Basically, this tree is grown in the same way as the peach, also thriving well with hens to keep the fallen fruit cleaned up. The idea of hens for eggs and trees for fruit all in the same space should appeal.

The nectarine needs a sunny open position with plenty of space, as it grows into quite a big tree. It needs a soil rich in organic matter, so it also needs mulch. Mulch, mulch and more mulch. The tree will grow faster, stronger, and fruit better and more abundantly than grown by any other method. And it will resist insect attack because of its natural health and vitality.

These trees seem to grow better on the hills and slopes with a bit of altitude than in a valley, and are well worth a place in the garden. Again, the calcium factor applies to this stone fruit. Prune lightly to obtain a good shape, then only surgery pruning.

Be sure to supply adequate water from fruit set to picking to ensure the size and quality of your fruit. The nectarine is very tasty, with quite a number of varieties to choose from. They store well in the freezer.

PEACH

The luscious peach is quite easily grown—their only drawback is that they are rather prone to bugs. However, grown organically we can combat most of these, simply because when grown in a soil that is rich in organic matter, they are less likely to occur.

When you buy and plant a young peach tree, remember the calcium factor. Allow it to grow and develop for a couple of years, taking off all flowers before they develop into fruit. Peaches can be rather precocious, but you need them to grow deep roots and strong branches first; the fruit needs to come a bit later. Prune out weak and unproductive growth.

If you have only a little space, the peach has been dwarfed to the extent it can be grown in a very large pot, yet the fruit is natural size. For me, I would choose a large older variety of tree, but that might create problems for you with growing space and picking. There are many hybrids to choose from, but I recommend you avoid very early varieties.

Peach trees respond to a good, deep mulch. They seem to prefer a well-mixed mulch, especially with some animal or poultry manure. If you have the room, or the situation, they grow very well in a hen run. One of the reasons for this is that any fruit that falls to the ground is quickly eaten by the hens. Fruit that falls early or easily is generally fruit that has some bugs in it. A healthy tree will normally hold healthy fruit until it is ripe, then it is handpicked. Impaired fruit falls easily. This is part of the tree's defence, but unfortunately, many of the bugs develop in the rotting fruit, then make their way back up the tree trunk to complete their cycle, ready for next year's fruit. By eating all the fruit, the hens break this cycle, so the trees greatly benefit. This works exceptionally well in a very well-drained deep-litter hen run. The litter is continually turned over by the hens and all fallen fruit is consumed, yet the tree is also deeply mulched with the hen droppings.

I used to run geese in my small wire-netted orchard of twenty mixed fruit, and this proved to be very beneficial. About forty peafowl and a mob of guinea fowl also frequented the orchard. The geese kept the grass and clover very short, plus they are very liberal with their droppings! The trees were also very heavily mulched.

Make sure the peach has adequate water from fruit set to picking. If the peach tree dries out the fruit is prone to splitting.

The flesh of a ripe, juicy, mouth-watering organically-grown freestone peach is quite superb, and more than worth a place in your garden.

PLUM

The tantalizingly tasty range of plums comes in many flavours, sizes, shapes, colours and seasons. Flavour varies a lot, but among them there is at least one for you. The Japanese varieties are popular, as are some of the English types. For me, no plum can surpass the Greengage; it is a uniquely flavoured fruit. When Treenie and I emigrated to Oz, I really regretted leaving our Cambridge Greengage trees.

Happily, you can have plum tree varieties fruiting from early spring literally to early winter. It has a very wide fruiting range without loss of flavour. If at all possible, try to have a tree fruiting in spring, summer and autumn, each with its different flavour and appeal. The plum should have a place in every garden as it is fuss free and easily grown.

Make sure that the soil is rich in organic matter and that it does not become waterlogged in the winter. Saturated winter soil in a cold climate is a 'no no' for every fruit that I know of. A little shelter from gales at flowering and fruiting time is beneficial, but not absolutely essential.

Keep the plum tree deeply mulched with straw, hay, or

whatever you can get, right out to beyond the drip line. Plums are heavy feeders with roots close to the surface, so abundant mulching is abundantly rewarded.

Because of their shallow roots, plum trees dislike any disturbance in the soil around them. No hoeing, no tillage at all, just deep mulch. Plum trees neither like nor need much pruning. Surgery pruning in the winter, such as trimming a torn limb or removing a branch that insists on growing downward, is okay, nothing more. Some of the English plum trees grow quite tall, but as the fruit grows and develops they weep downward with the weight of fruit, facilitating picking. Personally, I liked using a ladder.

Remember the calcium factor. Water is essential from fruit set to mature fruit at picking time. A lack of water can lead to the fruit splitting.

Plums have the advantage that they are easy to freeze and store. Many people now depend on the home freezer, and the plum is perfect for this. As with berry fruit, try letting them thaw as they cook.

HAZEL OR FILBERT NUT

This small tree can and should be grown in most gardens, not needing too much space for its generous crop of nuts.

The tree is a shrubby, bushy type of plant growing to approximately 4–5 m (12–15 feet), so it is not too big for the average garden. It likes a good fertile soil, well drained and rich in organic matter. The soil needs to be about pH neutral, or even a bit alkaline. It will thrive better if given some protection from strong winds, so planted in the vicinity of other shrubs, trees, the garage or a shed will suit it admirably.

Once again, this is a tree that thrives in deep mulch. How could it not? Mulch right out to the drip line, keep the mulch maintained, and you will smile when you harvest the fattest hazel nuts you have ever seen.

Water it in very dry weather and when the nut is forming, but overall this is a tough, tolerant, rewarding plant.

The hazel—as I always knew it, but the filbert in some countries—has separate male and female flowers on the same tree. The male flowers appear in the autumn, but do not produce pollen until spring when the female flowers open. Have a couple of varieties for cross-pollination.

The nuts ripen and fall to the ground in midsummer when they should be picked up and dried before storing. The nut is a fat little beauty with a delicious flavour, a flavour used in a whole lot of commercial foods.

Considering it is so easily grown, it is very underrated as a useful plant in the garden. A fresh, organically grown hazel nut is in a different zone from the imported commercial ones.

TEMPERATE/MILD CLIMATES
Occasional light winter frosts

AVOCADO

What an incredible food fruit this is. It is unusual in being a savoury, rather than a sweet fruit, and is not difficult to grow providing its cultural requirements are met.

Avocado prefers a moderately acid soil, but it is essential that it is deep, rich in organic matter and free draining. The avocado needs at least 1.5 m (5 feet) of well-drained top soil, and even beneath this the subsoil should be open and porous. The avocado is very susceptible to a nasty root rot fungus—phytophera—which thrives in wet, waterlogged, or even just poorly drained soils. Many growers plant the avocado on the hillsides, thus ensuring good drainage.

Another peculiarity of this plant is the pollination of its flower. Each flower contains both male and female sex organs, but unfortunately they emerge at different times. In a single tree this can mean poor, erratic fruiting, despite heavy flowering. To ensure full pollination we need to grow two or more of certain grouped varieties. Taking three common varieties of each group we find Hass, Wurtz and Hazzard will pollinate successfully together, as will Fuerte, Sharwill and Bacon. No ham!

In my own garden I planted Fuerte to fruit in May, Sharwill in late June, and Wurtz in early October. However, it was all a disaster. The trees grew, flowered heavily, even pollinated, and I watched the immature fruit fall onto the mulch because I was unable to meet their needs. My top soil was too shallow, and I could not supply anywhere near enough water. So, be warned. Keeping trees alive is a far cry from fruiting properly.

When you buy your grafted trees, you may need to protect the vulnerable green branches from the summer sun when first planted. To do this, paint the branches with a white *water* paint to prevent them from scorching on a scorching hot day! Seriously, sunburn can have a very detrimental effect on young avocado trees. As the plants gradually sun harden, the paint slowly disperses in the rain.

Avocado trees need a fairly sheltered position, or if exposed need careful staking for a couple of years. The roots are also vulnerable in the early stages of planting and growth, so keep the trees well mulched and well watered. Plant them at 5 m (15 feet) between trees. A triangle of three trees works well for mulch, watering and pollination. Mulch the whole area deeply and set up the water in the centre of the triangle if you are using a sprinkler.

Add gypsum to the soil once each year, spreading it liberally around the trees. Avocados have a large stone, so the calcium factor applies. I cannot stress enough how avocados need a soil rich in organic matter. I cannot place enough emphasis on how important mulch is for their health, vitality, and well-being. Organic matter in the soil will improve drainage while increasing water retention— that's Nature for you!

The trees have little need of pruning, other than the clean removal of storm-damaged branches, rubbing or splitting branches, and perhaps shaping. Avocado trees need some water all season, but most particularly from fruit set to picking. Then it should be a deep watering into moist mulch.

The fruit should be picked and ripened indoors, not left on the tree. If it takes more than seven to ten days to ripen, they have been picked too soon. Taking longer than this means the fruit is not mature enough and will lose quality if picked. So you test by picking a couple. When they are ready, you can hasten the process by placing a few in a brown paper bag with a ripe apple.

The avocado is rich in cholesterol-free oil. It is a very tasty, very nutritional and versatile package of super food.

CUSTARD APPLE

The custard apple is officially *Annona reticulata*, while the *Cherimoya*—known as the custard apple—is *Annona cherimolia*. However, they are so similar most of us would not know the difference. The major difference is that cherimolia is hardier, preferring the subtropics to the full tropics.

For me, they are all custard apples, and a sweeter, more delicious fruit would be hard to find. As the years have passed my tolerance for sugary sweet foods has dropped considerably, so unfortunately custard apples are now much too sweet for me.

Plant the trees in a deep soil rich in organic matter. Set the trees when any last frosts have finished, and the soil has warmed. Although attention is required the first season, once established the custard apple is a hardy tree. For the first season keep the tree well watered with deep watering. No wetting the surface only, but deep penetration. Now is also the time to establish the mulch. These trees need mulch to reach out beyond the drip line, so mulch, mulch, and even more mulch. Also the addition of animal or poultry manure is very beneficial. Only mulch can continue to enrich the soil, building up the organic matter.

Regular water is needed from when the fruit set until picking.

Custard apples are rather vulnerable to strong winds, so a bit of shelter is rewarded, but they need an open, sunny position. They can be grown 4–5 m (12–15 feet) apart, and seem to like their own company when grouped. The fruit is winter maturing and should be picked a few days before they are fully ripe.

LEMON

I think more questions have been asked about the sour old lemon than any other fruit, mostly because people are trying to grow it in a climate that is too cold, or it gets sick because they do not grow it organically. This is the organic culture for the lemon.

Choose an open sunny position, and avoid heavy clay soil. Stagnant, wet soil in winter is death for the lemon. The cause for an ailing lemon is often because of the wrong position in the wrong soil. Site it carefully.

Choose a lemon tree most suited to your area, and get a variety that will give you summer fruit as much as possible. Most fruit in the winter. When you set your tree into the soil, be sure that you leave no air pockets. Firm the soil carefully, and water well. If you are in an area of light frosts, wait until they are finished before planting. A mature tree has little problem with a light frost, but it can kill a newly planted tree.

Make sure the tree is staked before you set the tree. Take the tree to the stake, not the stake to the tree. Damaged roots can be a serious setback. If it has been planted a while and needs a stake, drive it in at an angle away from the roots.

The lemon is a shallow-rooted tree, with roots just below the surface. This means it is a poor competitor. It cannot even compete with grass, so make sure no other plants are growing within the drip line of the lemon tree, and this includes lawn. If there is one treatment all the citrus approve of and enjoy, it is mulch. I have pulled citrus trees back from the edge of death by removing all grass from around them, and then deep mulching them. In warm climates the cause of so much grief with lemons is the rampant grass kikuyu.

Never hoe or cultivate around lemon trees. Mulch them. Deep mulch is to citrus as water is to a fish. Never let the mulch touch the base of the trunk; make sure that at least 30 cm (1 foot) is clear because citrus are rather prone to collar rot. Before you add mulch each season sprinkle blood/bone and potash 8:1 all around the tree. All citrus like plenty of nitrogen, so give it this mix every three months throughout the growing season. Prune it in spring if necessary, removing branches that are rubbing on others, or are broken or crowded. Keep the centre of the tree open to the sun, rather than overcrowded with growth.

Water is an absolute necessity to the citrus if you want fruit. They need water all year, but most important is from fruit set to picking. A lack of water or irregular watering will result in the tree dropping fruit, plus split and distorted fruit. This is where a deep moist mulch saves so much water. All citrus respond very well to a regular kelp/fish foliar spray.

When harvesting the fruit, snip the slightly green, just-turning-yellow lemon off the tree with a piece of stalk attached. Store in a box of dry sawdust in a cool place and the fruit will ripen to yellow. This way the rind will be thinner and the fruit much juicier than if left on the tree. In the right climate, a garden should have a lemon tree, even if for no other reason than to help you realise just how sweet Washington Navel oranges are!

MANDARIN, GRAPEFRUIT, KUMQUAT, MULTI-GRAFTS

What more can I say. All citrus have the same requirements and all reward organic culture by being trouble-free to grow. Kumquats are terrible to eat fresh, but they make the best marmalade I have ever tasted. And I am a marmalade connoisseur! You can actually grow them in a large pot. They look very ornamental with flowers followed by tiny orange fruit.

You can now buy trees with up to eight different citrus grafted onto one tree. This may sound like a novelty, or a risky gimmick, but in actuality I think this is a very good idea. More often than not we get far too many lemons, oranges or grapefruit all at one time, and many are wasted. A tree that gives you enough to eat of many different varieties at differing times has a lot going for it. These trees are quite expensive, but this is the way I would go. They will respond to exactly the same organic culture as any other citrus, and deep mulch is exactly what they need. Be aware that a tree fruiting over a longer period of time will need constant blood/bone and potash 8:1. Also regular watering in a well-drained soil is a must. If you eliminate all stress in your multi-graft citrus tree, then you are unlikely to get any trouble.

Just make sure that all the grafts have well and truly taken when you buy the tree, and that they are strong in the grafted area. Be sure that the tree as a whole is high in energy. Just touch it, and stop thinking. A conscious gardener will 'feel' the energy.

ORANGE

Right on cue, we come to the orange tree. The organic culture for the lemon is basically the same for all citrus. Oranges like a soil rich in organic matter and well drained. In other words, a humus-rich soil.

The variety of orange depends a lot on your locality. Washington Navel is my choice. Stake firmly, but try to have the stakes removed from any citrus by the third year. They need to find their own strength, and constant or over-staking weakens any tree in the long run. Like all citrus, oranges can get a whole gamut of bugs and pests, but most are easily dealt with.

First and foremost, mulch, mulch, and more mulch. Have I said that before? This will give the plant the required health and vitality to repel and resist most invaders. A winter wash of white oil is not harmful to the tree, and affords protection in the spring. Neither does it offend my organic principles. A few leaf eaters are generally best ignored, but do keep an eye on things. Most fruit trees can live with a certain amount of pest bugs living on them. This is in the natural order of growth. Usually, in turn the pest attracts the predators, so Nature keeps it all in balance. To attempt to over control this with harsh chemicals is unnecessary and foolish.

When your citrus trees are young, especially the first couple years, take the fruit off the trees as soon as they have set. Give your tree a chance to spread out its roots, put strength into its branches and grow a bit of size. The modern hybrid citrus are so precocious they will tear their branches off with the weight of fruit on a first-year tree.

Water your orange tree exactly as I have outlined for lemons.

Keep your orange trees well away from the lawn. An orange tree in a lawn will keep alive—but it will not thrive. It is comparable to keeping a dog chained up. Neither tree nor dog can achieve their potential.

Make sure that the mulch is well away from the base of the trunk, and that it extends well beyond the drip line. Honestly, until you do it you have no idea of the incredible difference between ordinary culture and organic culture of plants. All fruiting plants, including citrus, reward you with fruit that has the vitality you need in your body.

PERSIMMON

This delicious fruit has the advantage that the trees come in large, semi-dwarf or dwarf sizes. This is one case where I recommend the dwarf varieties in smaller gardens, for it seems to favour their growth and personality. The trees are tolerant of soil conditions, but like all fruit trees they need a deep, well-drained soil rich in organic matter.

Its position should be sunny and open, but sheltered if possible. Plant the dwarf varieties at 3 m (9 feet) apart, adding another metre (yard) or two for the larger varieties.

There are two distinct types of persimmon. The astringent

varieties must be eaten when fully—and I do mean *fully*—ripe, having a delicious jelly-like fruit which is pleasantly aromatic. The non-astringent varieties are eaten firm and crisp like an apple, and are also delicious. Apparently the astringent varieties have a much higher tannin content in the skins and fruit, thus the need for full ripeness.

This is yet another tree that responds to a deep mulch. Mulch is the critical factor for a healthy fruiting tree, and nothing can replenish the trees' energy after fruiting like a soil rich in humus.

When I go to Japan each year in October giving my seminars, I am fortunate that this is the time of ripe persimmons. While I notice that they have many varieties, the only ones I have seen or eaten there are the non-astringent, crisp persimmons. Along the country roads many persimmon trees offer their fruit to the traveller, and I have greatly enjoyed partaking of them.

ALMOND NUT:

For some reason almond trees are not common, even in gardens where the climate is favourable, yet commercially the nut is grown and sold in huge quantities. So if you want your own organically-grown nuts, this is the way to proceed.

The rather lovely tree, with its beautiful spring flowers, likes a deep soil, freely drained, rich in organic matter. It is a deep-rooted tree when established, but mulch is still of value and importance. Anything that feeds the soil is feeding and strengthening the plants that grow on it. Give the almond tree an open sunny position, and when you plant the young tree, if it is a windy area, stake it for the first year or so. It will thrive better if given some protection from strong winds. The tree is basically easy to grow and pest free if grown with plenty of mulch, but it will need another tree in the vicinity for pollination. A smaller self-fertile almond, All-in-One, growing no more than 4 to 5 metres (12–15 feet), is probably the most garden- and gardener-friendly almond tree available.

The almond nut is a nutritional feast. Many nutritionists claim that around five almonds at a meal with your other food will provide all necessary proteins for an adult. Whether this is correct or not—people have metabolic differences—the fact is that the almond is a power pack of nutrition. And, dare I say it, a super-power pack if grown organically!

Warm/Hot Climates
No frost, no chill; a wet and dry season

Banana

For me, the supreme fruit is the humble banana. I cannot praise it highly enough, both as a fruit and a food. Beyond all doubt, this is my favourite fruit. I just love the energy of the banana plant; its tremendous power of growth, the abundant energy package of the fruit, even the tropical look of the plant. Obviously, I'm bananas over this superlative package of super food!

Bananas need a warm-to-hot, wet climate. There is an art to growing the banana successfully, but it is easy enough. I am serious when I say that if you do not like the banana plant, then reconsider growing it. It does require quite a lot of attention, and if you do it grudgingly, the plant will know. Sorry, but they like to be liked!

Bananas have a massive underground 'true' stem, from which suckers continuously emerge. The banana can tolerate a wide range of soils, but they need to be deep, organically rich, and very free draining. This is a must. Bananas suffer from the same phytophera root fungus as avocados, and are sometimes planted as distant companions in the same plot of ground. They can take a huge amount of water, and need a high rainfall, but free drainage is essential. A continuously moist soil is perfect for them, with the moisture freely moving.

The answer: mulch. Bananas go bananas over mulch. Mulch is the difference between mediocre and magnificent with bananas, so mulch deeply with all the mulch you can throw around them.

There are several varieties; actually there are over seven hundred of them, but only a few are easily available. The commercial variety is the Cavendish, growing to about 3 m (9 feet) tall. In my district gardeners are not allowed to grow Cavendish because of the disease risk. This suits me. I generally grow the far tastier Lady Fingers, Sugar Bananas, or the less common Red Daccas. These plants grow taller and stronger, and the flavour of these three varieties is excellent.

You begin by obtaining some small banana suckers, setting them about 2 m (6 feet) apart. The hole needs to be deep enough to bury the white, fleshy, unexposed part of the sucker, and it should be kept moist, not wet, for the first few months. The wet season is the best time to begin. The thick fleshy stem which grows above ground is really a pseudo-stem—this is the part you see—and grows very rapidly under ideal conditions. When the stem is fully grown, the underground true stem sends up a flowering stem inside the pseudo-stem. The first you know of this is when the rather beautiful flowers emerge.

As the flowers fall from the stem, hand after hand of tiny, immature bananas are revealed. Eventually the stem grows away from the tiny fruit, leaving only an attractive bell of male flowers on the end. These will not become fruit. When the bell has grown about 30 cm (1 foot) away from the last tiny hand of fruit, it should be cut and removed. I have been told that quite a few cultures cook and eat this, but I have never tried it.

After a few months, as the fruit grow and fill under your wonderful organic conditions along with plenty of water, it is advisable to pull a special plastic banana bag over the stem of fruit. This bag is generally blue or silver. It should be tied loosely to the stem, allowing air to flow over the fruit. The bags will offer the developing bananas protection from fruit bats, possums, parrots, and insects, while evenly maturing the fruit.

The huge, heavy bunches should be cut when the top fruit are just beginning to turn yellow, then hang them in a warm, dry shed, or, if you have a high ceiling, the kitchen. This is the best place, for you can take the bananas as they ripen, hurrying to eat more as they rapidly progress.

At this time, the whole pseudo-stem that has just fruited is cut down and chopped up around the plant for mulch. It is important not to have more than three 'stems' on the plant at a time. Let me explain. When one stem is cut, the replacement should be nearly ready to flower and fruit, with another about half grown; now there are two. As the flower opens on the advanced stem, so you allow another strong sucker to continue growing; there are now three stems.

Far too many gardens—and this is so common—have a sucker that someone planted and forgot. Several years later a crowded mess of stems are fighting for water and space, all clumped into a solid, untidy, non-productive mass.

The banana requires constant de-suckering with a sharp, narrow spade. You can get the special spade, or shape one for yourself, but it needs a very strong, heavy, rigid, sharp blade. Look after your bananas properly, and they will reward you with a staggering abundance of really outstanding, top quality fruit.

For me, the banana is truly the food of the Gods.

LITCHI

The litchi tree produces those yummy fruit that seem to be featured as a dessert in every Chinese restaurant. Believe me, raw is far better than tinned. The litchi is not the easiest tree to grow successfully, but if you are keen on the delicious fruit it is well worth the effort. It requires an abundance of water when young, also from fruit setting to eventual picking, yet it really hates a wet, stagnant soil. Once again, organic growing to the rescue! You need to provide a deep soil rich in organic matter, and there is no better way than organic culture. Mulch—that's the answer—never-ending mulch, covering the soil around the tree season after season, a deep mulch that reaches out beyond the drip line.

This tree prefers the soil to be a little acidic, and while it likes plenty of sun it needs some shade and shelter while it is young. It can tolerate a coolish winter, but no frost.

Buy a grafted, named variety that is most suited for your district. If you grow more than one tree, allow 5 m (15 feet) between trees. The litchi can develop into a handsome, good-sized tree under the right conditions.

When the tree is planted, make sure that the prepared hole is enriched with compost or rotted organic matter. As stated, it is vital to maintain water to a newly planted tree. Keep the mulch ahead of the tree's widening spread, and incorporate animal and poultry manure in with it. Litchi must have a cool, moist soil, so mulch, mulch, mulch!

This is another fruit with a stone, and unrealised by many growers, the calcium factor applies. With the acidic preference of the litchi, spread gypsum liberally around the tree each winter.

One disadvantage of the litchi is that its fruit all ripen in a few short weeks. This curtails your season of epicurean delight, but it is a season of excellence. The fruit should not be taken from the tree until fully ripe. At this stage the clusters of fruit should be snipped off, rather than pulled or picked. A mild pruning! Sadly, the fruit will not keep more than a few days, the soft reddish shells quickly becoming crisp, and the fruit deteriorating. They are best eaten fresh, but the fruit is easily removed from the skin, the stone taken out, and the tasty white flesh can be frozen.

MANGO

Although this grows into a huge tree, and is only for the bigger gardens, the fruit is so renowned for its delicious flavour that I simply had to include it. Seriously, this is not for the smaller garden. It looks small enough when you buy the new mango tree, but that is only the beginning.

One particular need for the mango tree is a dry spring, and with our current erratic weather, that is now hit or miss. A dry spring is needed to ensure flower set and subsequent fruit, for a wet spring facilitates a fungus that causes massive dropping of the tiny, newly set fruit. Over the last two decades, this fungus has run rampant throughout subtropical Oz.

The basic need of this tree is a hot, dry climate. It can easily withstand drought once it is established for it is a very deep-rooted tree with the ability to search out water. It thrives in the dry winter and spring followed by the true wet summer season. However, the new young tree needs care and attention at planting time. It will need constant deep watering, and a deep soil rich in organic matter. The ideal time to plant the mango tree is during the wet season.

Mulch is essential for the mango tree in its formative years, as deeply as you can apply it and reaching beyond the expanding drip line. As the tree gets really big, you can allow its own leaf fall and debris to gradually take over from the mulch, for the soil under the tree will now be in permanent shade. The mango is another fruit with a stone, so again the calcium factor applies. Use dolomite, spreading it liberally around the tree each winter.

Buy a grafted variety of mango. There are quite a lot available, but rather than buying a fancy type, get a proven, reliable mango that is most suitable for your district. The tree may require some initial pruning to ensure a good shape, but it needs little to none as it grows and develops. If a branch eventually starts growing through the kitchen window, you are allowed to remove it at the base!

Position the tree in a hot, sunny, open position and take care of the roots. Plant the young tree carefully, stake it taking the tree to the stake, not vice versa, and give it a deep soaking. Those roots need to be encouraged downward, so no light sprinklings on the surface. Be sure that the mango is a long way from your house, or instead of a branch through the kitchen window you really will have roots in your foundations.

Apart from being a superior fruit tree, the mango is also

a superb shade tree and a visual delight. New growth is a rich coppery-bronze, making a delightful contrast to the deep green foliage of a well-grown tree.

The fruit should be picked ripe, or very nearly so. You can buy handheld telescopic pickers that take one fruit at a time, reaching quite a height. Slow, but worth it. Some people say that you should eat the juicy mangos while in the bath . . . try the swimming pool!

PAWPAW (PAPAYA)

I often consider the pawpaw, or papaya as it is also known, a botanical marvel. Its speed of growth, combined with the abundance, large size, and superb qualities of its fruit, are little short of incredible.

Without any doubt this fruiting plant should be in every garden. It takes very little room, not a lot of attention, yet it produces prolifically. In good conditions a pawpaw commences fruiting within eighteen months of sowing the small, round, black seeds, and it will be anywhere from 1.5 m (4–6 feet) tall. Because of the speed of growth most growers plant them towards the end of summer. This enables the cooler winter to check their vigorous growth, inducing fruit on a less tall plant. However, it will continue to grow the following season, eventually reaching around 4 m (12 feet) high.

Pawpaws can be grown from seed, or they can be purchased as young plants. By far the easiest method for the average garden is to buy a couple of bisexual plants from your garden centre toward the end of summer. These are self-pollinating, so one plant alone is fine. You can buy red, yellow and orange varieties; my preference is the sweet flavour of the red.

Sowing the seed of a favoured pawpaw works well, providing the seed is fresh. It will not keep and remain viable. Wash the seed when you take it from the fruit, and sow into the soil of the intended growing site, or sow the seeds in small pots no more than 2.5 cm (1 inch) deep. The first seedlings to emerge are generally male plants.

Only one needs to be kept. A week or so later the female seedlings emerge, and the required number of fruiting plants should be kept. I would like to emphasise that this is a generalisation for sexing the plants, and not an infallible method. The only certain method is flowering time. Males flower in clusters on thin stems, while the females flower at the trunk, singly. For pollination, one male to eight female plants is adequate.

All this is simple enough, but it does require conscious observation of the seedlings to determine the male plants, and the time lag before the females arrive. Being conscious of the plant, aware of its tremendous energy as it grows, opens you to the reasons why this plant has fruit with such amazing qualities. If you would like to do a little research on the pawpaw, you will find that it offers a cure for many human ailments.

When you set the young plants in late summer, make sure that they are going into a soil rich in organic matter, with very good drainage. They prefer a neutral soil, around pH 6.5–7.0. They are not keen on too much acidity. Pawpaws are sun lovers; this is essential, and they will thrive in the same conditions as for bananas. They are lovers of deep rich mulch, and with many of their roots close to the surface, mulch should also be considered as essential. They like the soil to be cool and continually moist; only mulch can maintain this condition.

Water your pawpaws frequently. They will mostly be growing fruit all the year round. In the full tropics they will continue to develop their fruit all winter, but in cooler regions in the subtropics they can come to a standstill, waiting for the warmer weather. They cannot tolerate cold weather, and frost will ruin them. If a favoured mature plant becomes too big and unwieldy, it may be cut down to about 60 cm (2 feet) above ground. Cut a plastic bottle, or upturned can to fit over the stump to prevent entry of water into the hollow stem and any subsequent rot. The plant will now grow several stems, gaining a new lease on life.

Pawpaws are not long-lived like trees, but many will last

up to ten years, especially if cut down and regrown. No matter what variety you grow, the flavour will vary according to the soil conditions—mulched are superior—and the climate. Generally, the warmer the winter, the faster and sweeter it will develop the fruit. You owe it to yourself to grow the very tasty, fabulous pawpaw, for their healing qualities are, indeed, no less than fabulous.

MACADAMIA NUT

How nice to grow a nut tree indigenous to Oz, even if the Hawaiians had to show us how to do it. Once known as the Queensland Bopple nut, the popular macadamia now enjoys worldwide appeal. Most of the hybridisation has been to reduce the thickness of the once tough, almost impenetrable shell, and to fatten the nut. This has proven to be very successful. I consider it among the best of the nuts, with a rich, pleasantly sweet flavour.

The macadamia originated in Queensland, so that indicates its climatic preference. It dislikes frosts, although a mature tree is able to tolerate light frosts, and it dislikes being exposed to cold winter winds. Shelter is needed for the first few years of a young tree's life. It likes a sunny position, with an open, well-drained, slightly acidic soil rich in organic matter. It responds to mulch by growing pest free, producing larger, better quality nuts.

When you plant your young macadamia in early spring it may need to be staked if it is in an exposed position. Incorporate plenty of organic matter with it at planting time, and mulch it deeply. Keep mulching to beyond the drip line, persisting with this until the tree grows big enough to supply its own mulch with leaf drop and debris. Even then, keeping it mulched is the best way to feed the soil and tree while maintaining moisture.

When selecting your tree, you will learn that there are two basic species, each with their own varieties. *M. tetraphylla* has a rough, knobbly-shelled, sweet nut, and is best eaten fresh. These trees are more suited to cooler areas. *M. integrifolia* is a smooth-shelled nut, more easily extracted, and is the nut that has been commercialised for roasting and packaging. It prefers a warmer location.

Give the new tree plenty of water when you set it, and keep it well watered for the first year. Pruning should be light, aimed at producing an open, well-shaped tree in the initial stages of growth. The macadamia tree can grow quite large, so be prepared for its eventual size. Give this tree the attention it deserves and you will be amply rewarded.

When the nuts fall onto your mulch, gather them weekly. Moisture, rats and bandicoots will spoil them. Remove the fleshy green husks as soon as they are gathered, and dry the nuts on a wire rack for a couple of weeks before storing. Be sure they are properly dried. Your efforts will give you a harvest of rich nuts—a valuable food—lasting until the next season's nuts. A squirrel would go nuts over these!

The nuts can be opened with a number of clever, specially designed macadamia nut crackers, or even a home vice. Please, don't hammer them. It wrecks the beautiful nut and is unnecessary.

WATERING FOR FRUITING TREES

The principle of watering from fruit set to picking includes all fruit trees, soft fruit and fruiting vegetables. A fruit is basically packaged water and nutrients, mostly designed to be tasty enough that some passing creature will take the fruit, eat it, and pass the all important seed at some reasonable distance, thus ensuring the survival of the species. We exploit this—and cheat the system!

However, regular watering from fruit set to picking does not mean that prior to fruiting they may be neglected. It simply means that during the time of growing fruit the plants need for water increases substantially.

One of the most important times for watering is when the fruit trees are planted. This includes soft fruit. The root system is vulnerable at this stage, and sometimes even inadequate. The roots should always be untangled if they are root-bound, even trimmed, and planted so that the all important roots can easily grow into the soil. I have seen pot-bound roots going round and round the pot continue in this pattern when set out in good soil, causing the tree to eventually fall over and die.

Soft fruit will quickly become established, just keep them well-watered in the first season, and during fruit set.

The first season for fruit trees is critical. All precocious trees should be stripped of fruit for the first two years while they grow a deep, or spreading root base for further years. Unseen, the roots are the all important factor that need to be given full attention. I have seen gardeners proudly display the large amount of fruit on a first-year lemon. At the end of the season, broken branches on an obviously exhausted tree infested with aphid was no longer a cause for pride. The first season of growth is about roots and tree vigour, nothing else. Deep watering is essential, applied often enough to keep a thick mulch constantly moist.

The second season you can ease back on the watering, but when water is required it must be a deep soaking. This is the second year of root and tree vigour development, and in a soil rich in organic matter, you are building a foundation for many years of trouble-free fruiting.

By the third season the tree should be well-established, able to find water in the subsoil, or having a network of roots that are efficient at taking surface water, depending on the species of fruit tree.

Always mulch your fruiting trees, consider it as essential as soil. Never force your trees to compete with grass or weeds for water and nutrients. In times of drought and dry heat you will need to give more water, in cold dry times considerably less.

If your fruit trees are in a fairly sheltered position, they will need less water than trees exposed to the full wind. Hot sun plus wind quickly dries out the soil and leaves, thus putting the tree in stress. You need to remember that apart from the macadamia, none of the fruit trees we grow are endemic to Oz, mostly coming from wetter, cooler countries, or some of the world's rain forests. Our Oz climate can be very suitable, and equally very stressful, for some of these fruit-bearing trees. It is the task, or joy, of the conscious gardener to make the conditions as suitable and supportive as we possibly can. With water becoming increasingly scarce in our country of climatic extremes, deep water to establish an efficient root system in the trees is an intelligent way to save water. A well-established tree is mostly a survivor. There are worse things than losing a single season's crop in a drought if the tree easily survives for another year.

Water and mulch—mulch and water—never think of one without the other. This is the way to consciously and intelligently grow fruit.

Enjoy!

CHAPTER
12

CACKLEBERRIES

W E CANNOT LEAVE the topic of fruit without including what is probably the most important fruit in the world— cackleberries. What, you may ask, are cackleberries? Well . . . I'll tell you. Cackleberries (eggs) are the fruit from the humble hen—a package of protein and nutrients all wrapped in a clean protective shell and delivered approximately once every twenty-six hours. When the fruit is delivered, a loud cackle announces its arrival. How's that for service? Most trees give fruit once a year; a hen offers it almost, not quite, daily. She does take some time off for moulting!

In Oz the hen is known as a chook, short for chicken, but here I will call a hen a hen. First, let me explain the terminology. When a young bird hatches from the egg, it is a chick. Collectively, even when adults, they become known as chickens, poultry, or fowl. However, as they grow to a few months of age, the sexual differences become apparent. The females become pullets, remaining pullets until they begin to lay eggs, at which point they become hens. The young males are known as cockerels, and are normally eaten. If they are a meat-and-egg breed, they are used for human consumption. If they are a thinner, lean, egg-only breed, they are used in zoos, laboratories and such places, as food for animals. If a good specimen is kept for breeding purposes and is placed with some hens, he is mostly called a rooster.

Having said all this, I might as well add that 'all' the commercial chickens we consume in the Western World are genetically altered hybrids. They are genetically altered to put weight on baby chickens at an entirely unnatural speed. The less said the better! The pure flesh of an organically reared barnyard fowl is now a rarity that only a country breeder can enjoy. So-called free range and organic chickens are also genetically altered, but they are not fed with the usual gamut of growth stimulants, hormones and antibiotics.

So, now we know what we are talking about. Having kept hens for many years, I can share with you the very best way to do this. You can, in effect, have true organic eggs, and eat pure and natural chicken meat in the way that our grandparents did. Isn't it amazing—we now have to go backwards to go forward! However, if you want the meat you will need to do further research, for in this book I am concerned only with the production of top quality cackleberries.

LOCATING THE HENHOUSE

If you have a few trees and shrubs in your garden, you have room for some hens. I would like you to seriously consider the idea of hens. They are easy to keep, take up very little room, yet they offer so much. Quite apart from the daily cackleberries, you have an annual supply of manure—and that is a bonus. Six hens is the ideal number. They are flock birds, so they like and need their own type for company, and six hens will supply a family. If there are only two of you, well, you will have some cackleberries to sell or barter with.

Imagine the rewards they give for just a little attention. You can begin each day with a drop of gold, sunny side up, fried in olive oil or ghee. The yolk will be golden instead of the pale, sickly yellow of commercial eggs. Even if the commercial eggs have the golden colour, it will be the result of food dye fed to the hens. The albumen will stay firm and close to the yolk in your fresh cackleberries, instead of spreading halfway across the pan as a stale egg does. Your hens will be kept from chicks or point-of-lay pullets, with a proper regard for their needs. You will be rewarded with eggs of a vitality that cannot be achieved under commercial conditions.

Imagine a small wire cage just over half a metre square, automatic food and water supplies, with constant antibiotics added to keep the wretched hens alive. Four or five hens are crammed into each cage. Each egg rolls away as it is laid, and the hens have many hours of artificial light to induce more egg laying. In twelve-to-eighteen months the hens are finished, exhausted by the unnaturally forced egg production. There are even egg factories today that have an electrified wire along the back of the cage. If the poor birds should have the temerity to step away from the egg stimulating food, to have a brief spell at the back, it gets a mild shock that propels it forward again to begin stress eating . . . and to produce more eggs! Such egg production produces eggs that contain the energy of stress and discord, and we eat them.

For the family that wants fresh eggs, there is a way to keep hens in almost any situation where you have a garden or backyard. If you only have room for a shed, that's fine. You can keep half-a-dozen laying hens for your family.

There are several ways of keeping hens, but the system I am going to outline is the easiest, safest and most hassle free. This is the deep litter system, basically a shed containing deep litter. With attention to detail this is very successful, resulting in an enjoyable hen/human relationship where each benefits from the other. You will get a visual idea from the diagram how the deep-litter shed could look.

It need be no larger than a garden shed, about 1.80m cubed (6 x 6 feet) for half-a-dozen hens. It is essential for the hens to receive plenty of fresh air and some sunshine, yet they must be protected from excess sun/heat and cold winds. You will see in the diagram the front has wire netting over the nest boxes to allow light and air to flow in. Over the front on the outside is an angled overhanging roof. This is made of either horticulture glass, polycarbonate, or it could be a thick clear plastic sheeting, to be replaced when necessary.

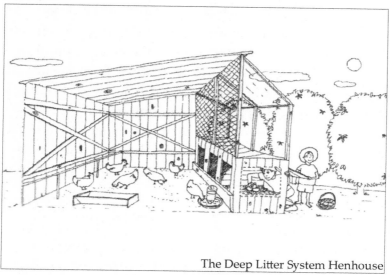

The Deep Litter System Henhouse

Notice also there is a row of shrubs to break the wind. We need to allow sun, air and light to enter, but wind sweeping in constantly will drop egg production as the hens become chilled and unhappy.

There are two very different attitudes to keeping hens and preparing their home; one is that anything will do, which will harvest disappointment; the other is to build or convert the shed properly with attention to detail, harvesting the full potential of your hens. You need not follow the design exactly so long as you meet the basic needs and requirements of your laying hens.

A deep-litter shed has the advantage of being compact and neat. The hens like it and it takes little space. A rewarding advantage lies in the fact that you get not only eggs for the family, but manure for the garden, either as direct mulch, or for the compost heap. When the shed is ready, spread a fair bit of lime over the compacted earth floor of the shed. Note it must be an earth floor, not concrete.

Next, spread a 25 cm (9 inch) layer of wood shavings, short straw, pine sawdust, hay, even dry leaves or any available dry mulching material, or a mixture of them. Hardwood sawdust is all right but not as beneficial as pine. Basically, use any dry litter that you can get so long as the hens can scratch it around and turn it over.

The deep-litter system works via micro organic life within the litter, constantly breaking down the hens' droppings into friable humic material. The hens constantly scratch the litter over, allowing oxygen to reach deeply into the materials. This results in a fast breakdown of droppings. It can only work while it is kept dry. This is very important. If rain can blow into the shed then it will all become a sodden, stinking mess. Dry deep litter is the key to success.

CONSIDER THEIR COMFORT

The shed will need perches for the hens at night. Do not make these too small as it can lead to feet deformities. An ideal size is 5 cm (2 inches) square. The perches should all be on the same level, about 45–60 cm (1.6–2 feet) high. Hens like to roost on the highest perch, so if they are all on the same level it will prevent a regular evening squabble about who gets the top perch. The nighttime droppings under the perches should be raked into the rest of the deep litter daily. It takes but moments! If left, it turns into a smelly area of potential mite infection.

They will need constant fresh water, essential for clean-tasting eggs. The way you supply the water is important to the welfare of the deep litter. There are many types and brands of water fountains for hens on the market, so I suggest you have a look at some. Choose a type where you can see the water level, so that the hens will not run out of water just after you leave for work one morning. It is easiest to have the water installed with an automatic system. Wherever the drink fountain is situated, dig at least a bucket-sized hole beneath it and fill it with gravel or small brick rubble with a sprinkling of soil over the top. This will allow all slopped water to soak away quickly, instead of creating an ever-spreading area of a foul, stinking mess. Also, the water must always be clean of dirt and droppings.

Another important aspect is the grit box. This should be big, and deep enough for the hens to scratch in without scattering and losing the grit. Grit is essential for the efficient digestion of food, especially grains. Crushed oyster shell is one of the best, but there are plenty of brands on the market.

NEST BOXES

Probably the most important fitting in the laying hen house is the nest boxes. These can be totally inside the shed, or on an outside wall with the hen holes on the inside, as illustrated in the deep-litter house. As with the perches, it is better to keep all the nest boxes at one level, otherwise they will scramble and squabble for the top ones. For six hens, three nest boxes will be enough. If you raise the nest boxes off the floor 60 cm (2 feet) it will allow more floor space for the hens to scratch around in without disturbing the hens in the nest boxes. Hens like to lay their eggs in dark places, so face the nest box entrances toward the darkest part of the shed. The best size for the boxes is 35.5 cm (14 inches) cubed with a retaining board along the entrance 10 cm (4 inches) high to keep the nesting material inside.

Keep a nice soft layer of straw or hay inside the nest boxes to prevent egg breakage. When a hen sees and tastes a broken egg she will learn, over a period of time, the bad habit of deliberately breaking them. Nest boxes in semi-dark help to prevent this. One of the more common causes of broken eggs is failure to collect them regularly. Leaving them heaped in a nest box is an open invitation for trouble.

Any handyman or woman can make a 60–90 cm (2–3 feet) feeding trough from some good boards as illustrated. Or you can buy a continuous feeder that will hold a reserve of food.

The shed will need to be vermin proof. Not only are rats and mice undesirable, but they will attract their predators. A shed that is not fully secure will allow entry for snakes and monitors. A carpet snake (python) can get a large body through a very small hole, and they are easily capable of killing and eating one of your hens—and it is always the best layer! Monitors are very powerful reptiles and can claw their way into and through a flimsy, insecure shed. Equally, foxes are smart and resourceful and will certainly test every weakness in your shed. In America, you can add the super-smart raccoons to the list of dedicated chicken killers, as well as coyotes, which can be a problem in many areas. Build strong, build well. If you are in a very cold or very hot region, you would be better off building with timber as a buffer against the extremes. Thin galvanised iron sheds can be very cold and/or very hot if they are located in an unprotected place. If you live in the cold or tropical regions I recommend that you choose a winter sunny place in the cold area, and a well-shaded area in the tropics.

STOCKING YOUR HENHOUSE

Having built your super henhouse, the next step is to get the hens. For the backyard hen keeper the easiest way is to buy pullets that are on the point of lay from a first-class breeder. The breed you choose needs to be carefully decided. If you are in a cold climate a black bird such as the Austrolorp is hard to beat, both for hardiness and egg production. However, some black-coloured fowl in a hot climate seem to get more heat stressed, even in the shade. Although the Austrolorp has black feathers, it has white flesh, and has the advantage of being very good for the table.

Another fine heavy breed is the Rhode Island Red. It lays well, is hardy and has a dual purpose for meat. If you have no interest or intention of eating your older hens, then a light breed like the White Leghorn is most suitable. Leghorns lay well and, although not as calm and placid as the heavier breeds, are perfect for the deep-litter shed.

Of course, there are many varieties to choose from; with a little study, you will make the choice that most suits you. If it helps, I have kept Brown Leghorns in New South Wales, and they were excellent. My personal favourite hen is the White Sussex. This is a heavy breed, calm, a very good layer of large cackleberries, and when, after a surprising number of years her laying time finally ends, makes a very good meal as a fitting end to her life. For these older breeds you would need to find a reputable breeder from a Poultry Society in your locality.

KEEP THEM SAFE AND COMFORTABLE

This may make you smile, but when you enter your deep-litter house always first give a knock on the door. This will prepare them for the door to open without the sudden shock of the unexpected. How often as a boy, my friend and I jumped into his father's deep-litter house and watched the resulting explosion of panic and feathers. Not to our credit! You knock, wait a few seconds, and the birds will be calm and undisturbed when you walk in.

Your first consideration is to keep your hens contented and happy. They need to become familiar with you and your ways, learning that you are a friend and supportive of them. Give your hens lavish helpings of love and understanding. Talk to them while you are with them, moving slowly and calmly. I had a retired friend who delighted in spending hours with his backyard hens. They were so tame they would feed from his hands and settle onto his arms, snuggling close to his body. They were his retirement hobby.

The hens in a deep-litter house do not go outside. The shed protects them from your dogs, stray dogs, feral dogs and the various hawks and eagles that are very efficient chicken killers. It is possible to build an outdoor run for them which is attached to the shed, and even to let them free range from about three o'clock each afternoon, but from my experience it holds the risk of losing a few hens. The hen environment should be as stress free as possible. Less stress means more cackleberries. However, if they have no outdoor run and/or range, this means that they are dependent on you for all their green food.

I have seen miserable backyard hens in a small wire enclosure which is mud in the wet weather and dust when it is dry. When I asked one such owner how the hens got green food, I was told that they were outside birds and got their own. In other words, they did not get any. Please, if you are not prepared to keep hens properly, simply buy your eggs from your local organic produce shop.

Feeding Methods for Health and Eggs

Green food is of major importance to the colour and quality of the eggs. It will put the gold in the cackleberries and the red in the hen's comb. Try to grow a succession of cabbages for them in a small patch of your vegetable garden, or grow enough green produce to include the needs of your hens. You can hang a cabbage in the shed so that the hens are compelled to jump up to peck it, thus getting their much-needed exercise at the same time. Most green food will be eaten, including some lawn clippings. Weeds can be fed to them with great advantage. Put lettuce leaves, left-over salad, and any green scraps in a mesh bag and hang it so they have to jump for it.

The basic ration for your hens is simple. After you have spread the droppings under the perches each morning, throw a good of handful of wheat per hen, scattering it over all the deep litter. They will spend hours scratching happily for the grain, turning the litter over and over. You can substitute maize or other seed such as buckwheat or millet if you so desire. For their evening meal you can make a mash using all your edible household scraps, cooked or uncooked. Combine the mash with some bran and a little specially-blended layers meal. Aim at feeding 60 g (2 ounces) per hen of grain in the morning and 90 g (3 ounces) of mash in the evening. Keep the mash to a crumbly moistness. Green food will complete the diet. If you do not like the idea of feeding a commercial food because of the additives, you may find an organic supply, or you can try the following method I devised and used over many years of keeping hens.

For six hens you will need two or three buckets. Soak a quarter bucket of wheat, just barely covered in water. This will swell and double in volume. Stir and mix it morning and night to keep it aerated. Depending on your climate, this will sprout in 1 to 4 days. The wheat is ready as soon as the first white shoots appear. Be careful not to have the mix too wet or too dry; aim to keep it very moist.

For the necessary extra protein, mix at the rate of one handful of meat-meal to four handfuls of sprouted wheat. Mix and use at each mealtime. Remember, an egg is a package of protein. As you use the sprouts, start another lot sprouting in another bucket or bowl. A large bowl is better than a bucket because it gives you a greater surface area for oxygenation. Laying hens will thrive and egg production will improve on sprouted wheat and meat-meal. Do not use fish-meal. Its overpowering flavour will taint the eggs. If the idea of meat-meal turns you off, or it is unobtainable, I suggest you try sprouting a parrot seed mix instead of wheat. This mix is a variety of big seeds which will almost certainly have a higher nutritional and protein content than wheat alone. Also, simply by sprouting wheat or a parrot seed mix, the available protein content rises remarkably. You can buy parrot seed mix in bulk bags.

The deep-litter can be added to when necessary to keep a good depth for the microorganisms. If properly maintained it will only need to be emptied out once or twice a year. Always leave about half a barrow of old litter to impregnate the new litter with the required microorganisms. The old litter is excellent for the garden, completing the cycle of fertility by going back onto the soil.

With the deep litter system of half-a-dozen hens in a small garden, there is no need for a rooster. He is required for breeding, fertilising the eggs. The eggs your hens will lay are full of nutrition, but with no rooster the eggs are not fertile. For some people this is important, as they do not like the idea of a developing chick in the egg they plan to eat. For human consumption, we do not need to eat fertilised eggs. Not only that, the rooster is a very virile bird, and with less than ten-to-twelve hens per rooster, the hens will be so 'sexually harassed' that egg production will decline. Another serious drawback is the rooster's habit of greeting the dawn! For the country dweller with no close neighbours, this is a rather pleasant, familiar sound, but in the suburbs it is not appreciated. The cackle of a hen delivering its egg is neither prolonged nor overly loud, and is muffled by the shed. For a rooster with a big chest, the shed becomes an amplifier!

Be aware of your climate, and put the shed in the sun and shade, or shade only, accordingly. Better to be too cool rather than too hot. If it is too hot, insulate the inner walls and have the open section of netting facing away from the direct sun. The site of your hens' shed is important.

THE FINE QUALITIES OF A HEALTHY HEN

The hen will prove to be an intelligent bird if respected and kept with an appreciation of her finer qualities. If you consciously care for your birds they can excel. Imagine the supreme laying hen. Her eyes are bright and bold, set well up in her head. Her comb is bright red in colour and fine in texture. Her small face feathers are tight and smooth, her neck is fine with sleek feathering and the plumage is silky. Her lower legs—shanks—are smooth, with the scales small and tight. Her pelvic bones are well-shaped and covered in soft flesh. If she is in full lay, two fingers can be placed between those pelvic bones. Her moulting season will be short and she will be an active bird, rising early and roosting late. She will lay in excess of two hundred eggs a year, and can lay well for up to eight years in accordance with conditions and breed.

At the other end of the scale is a very different and an all-too-common story. This is the poor hen that, forced into an unnatural environment, is weak and debilitated. She will have a dull eye and her face will be wrinkled and coarse. Her comb will be thick, limp, and look anaemic. Her head, skin, and neck will all feel thick. Her feathers will be loose, constantly falling. Her shanks will have large coarse scales, often raised with scaly leg parasite. She will be covered with lice and body vermin. Her vent will have dirty feathers around it and her pelvic bones will be gristly. She will rise late and roost early, with a long moulting season. Her egg production will be low and of poorer quality.

You see here what to look for in a laying hen, and what to avoid. Some people buy used-up hens from the commercial factories, hoping to give them a better life in exchange for eggs. This can work, but the commercial hens have been de-beaked to stop them from feather pecking in their crowded conditions, thus they are never able to peck for grain in a natural way. I applaud the intentions, but the results can be disappointing in a deep-litter shed. The best place for 'crook chook' rescue is down on the farm in free-range conditions.

Keep hens that make you feel good just looking at them, for they reflect your own skills and care. Give you and your family the opportunity to enjoy the ultimate in quality homegrown food—the humble egg—a supreme package of protein and nutrition.

If you have children, get them involved. The henhouse is a great way to introduce children to responsibility, caring for some creatures that depend on them for their welfare. However, only do this if the child enjoys the experience. Forcing a child will produce a counter effect, and lower the egg production of unhappy hens.

The production of organic cackleberries completes the organic garden. A self-contained cycle of natural fertility becomes possible.

CHAPTER

13

OBSERVATIONS OF A
CONSCIOUS GARDENER

M Y GREAT RULE OF GARDENING is observation and application. Of course, this is equally applicable in our daily lives. Let me give you a good example of what I mean.

When visiting England one year I visited an elderly woman I knew who had made a deep impression on me during my adolescent years. She was that rare personification of 'whole-hearted goodness'.

As we walked into her big, rambling, overgrown garden she told me about her five very large old apple trees. She told me how two of them were attacked by codling moth maggots in the fruit every year, while the other three trees had fruit of excellent quality. It was always the same two trees that suffered codling moth maggots.

Our discussion moved on as we continued walking around her garden. I mentioned the properties of compost and mulch. I told her that if a fruit tree has its potential need of nutrients fully realised, then it acquires a greater immunity to insect pests and disease. I continued on, telling her about the relationship between apple trees and mycorhiza fungi.

She listened intently, becoming quite excited. Clutching my

arm, she led me to the scattered apple trees. Under three of the trees she had a large, long-established compost/rubbish heap, while under the remaining two trees there was nothing but grass. I hardly need say which trees were attacked by the codling moth each year!

Observation and application: in all those many years she had never once observed that it was the trees with the compost heaps that were immune to the codling moth. Their roots were permanently engaged with a whole spectrum of nutrients, along with the essential mycorhiza.

UNSEEN CONNECTIONS

Observation goes with being aware and conscious. As I walk my garden I am well aware that my eyes have seen it all—or think they have—and that it is the brain in its world of separation that conjures up such stupid thoughts. Fortunately, I know better. I know that eyes and brain see only the surface of life, and although they, too, are capable of keen observation, it takes something extra to penetrate beneath the surface. The eyes of my elderly friend had seen the compost heaps under the thriving trees countless times, and her brain had no choice but to register this, but the wholistic connection was missing.

This is where conscious observation is different. When you are observing from a wholistic viewpoint, you instantly see the more non-apparent connections. The brain may well see the connection between what it perceives as random parts, but the open heart sees everything as whole, making observations that the brain cannot grasp. The brain needs to understand what it sees, while the open heart already 'knows' what it sees. This is the way Nature works. Animals see holistically through the eyes of intelligence; they have to if they are to survive. We see separation through the eyes of the intellect, assuming our survival is not threatened.

Water Smart Plant

In my garden, I have a number of *Brugmansias*. In Oz these seem to be stuck with the name *Datura*, but the *Datura* is a different plant, smaller and less robust, with trumpet flowers pointing up rather than hanging down.

The *Brugmansia*—also known as Angel's Trumpets—grows into a large shrub, about 3 m (9 feet) tall and as far across. The more common variety has pure white flowers, but I also have apricot, pink, almost-red, and lemon yellow, all powerfully fragrant during the evening and night.

Brugmansia has the endearing habit of flowering during almost every wet spell, maybe three-to-six times a year. It really enjoys rain and shade, but when there is a long dry spell, it has no trouble in dropping its leaves and going dormant. I have observed these plants right on the edge of the bush growing in poor soil and competing for moisture with the gum trees. At times they have been nine months without leaves, then along comes the rain, and they are in flower within weeks. It's a very rewarding plant.

In Oz we are more and more threatened by a lack of water. It is the driest continent in the world, yet coastal people have taken water very much for granted, wasting it on lawns and in countless gardens. Of course we all like a green lawn, but grass is very capable of surviving a drought and it is not necessary to water it. With our increasingly warmer and drier climatic trend we are required to grow plants that are easily able to survive in the garden. Of course, this is made easier by having a soil rich in organic matter, the very foundation of moisture retention and soil fertility.

Television Impact

In Oz, we have television programmes about gardening. Over the last two decades this has had a great impact on the people of Oz. I read recently that gardening is now the number one hobby in Oz. I think this is marvellous, but unfortunately, some of these programmes have created trends in the garden, similar to fashion in clothing. One of those trends was the 'tropical look'. It is easily possible to create a tropical look without using thirsty plants, but the reality is that a great many 'tropical' gardens suddenly became huge consumers of water. Most gardeners use far more water in the garden than in the house.

Another trend is colour coordination throughout the garden. I walked in one of these, escorted by the proud garden owner. As we conversed it became apparent that she did not particularly like the plants she was growing, but she had to have them to coordinate the colour. This is not gardening and she was not a gardener. This is fashion following. This is an attempt to extend a colour coordinated interior of the house into the garden. It does not impress me.

I grow plants in my garden because I admire them, because they excite me, stimulate me, enchant me, charm me, but never because I want a matching set! I look for plants that I want to share the precious space of my garden with, not because they have a certain colour that I must have. I am perfectly open to the fact that a garden of colour coordination is done by some gardeners who love the results, but these are the few, rather than the many. Personally, I don't care if red flowers are next to yellow, or purple, so long as I love the plants and their energy. I have yet to hear a single complaint from Nature!

My whole point here is to be true to yourself in your garden. Grow the plants that you most enjoy. And if those plants do not suit the changing climate, then visit the garden centres and botanical gardens and familiarise yourself with a far wider range of plants which have a potential to grow in your garden conditions. I actually read about a suburban garden owner who followed garden fashion to the extent of demolishing the whole garden every five or six years to follow the next trend. Apparently, he hated the latest trend, but put it in anyway; he felt he had to if he was to 'be with it' as a gardener.

GOOD NEIGHBOURS

Observation in my garden has clearly shown that there are plants that do not thrive in the company of certain other plants. Roses, for example, like garlic and chives near them and benefit from them, but they really do not like tulip bulbs. This is generally caused by the roots exuding certain substances into the surrounding soil that suits some plants and disturbs others. I have an unusual fragrant oleander growing next to a wild hibiscus, and it is not happy with the situation. The energy of the hibiscus is strong, wild and unrestrained, while the energy of the fragrant oleander is not at all vigorous. This is what I call a mismatch. This autumn I shall move the fragrant oleander and look for a more suitable neighbour. Of course, most oleanders are strong and vigorous, but like the wild hibiscus they are not fragrant. This oleander has paid a price for its fragrance.

It is a good idea to observe the plants in your garden, and if you have an ailing plant notice who its neighbour is. Incompatible plant energy is far more common than is realised. Whereas science always wants a physical reason it can understand and relate to, the field of energy that surrounds each plant is not easily measured by conventional means. Although I have never used it, I am sure Kirlian photography would show the energy field to which I refer.

A perfect example is the distressed energy of all seedlings when planted; one moment growing happily, then suddenly pulled out and replanted in a different place. The average gardener is oblivious to the distress that is now emanating from the tiny plants. Using the individual containers with each seedling in its own compartment has done a lot to alleviate this. For the conscious gardener, *learn to feel* the energy of plants. *With the feeling comes the intuitive solution to their distress.*

I continue to practise this, being with and feeling the energy. Then I apply what I have observed. Naturally enough, most plants grow best in groups of their own species, rather than one alone.

Mine is more a one-alone garden than in groups, but I have both. Roses definitely like their own company. Also, you can prepare the soil for a group more easily than a single one, especially if, like the rose, it needs mycorhiza fungi among the roots. I have observed that strong vigorous plants enjoy going it alone, while plants that are more delicate, without much vigour, are far better in groups.

This is one point where groups and colour coordination combine. It takes little observation to see that a bed of roses set in groups of five of the same colour and variety, with an overall regard for an even height, look far better than a bed with all different colours and sizes. For me, it is all about consciously observing what works, what appeals, what excites, what stimulates you, and applying it—rather than what you should do.

The Subconscious

Subconscious gardening is the alternative to conscious gardening. This is the way of most gardeners, but it does not mean or imply less skill or ability.

Let me very briefly explain the subconscious. We humans live our daily lives functioning about ninety percent of the time from our subconscious state. The word 'sub' means secondary in rank, less than, falling short of. In other words, by living subconsciously we are falling short of the potential to be found in living fully conscious.

Our subconsciousness is rather like the hardware programme in a computer. We might know that there is a lot of undesirable and messy stuff in the programme, but knowing it does not remove it. From the very early stages of conception our subconsciousness is beginning to build its programme. Within twenty-five days of conception a group of cells come together and start beating—this is the embryonic heart, the result of consciousness. Yet it is the function of the subconscious that will monitor the heart and keep it beating, long before birth.

All the emotional stress, anxiety, anger, frustration and negative reactions of the parents are imprinted into the developing subconscious of the embryonic child. Add to this the reactions of the embryonic child to the negative stress of the parents, and a brew of complex emotional confusion is all indelibly recorded in the subconscious hardware of the nucleus of a child. The trauma of birth is recorded, and the child's ways of dealing with life, based on the early parental influence, are added to the subconscious confusion as the child grows.

The life we live is then based in and from this complicated, emotional subconscious conditioning. Considering all this, most of us do well!

This gets interesting. Although our subconscious acts *in* the moment, it never acts *from* the moment, always from the past. So we repeat old patterns over and over, creating and developing deeply ingrained emotional, mental and physical habits. History repeats itself! None of this is bad or wrong, but there can be no true freedom in this. The subconscious is a prison in which we live. Of course it breathes for us and keeps our physical body functioning without our conscious awareness, but equally it can make us very sick without our consciously realising that a certain habit is potentially fatal. And many are . . . especially repetitive criticism and angry thought habits.

SUBCONSCIOUS GARDENING

You can begin to see why conscious gardening offers so much more than just gardening in a more aware way. It offers you a path to a greater reality, and that greater reality is your own full consciousness. Nothing is more exciting or fulfilling than to consciously come into the moment. It is the only place of *participating* in life, instead of being the *onlooker.*

The subconscious gardener can have all the skills, everything in fact that is needed to be an excellent gardener, but consciously 'being with' the energy of Nature will always remain elusive and unreachable. I have had a few people tell me that it would not be possible to get more enjoyment from the garden than they do, and I respect this, but that is rather like saying 'what I have never experienced has nothing to offer me.' If we stayed with the experiences of our childhood, never adding the richness of adult experience to our lives, our life and living would be severely depleted, reduced to a subordinate experience.

The garden is one of the most feasible and possible ways and means of entering the richness of the moment. It takes practise. As I have said, I am still practising, and I expect to practice for the rest of my life. As I bring my focus ever more into the conscious moment, so I experience the richness of life to an ever-increasing degree.

There is so much more to this—I have merely skimmed the surface, but enough, I hope, to whet your appetite. Subconscious gardening will allow you to have a magnificent garden, but there will be dimensions of that magnificence that will elude you. Just as an optical lens can clarify poor vision, so conscious gardening can reveal far more than is subconsciously available. Try it for yourself.

PESTS AND WEEDS

Observation will reveal so many things in the garden. You will notice that if you have a plant with aphids, or some other pest, the plant is not healthy. Rarely does a healthy plant get pests or diseases. We are the same. If health has been paramount in our life with a lifestyle that has been supportive of health, we seldom get sick. We treat the plant by getting rid of the insect pests, then we treat the sick soil that is supporting a sick plant. You cannot have a depleted, impoverished soil and grow the desirable, often exotic species of plants we want to grow in a garden. In Nature, many species of plants colonise impoverished soil, thriving on it, but the residue of those plants will always contain the nutrients or minerals that are missing from the soil. We mostly call these plants weeds.

When I was farming in Tasmania, many hectares (acres) of one of my new pastures became covered in sorrel. With observation I learned that the soil was deficient in calcium, and of course, Sorrel was rich in it. This is the way of Nature. Thistles are rich in iron, so thrive in iron deficient soil, even daisies in the lawn are there for a purpose. If, in your garden, you have an infestation by a particular type of weed plant, have a tissue sample of the weed tested for its major elements. Almost certainly your soil will be deficient in them. If you add that element to the soil the weed will have less vigour, often gradually dying out.

It is ironic that the weeds in my garden are sometimes avocado or mango seedlings, with masses of pawpaw seedlings, all following in the wake of spreading my old compost. I do not have hot compost with a heat capable of cooking large seeds. My compost is added very slowly from the kitchen, taking a year to fill a one metre square section of my two side-by-side compost bins. That one is then forked into the empty bin along side, and it does heat up a bit but not enough to cook avocados and mangos.

SUBSOIL

I mentioned in one of the earlier chapters about our garden being built of subsoil from the house extension. Today, when a house is built, the trend is to then buy truckloads of fertile topsoil to spread all over the garden. I have even heard people say that you cannot have a garden without this. What total rubbish. There is no soil that is incapable of being developed into a reasonable soil, and eventually into a good soil. It may take time and work, but it can be done. I have known true gardeners who have built a magnificent garden on rock, simply by adding layer after layer of various types of mulch, not by buying topsoil.

My garden is half the age of our time living here. We had been here nine years when the house was doubled in size, and I laid out a new garden. Eleven years of deep mulch are well on the way to transforming the subsoil. Most, not all, subsoil is depleted. Mine was almost zero in organic matter, and was very substandard soil. But the garden growing on that soil—and the years of mulch—is anything but substandard.

There is a problem with buying topsoil. When you set your plants they are in a soil of a particular pH, yet as soon as their roots penetrate deeply into the natural soil of your garden, they encounter not only a different pH, but also a soil of different qualities and energy. Sometimes this is not a problem, sometimes it creates very complex problems.

Generally the imported topsoil is spread no more than 15–30 ml (6–12 inches) in depth, depending on how much money is available after building the house. Many landscapers insist that you must have this imported topsoil—it certainly makes their job easier and more spectacular—but this is a short-term view. I have looked at some of these landscaped gardens three years down the track, and they are a disaster. Not only were they created for garden owners who had no idea how to maintain them, but the plants they chose were suitable only for the imported topsoil, not the true soil of the location.

An Exercise In Futility

Let me give you a good example of what I mean. Around twenty-something years ago, I was talking to a farmer who was telling me that his farm neighbour was about to seed a field with alfalfa.

"But that's ridiculous," I exclaimed. "His soil is really acidic, and alfalfa needs an alkaline soil."

"Ah, but he is putting a ton an acre (2 tonnes per hectare) of lime on the field, so it will be all right."

I sighed. "Tell him I said he is wasting his money. The alfalfa will grow and even look good for the first year, but it will have vanished by the end of the third year."

This is exactly what happened. While the roots were immature they engaged the lime, meeting their needs. But as the long-lived, deep-rooted alfalfa continued to grow, its roots plunging down 2 metres (6 feet), it was unable to survive in the very acidic soil. As with imported topsoil, changing the surface is entirely superficial; it is the whole soil profile that will determine what can be grown in a soil.

I have been told that most landscape gardeners check the pH of the imported topsoil to make sure it is around neutral. I respect this, but if the garden has a pH 5.0, which is common in Oz, the plants are still going to get a shock capable of killing them when their roots engage the true soil.

Please do not get the idea that I have a vendetta against garden landscapers. Some of their designs and the implementation of them leave me almost breathless with admiration, some are truly brilliant. Like every profession, there are those who know their job thoroughly and are very particular about details, and there are those who are less scrupulous, learning as they go.

PREPARATION

The first and most important thing to do for a new garden where bulldozers and machinery have been working, and the site is now cleared and ready for the garden, is to aerate the soil. Have a chart of your underground pipes and cables available, and over as much of the ground as possible have a small mechanised ripper rip into the soil, not to turn it over, but to erase the deep compaction. All flood-water drains that are necessary should be laid at this time, and they usually are, but it is so easy for a few loads of imported topsoil to bury a problem for later years.

Trees and shrubs, in fact most plants, do not like subsoil compaction. They grow well for a few years under the false impetus of imported topsoil, then they hit the subsoil compaction and a slow decline sets in. Some large trees can penetrate this, but those trees are invariably large and powerful, with roots that can jeopardise the drains and even the very foundation of your house.

I am not saying that all imported topsoil is bad. On the contrary, I have seen it used to great advantage on many occasions, but I am saying that topsoil for the sake of no more than easiness is a poor investment, both in energy and for the future of your garden. Another reason that some landscapers like it is for instant results. And they get the kudos! No true gardener expects to have an instant garden. A garden owner might want this, but they are not a gardener. The gardens I visit where the gardener proudly tells you that it has taken ten or fifteen years to grow into this, is a gardener who has enjoyed every moment of the growing, ever-changing canvas of their garden. No gardener of the past expected an instant garden. This is a result of television's entertainment 'garden makeover,' as opposed to the 'real gardening' that can also be viewed on television.

PARAMAGNETIC ENERGY

When the great heap of subsoil was spread over my garden, I am sad to say it was not much poorer than the soil it went onto. When you have a garden on a ridge in an area of fairly high rainfall, you have to accept that all the organic matter and nutrients will have had millennium of being washed down to the flats below. Despite this, the poor top soil and the very substandard subsoil all came from the same area, so there was no conflict in earth energy. However, one of the factors I recognised and addressed in the soil and subsoil that made up my garden was the lack of paramagnetic resonance in the soil. I am aware of mentioning this earlier, but I consider it important enough to expand upon.

All matter is energy. All soil is energy, but not all soil is of equal energy, not by a long shot. One of the factors determining soil energy is the density and composition of the mineral particles in the soil, and of the paramagnetic charge they contain. Interestingly, because energy is affected by the fields of consciousness that surround it, a consciously focused gardener will be constantly and beneficially affecting the energy of the soil in his or her garden. However, with or without a conscious gardener, the paramagnetic energy of the soil is paramount to the growth and well-being of plants.

To address this lack in my garden, I spread a tonne (ton) of crushed volcanic lava over all the garden soil where I grow plants, except the bush area. Crushed volcanic lava has a very high paramagnetic energy. Within a year the results were apparent. I had not really improved the soil, but I had increased its energetic resonance, and by so doing, not only did it improve plant growth but the micro organic soil life also received the benefit of increased energy. In other words, by increasing the energy of the soil I created the conditions whereby the soil could continue to increase its own energy on many different levels.

I have walked in gardens that lack this paramagnetic energy, gardens that are often flourishing. Sometimes that flourish is based in chemical stimulants and will be short term; other times I have sensed the very slow, gradual erosion of this vital energy. Personally, I recommend the application of crushed minerals on every garden, because even the very best soil, rich in organic matter, is very much improved by it.

In worldwide agriculture today the de-mineralisation of soils, along with the loss of paramagnetic energy, has become a major problem, and mostly an unrecognised one. It is the more visionary soil environmentalists that attempt to address this issue, meeting resistance all the way from short-term, profit-based agribusiness.

TERRACING

Having created a new garden every time I have moved, I am now enjoying the rewards of watching my garden develop and mature. Moving can be stimulating, but moving every ten or twelve years has denied me seeing the fruits of my labour.

When our house was extended, and all that subsoil dumped

in a nearby heap, I had a bobcat contractor come in to spread it around. I have mentioned that we are on a mountain ridge, meaning there are very few flat areas in our garden. Previous to this, I had based my garden on a slope. I had the garden area terraced with the subsoil, turning the slope into a few wide, level shelves of soil.

Take it from me, avoid gardening on a slope. This is not to say it is impossible, far from it, but it only works well if the slope is permanently planted with well-mulched perennial plants. A bank of well-chosen plants can look magnificent, but this is not a place for regular walking unless you have winding paths carved into the slope. I am referring to a garden slope where the soil is regularly worked over.

I have a steep bank on which I tried to grow one plant species after another, all to no avail. They would grow for a few years, then fade away. Finally I planted a single *Euphorbia millii*, the crown of thorns, and it grew and thrived. That one plant gave me enough cuttings to cover the whole slope. Now the slope has been transformed from an eyesore to a prickly mass of green leaves and vivid red flowers all year round.

Especially avoid having a sloping vegetable garden. Even a gentle slope will gradually relocate the soil from the top of the slope to the bottom. I know because I tried it in Tasmania. No matter how careful I was, by the end of the year I had to take barrow loads of soil back to the top of the slope. And of course, the soil that moves down the slope is the most fertile soil, so the plants at the lower end of the slope grow twice as big as the plants at the top of the slope. All in all it is very dissatisfying.

If your working garden has slopes, and it is at all possible, have it terraced into wide shelves. Once the initial work is done, you will never regret it. Fertile soil stays where you create it, mulch no longer creeps away, and heavy rain soaks in instead of running off. If it is at all possible, a terraced garden is so very much easier, altogether better, and far more efficient than actively gardening on a slope.

DOGS IN THE GARDEN

I have had people ask me how they can have a beautiful garden as well as their boisterous dogs. My answer: with extreme difficulty!

Basically, large dogs and beautiful gardens seldom go together. Large, elderly dogs, yes; but large, young and boisterous, no. And unfortunately, before the dogs get elderly and lazy, first they are young and energetic!

I know, I know, you have large young dogs and a beautiful garden. Great! I'm happy for you, but you are the exception. Many dogs like to dig, for any number of reasons: hiding bones, boredom, for the exciting smells in the earth, to release energy, the sheer hell of it. The reasons are many, but the results are the same—a destroyed garden. Small dogs in the garden are generally not so much of a problem, although many of the terrier breeds attempt to terrorise the garden plants!

Dogs are like humans, they differ greatly. We kept Great Danes in our large garden in Tasmania, and they did no harm to the garden at all. Large placid breeds are unlikely to be a problem. Excitable or more temperamental breeds can easily ruin a garden and keep it ruined. In my experience, the type of dog that is happy to be at home is not usually a problem in the garden, but the breeds that like to wander, work, and/or hunt often suffer from acute frustration and boredom; then the garden suffers.

As a garden lover and gardener who also likes dogs and cats, I would study carefully the characteristics of the breed of dog I favoured, and have both the dog and the garden. But I would only have a breed of dog that I had personally seen at peace in an unmolested garden. This does not give a guarantee of a dog that will not damage your garden, but it certainly makes the odds favourable.

It is not really so much a choice of dog or garden; it is more about being very careful in your selection of dog, rather than being attached to a certain breed, no matter what. I have seen many gardens completely trashed by several large, frustrated dogs that wanted nothing more than to get out and run—so exercise is a big factor. The dog that is truly exercised morning and evening is less likely to trash the garden.

AND CATS

Obviously, cats do not ruin the garden. The worst that can happen is cat poo—ugh—getting on your hands from the loose soil in the vegetable garden, and even that is not fatal. The problem with cats in the garden is their habit of killing birds, animals, and other creatures. They kill.

Okay, I know, here we go again; your cat does not kill animals or birds! You 'know' this, do you? Your cat does not go out at night? Any cat that goes out and stays out at night is a killer. It is their nature. I value the wildlife in our garden to the extent that my two cats are strictly indoor cats. The small finches on the edge of shrubs, often just out of sight, are one of the first victims, as are the tiny skinks (lizards) that I so enjoy. At night, cats kill huge numbers of small, rare marsupials, like the beautiful, useful carnivorous *Antechinus*, mostly called a mouse or rat by those ignorant of our Oz animals. When your cat leaves a brush-tailed *Phascogale* lying on the lawn dead, it is very distressing. In Oz, cats and foxes pose by far the greatest threat to our small indigenous species.

Most cat owners claim their cats don't kill birds and animals, but the facts of the situation indicate otherwise. With few exceptions, the family pet cat is transformed into a savage killer when alone outside at night. I will welcome the day when legislation compels all cat owners to keep their cats indoors during the hours of darkness, and I am a cat lover.

There are now brilliant outdoor modular units available for cats, where, at will they can move from indoors to the outdoor unit with all its varying items of interest. When introduced to the system as a kitten, they are active and deeply contented.

Just as a conscious gardener becomes aware of the garden at a deeper level, so the person who is a conscious pet owner should be more aware of the reality of their pets, rather than living with them in a vague and emotional fog of delusion.

OBSERVATION AND APPLICATION

Let me share one last story that really sums up the power of observing, then applying what has been deduced. One morning, many years ago, I was harrowing (like raking from a tractor) the pasture on the highest hills on our farm in Tasmania, when I stopped for lunch. It was the usual practice to harrow the pastures each autumn, thus spreading the summer's cow pats (dung) over all the surrounding grass as a fertiliser.

I stopped the tractor, and, getting off, I quickly ate my sandwiches. As I did so, I idly kicked a dry cow pat which was just under my fence, on the edge of the surrounding forest. As the cow pat rolled over, an exposed earthworm slithered away. As I watched it, I realised that I had not noticed any under the cow pats on the pasture. I walked along the fence and kicked a dozen or so cow pats and saw a few more earthworms. I then walked onto my pasture and kicked probably a hundred cow pats, but I did not see a single earthworm.

This puzzled me. Earthworms are a farmer's best friend, and I knew that I needed them in the pasture. Why were there none where I wanted them? Instead of getting back on the tractor, I sat down and dredged from my memory everything I knew about earthworms.

Tasmania's main rainfall is in the winter. Earthworms need an abundance of organic matter in which to breed, and they breed when the soil is wettest—winter. So . . . if I harrow the pasture, spreading all the cow pats in the autumn which is the normal farming practice, I am spreading and demolishing the very heaps of organic matter (cow dung) that the earthworms need to breed in.

If this is so, how can I, or any other farmer, increase our earthworm numbers? We can't.

This was my observation and deduction. I stopped harrowing and, taking the tractor and harrows back to the farmstead, I explained my reasoning about the earthworms to Treenie. I told her I intended to leave the cow pats in place all winter; then, in spring, when the earthworms had retreated back into deeper soil, I would harrow the pasture, spreading the cow pats. She gave my idea her approval.

That winter I saw a few earthworms under the maturing cow pats, before doing the spring harrowing. I continued this for the next year, and the earthworms were now multiplying rapidly. The third year we witnessed such an explosion in earthworm numbers that they completely transformed the soil on our farm. By spring, the cow pats were mostly spread out and buried. Without ever intending it, this observation and its application propelled me into becoming one of the leading, pioneer organic farmers in Tasmania. I could write a lot of stories about that!

A FEW WORDS ABOUT LAWNS

I N MANY—TOO MANY—GARDENS, the lawn is the dominating
feature. In large gardens, this can work very well; but in smaller
gardens, it is a sign that either children or a dog live there, or both,
or this is not the garden of a gardener. For some people the lawn
is essential, while some cannot think of any better way of utilising
the space. Some unimaginative people have a square or rectangular
lawn, while others have a lawn that meanders among the shrubs
and trees in a more creative way.

I am not looking at any of this as right or wrong. The garden
lawn is a well-established concept for most garden owners, and
how it is applied is their business, not mine. All I intend to address
here is the fate of what is probably the most mistreated area in the
whole garden—the humble lawn.

Some gardeners love their lawn, and could probably teach me
a thing or two about it, yet there are garden owners who hate the
lawn, finding that it represents a weekend battle between grass, the
mower, and the person.

I differentiate between gardeners and garden owners only
because a true gardener would not have a lawn they did not want.

They would deeply mulch the lawn and turn it into a flowering shrubbery or a rose bed, whatever appealed to them. A garden owner tends to put up with what they have, unsure of how to change it, or even if they can. This suggests that a garden owner would get far more satisfaction from their garden if they became a 'conscious' gardener.

In suburbia, the lawn is all too often weed infested and patchy, looking rather like a green, threadbare carpet that somebody forgot to take to the local rubbish tip. At the other extreme, it may be manicured and pampered, a prized possession you are only grudgingly allowed to walk on. Seldom is there any real conscious connection between the gardener and their lawn; generally it is very much taken for granted. And not unnaturally so, for the lawn is such a common item that it seldom excites us, or attracts our attention in the way of a beautiful flower.

To Have or Not to Have?

That is the question. A sensible starting point with the lawn is to first ascertain whether or not you really want one. An unwanted lawn seldom thrives in the way of an appreciated lawn. Consciousness— remember? Be honest about this, because if you do not want a lawn, having it simply because you can think of no alternative, then you and the lawn are going to negate each other to the detriment of both. Not wanting a lawn is not an offence. It does not imply that you are a Nature hater, automatically qualifying for the hit list of Pan! Seriously, if the lawn is no more than an inconvenient cover to the soil, then I suggest that you reconsider having or keeping it. Imagine . . . no more weekend battles with the lawnmower. Tempting? No more unsightly bare patches in the lawn, no more weeds, no more guilt at snoozing when you should be cutting the lawn. No more sweat and tears over a reluctant or temperamental lawnmower. Tempting?

If this is you, a wiser approach, both for peace of mind and personal comfort, would be to consider the merits of sealing the offending part of the garden with clay pavers, or perhaps a swimming pool would fit nicely into it, or a large trampoline for the kids. The area could be paved with an intricate brick design, tastefully planted with small flowering shrubs in soil pockets or in tubs. It could be a hard-wearing, clean-surfaced play area, or a pergola-covered patio, complete with barbecue. Or, best of all, it could be a beautiful goldfish pond, complete with waterfall and water lilies.

Such an approach could re-enhance your appreciation of the garden, encouraging you to use the area that was once lawn for a collection of bonsai or bamboo, or perhaps a bush-house or glasshouse to house a collection of exotic plants. The ideas for using the space in a way that honours you and your interests are numerous, but you will need to act on it. This is not the time for procrastination.

WHAT IS A LAWN?

For many gardeners, the lawn is a must. Just as you have brandy sauce with Christmas pudding, so you have a lawn with the garden!

Green and mellow, a well-kept lawn provides a perfect setting for a mulched rose bed, or a flowering shrubbery, or a bed of perennial flowers in the greater framework of the garden. Easy on the eyes in bright sunny weather, the lawn presents a perfect environment for relaxing beneath the softly rippling shade of a favourite tree.

Consider first, what is a lawn? Ideally, in a cool climate a lawn consists of a blend of two or three suitable grasses and a legume which is short, creeping, and can thrive with regular mowing. In a subtropical climate it is probably better to have a lawn with a single superior grass, such as Sir Walter. White clover is the superior legume for lawns, but it prefers a mild, cool or cold climate. In the subtropics and tropics it grows mainly in the winter, fading out in the heat.

The climate, sunlight, and soil pH will determine the content of your lawn, even the weeds! A lawn that has areas in semi-shade or full shade for much of the day will need to have a grass capable of growing in this. It is a common sight to see good lawns that become very sparse under the influence of trees. Some people think that the lawn is losing its moisture to the tree, and this can happen, but all too often sunlight is the determining factor. Do not be afraid to have a lawn with one type of grass in the full sun, another type for semi-shade and even another for full shade. If you were to choose two or three suitable types of buffalo grass in the subtropics you would hardly notice the difference, but in a cooler climate you would probably need different species. Different grass species flourishing well looks far better than a single, unhappy, struggling species.

Personally, if I had lawn under trees with permanent shade, I would explore the many different native grasses that could thrive under those conditions, try a number of different species, and leave the area uncut to enjoy the grasses when they flowered, to have wild grass instead of lawn.

LAWN LEGUME

Before I go further about the grass, let me address the issue of a legume in the lawn. So many garden owners and quite a few gardeners attempt to have a lawn that is entirely grass. This is not natural in Nature. It is natural that where grasses grow there are companion plants. Under natural rhythms the grass comes into its season, then declines, while the companions come into their season and decline. And so it goes through the seasons in a rhythm determined by the climate. Under natural circumstances the companion plants are supportive of each other, and invariably a few leguminous plant species are involved in this. It is only where human interference has intervened that you get competitive weed plants.

In America I have seen hundreds of gardens where the entire garden is lawn, or perhaps I should say grass, for the lawn is totally grass. Not only that, but I have seen the prolific lawn care contractors who cut these lawns, spraying them to deliberately kill the white clover. And this is called care! White clover is the most supportive plant for grass possible. As a legume, white clover is creating and supplying the soil with a continuous supply of nitrogen via its root nodulation. The lawn grass utilises this nitrogen which is so freely supplied, a vital nutrient necessary for both health and colour. Again, this is the way of Nature.

If you have a cool/cold climate that will easily support white clover growing in the lawn, then encourage the white clover to grow. Your lawn will be stronger, more drought resistant, and healthier as a result. Where the climate is too warm for lawn legumes, a variety of buffalo is a good, capable grass.

There are, of course, many clovers. Some are annual, reseeding themselves, and some are biennial, not lasting long. Some are tall, like red clover, but a lawn needs the low creeping, white clover. I have emphasised 'white' clover because this is by far the superior perennial clover to grow and encourage for the benefit of your lawn.

The Basics

For a few moments consider the downtrodden lawn, and it always is down! If it is your intention to cultivate a lawn that you can be proud of, one which feels full of 'zing,' a lawn you can 'consciously' enjoy, then you must understand the principles on which this must be based. The bare patches, the mossy areas, the weeds, they all tell a story. Your lawn must be able to develop a proper, deep, root system, and equally the aerobic soil life must be able to breathe. Not too much to ask, is it?

Grass and clover both have a basic need to plunge their roots deep into the soil for moisture and nutrients. If you allowed a patch of lawn to grow to full height, the root system would grow correspondingly deeper, maintaining a balance between roots and foliage. If you were to then cut that patch of lawn, reducing it to a normal lawn height, a corresponding amount of root would die.

Keeping your lawn continually short enforces a short, considerably weakened root system. These roots are denied the ability to plunge deep into the soil, mining it for nutrients and moisture. This means, in effect, that either you are required to feed and water the lawn on a regular basis, or you have to find a way of growing a stronger, more deeply rooted, and self-fertilising lawn. Happily, this is easily done for a conscious organic gardener!

Although a lawn needs to be cut, a balance must be found. I have given a lot of lawns a careful scrutiny. My focus was their height and how this compared with the condition of the lawn. Without exception, lawns which were regularly cut too short, with all clippings collected and dumped, were problem lawns. Most of these were cut and maintained at about 2–3 cm (1 inch). This is far too short. A lawn should be cut and maintained at a height no lower than 5–6 cm (2–2 ½ inches).

This will allow the grass and clover to grow thicker, quickly allowing a deeper penetration of the roots, thus overrunning and overwhelming any weeds growing in the lawn.

LAWN CLIPPINGS

Strange as it may seem, I know of keen gardeners who have a lawn mainly because they want to use the lawn clippings. These are gardeners who are always scrounging for mulch, and the lawn is a good supplier. While I accept that the organic gardener has endless uses for the grass and clover clippings, nevertheless you have to 'consciously' consider the lawn and the soil on which it is growing.

As a conscious gardener you are growing your lawn organically. If you remove all the lawn clippings to use elsewhere in the garden, you are going to starve the lawn to feed the vegetables or flowers. This is not a good idea. Once you engage in this practice, the lawn will steadily deteriorate as the soil beneath the lawn becomes depleted in organic matter. And it does matter! Very quickly the lawn will produce weedy, seedy clippings, instead of clippings filled with nitrogen-rich clover. This defeats the purpose of the exercise. Yet some gardeners continue with their subconscious habit, not observing the clear signals from the lawn.

You can rectify this in several ways, feeding both the lawn and the rest of the garden. You can remove all the lawn clippings for one season of growth, allowing it to fall back onto the lawn during the following season. Equally, you can do this bi-monthly, one month on the lawn and one month on the garden. If you have several lawns it is easy to work out a rotating system whereby you let one lawn feed itself while the rest supply you with mulch to feed the garden.

However you choose to do it, remember that the clippings left on the grass are going to need time to break down and enter the soil. If you allow one clipping to fall on the lawn and one off, you will collect the one on each time because it will not have had time to decay into the lower profile of the lawn. This will not work. I suggest that three months on and three months off is a good balance if you are a gardener who wants the lawn clippings.

Personally, I have a mulching mower, so it all returns to the lawn. I never water the lawn, never cut it too short, never weed it or fertilise it. Everything the lawn needs it grows, except for a scattering of dolomite every year or so. If there is a drought it goes dry and brown, and I do not mind. It's still alive, and when it rains it springs into life with enormous vigour. I enjoy my lawn, and it enjoys me!

THE SOIL UNDER THE LAWN

If you intend to fertilise your lawn—and if you take clippings off you will need to—I suggest you use a handful of blood and bone per square metre (yard) of lawn, applying it once a month throughout the lawn's season of growth. Bypass all the chemical stimulants. They offer short-term growth with long-term soil life damage.

Under natural conditions the season of growth is dictated by the climate, but with a watering system this is overridden. It is natural for grass to have a season of growth and a time of rest, but with irrigation systems it is all grow, grow, grow, unless you have a cold, frosty winter. Allow your lawn its time of rest. Not many parts of the world have a climate of continuous all-year-round growth, and practically all that do are covered in dense rainforest.

With a lawn regularly cut too short, the resulting short, weakened root system imposes severe restrictions on the plant and soil life. A poorly maintained lawn can effectively seal the soil, causing compaction and sourness, with gradually increasing acidity. In other words, problems! When this happens, Nature, in her wisdom, calls in the deep-rooted aggressive weeds to plunge their roots into the subsoil, breaking loose the deeper minerals and nutrients that the grass cannot reach.

These deep-rooted weeds also break the compaction, but by now the lawn is a mess. Some garden owners then buy a toxic poison to spray onto the weeds, jeopardising the health of themselves, the family, and the soil life, but of course, as a conscious gardener you avoid all such pitfalls.

Remember, there is soil under the lawn, and how you treat the lawn is also how you are treating the soil and the soil life. The lawn can only be as good as the conditions you create for it.

Lawn Assistance

In the various places I have lived, I have created lawn from pasture simply by mowing it. I have restored weed patches with grass, called a lawn, simply by cutting high, allowing the grass and clover to again become dominant, and leaving all the clippings on the soil to feed and replenish the organic matter in the soil. Given the chance, clover and grass will out-perform most of the weeds, especially with regular mowing at a fair and proper height.

However, assistance is often required. Spiking the lawn can have an amazing effect when it is compacted by feet. To do this you use a normal garden fork, driving it into a *very moist* lawn to half the tines depth. You do this over all the lawn or the areas that need it, with as close and regular spacing as your energy will allow. Failing this, hire a good lawn spiker from your garden centre.

Next, sprinkle dolomite over the lawn at approximately three handfuls to each square metre (yard) and rake it in with a strong, long-toothed rake, thus ensuring that some will fall down the spike holes. If your soil is alkaline, use gypsum at the same rate.

In these two operations you have let oxygen into the soil to generate a better exchange of soil gases, and have introduced the cation minerals calcium and magnesium into the soil to reduce acidity, thus releasing some of the complex mineral nutrients.

If there is moss in your lawn it should be raked with extra vigour. Moss indicates a lack of drainage, creating dampness and acidity. It may be necessary to resow a lawn mixture after a bad infestation of moss, but be sure to improve the drainage and add the dolomite. I have seen the most beautiful moss gardens under large trees in Japan, where the conditions were encouraged for the growth of moss instead of grass.

Weeds in the lawn are best pulled by hand, using a special hand tool to ease the roots out of the soil. You can touch them with a weed stick if they are very numerous, or you find the task too overwhelming, but be very careful how you use it. It is poison, death to frogs of the night.

Beginning with Turf

A word may be in order here for those who are about to put in their first lawn. Turfing the lawn has become increasingly popular, despite it being much more expensive. The main advantage is that you have an instant lawn, alleviating any risk of erosion in a heavy rain, and it is very satisfying to have the lawn completed and actually growing by the end of a day's work. It also smothers immature weeds that are in the ground. However, I cannot stress enough the need for top quality turf, preferably with named varieties, or variety, of grass that have been cut at the correct thickness. Beware of cheap turf. It will be weedy, thin, and nasty.

The soil conditions will need to be well prepared for either turf or seed. Prepare carefully, do not rush the job. If you make errors you will have a very long time to regret it.

For turf, the main requirement is to ensure that the soil is level, without humps and hollows. You will need to ensure that the drainage is adequate, and that you have plenty of help on the day of laying turf. Do not lay turf in hot, dry weather. You will need to water it the first two to three weeks unless it rains daily, but despite this, a very hot day will add considerable stress to the turf.

Remember, the grass has just had most of its roots sliced off. The portion you buy should have enough roots to start growing new ones, while the portion left on the turf farm should have enough roots left in the ground that it can grow a whole new crop of foliage. It is this that encourages a very few less scrupulous turf growers to slice the turf you buy too thinly. However, with any reputable turf farm, this should not happen.

Lay the turf rolls as close together as possible, and pat them down flat to the soil, do not roll. Some gardeners roll their turf, but it will mostly move in the direction you are rolling. A heavy roll on a slope is an absolute no-no. This is not a good practice. It came about because of the hurry, hurry, hurry syndrome. A quarter of a railway sleeper (tie), with a handle fixed on so you can lift it up and whack it down, does the job perfectly. Failing that, a heavy shovel— not a spade—whacked vigorously onto the turf is okay. The time you spend preparing the job and doing it correctly will be far less than the time spent regretting it for an ill-prepared job.

Seeding Your Lawn

I repeat, prepare carefully. Get advice on the best seed mix from your local garden centre. They know your conditions and should know what they are talking about. If it is a cooler climate, add some white clover seed to the mix.

Months before you intend to sow—and this will depend on your climate—cultivate and level the ground where you intend to sow the lawn. Water it well, encouraging all the weed seeds to germinate and grow. Now is the time to assure adequate drainage.

Generally, autumn is the best sowing time for hot dry climates, while spring is most suited to cool cold. However, before then try to have had the soil cultivated and weed seeds germinated and growing a couple of times before you get to the time of finally levelling and preparing the soil. All the weeds that grow before sowing time are weeds that you will not have in the new lawn.

Incorporate plenty of organic matter into the soil, boosting its humus, and give it plenty of blood and bone, and slow-acting sheep manure.

By now you should have found all the humps and hollows from your hand cultivating and watering. Watering will always reveal the undulations in ground that is not level. Your soil should be level and well raked, with a fine tilth on the surface. Sow the variety of lawn seed at the rate suggested by your local garden centre. You can often borrow or hire a grass seed sower from the garden centre, and this makes for an even sowing. Failing this, and you are sowing by hand, try to sow the seed as evenly as you possibly can. Divide the seed into two portions. Sow one lot by walking up and down the area to be lawn, and the other portion by walking back and forth. Not too thick, not too thin, but evenly.

Try to make sure that no flooding rain is forecast, and that the day of sowing is not windy. Wind can scatter the seed all over the place. Once it is sown, keep people and pets off of it, and keep it moist, not saturated.

When the grass is growing well and is about 10 cm (4 inches) high, mow it with care with a mower that has sharp blades. Blunt, damaged blades can tear new grass out of the soil. Once it is established allow all the clippings to fall back on the grass for the first season. However, be sure that your mower does not leave the grass clippings in a thick swathe (row) which can smother the grass under it. This is not uncommon.

Water wisely. Be conscious of your lawn.

CHAPTER 15

HOMEMADE SPRAYS AND HELPFUL HINTS

ORGANIC INSECT SPRAY

Some people may find this a bit repugnant because you use the insect you want to repel as the basis for the spray. Despite this, it is very effective, and harmless to other insects. Catch a teaspoon of the species of insect that you want to get rid of and liquidise it in a cup of water. Stand this in the sun for one day, strain it through an old stocking and mix it with 4.5 litres (1 gallon) of water. This is now pathogenically potent for the insect that is a pest, and is a powerful repellent on an energetic level. Do not use a mixture of insects—one species only, e.g., cabbage caterpillar only, or aphids only, and use it only for that species. Use it whenever or wherever it is necessary.

GARLIC SPRAY

This is good for small insects and general plant protection. Use 90 g (approx 3 ounces) of garlic bulbs. Chop them up and mix with 2 teaspoons of liquid paraffin or kerosene. Soak for 48 hours then add 600 ml (1 pint) of warm water, and 15 g (½ ounce) of good oil-base soap. Store it in a bottle. To use it, strain it and use at approximately 2.5 ml to 1 litre of water.

RHUBARB SPRAY

This is a safe and easy spray to use on small insects. Cut up 1.5 kg (3 lbs) of rhubarb leaves and boil them in 3.5 litres (6 pints) of water for 30 minutes, then allow them to cool. Mix 125 g (4 ounces) of soft soap in 2.5 litres (4 pints) of hot water. When cool, strain and blend the mixture.

DERRIS SPRAY

This is an effective insect spray, harmless to humans but deadly to fish. Keep this spray well away from ponds and rivers. You need 60 g (2 ounces) of derris powder, 120 g (4 ounces) of soft soap, and 22.5 litres (5 gallons) of water. Dissolve the soap in 4.5 litres (1 gallon) of water. Add derris to the soap solution. Stir vigorously and add the remaining 13.5 litres (3 gallons) of water. Use as necessary.

SALT SPRAY

This is a safe simple control for cabbage white butterfly, and other pests. You need 125 g (4 ounces) of salt, 9 litres (2 gallons) of water, and 25 g (1 ounce) of soft soap flakes. Mix and use.

CHIVE TEA SPRAY

This is for scab and mildew fungi. Use dried chives. Do not boil, but instead pour 600 ml (1 pint) of boiling water over the dried chives and leave them to infuse for one hour. Strain. Dilute 1 part chive tea spray to 2 parts water.

BORDEAUX MIXTURE

This is a fungicide spray. For use on dormant, bare, winter trees, it is to be used just prior to leaf and/or bud burst. Stir 90 g (3 ounces) of copper sulphate into 4.5 litres (1 gallon) of boiling water. Leave overnight. The next day mix 125 g (4 ounces) of washing soda with 4.5 litres (1 gallon) of cold water. Mix together and use immediately. *Never* use this mixture on any tree while in leaf.

An Animal Repellent

This is to deter possums, squirrels, even porcupines and such, from fruit trees. Mix together a quantity of Vaseline and pure Camphor oil. Smear this along the branches where the animals like to climb at night. The animals do not like the smell, and try to avoid getting it on themselves. If the tree is isolated, smear it up and around the trunk.

Helpful Hints

◆ Dipel HG is an excellent biological control for the infamous cabbage white butterfly caterpillar. The product contains the living spores and endotoxin of the bacteria *Bacillus thurengiensis*. It is harmless to other insects, including predator insects.

◆ Do not hoe or thin rows of seedling plants in hot sunny weather. They get scorched and their growth will be retarded. Choose a dull, cloudy day and all will be well.

◆ It is a good idea to save your own vegetable seeds. Many are easy. Allow one cabbage to seed. Tie a ventilated polythene bag over the flower head and catch the seeds in it. Always keep the biggest and the best for seed . . . the biggest tomato, sweet corn, peas, beans, pumpkin. Saving seed can save you money, and you avoid the poisons that dress many commercial seeds.

◆ If you have any trouble getting your own seeds to grow, try sprinkling a little pepper along the drill with the seed. If you listen carefully you will hear the bugs sneezing!

◆ When sowing any types of seeds always sow into a moist drill. It helps avoid light seeds blowing in the wind, and gives them moisture as soon as the seed is raked over.

- Many organic gardeners never thin the plants in the drills at all. They find that a rich, living organic soil can easily support the crowded vegetables. However, sow the seed thinly. This does help the elderly and people with back trouble.

- It is better to set young seedlings out in the evenings, even though slugs and snails will need controlling, or choose a dull day. Setting young seedlings out in the blazing sun often causes rapid transpiration and dehydration.

- After staking tomato plants, tie the strings on the stakes when you have some spare time. The strings will be ready and waiting as the plant grows and reaches them. You may be busy then!

- When harvesting crops, never store apples with, or close to, carrots and other root crops. The flavour will be affected.

- Eggshells are a good source of calcium and magnesium to add to the compost heap, or to the mulch. You can even crush and smash them to feed to your hens, but make sure the eggshells are unrecognisable.

- When poaching fish, try wrapping it in fennel leaves to avoid the smell in the kitchen. The fennel will not flavour the fish.

- Work with Nature, not against her.

- In America you can buy ladybirds (ladybugs) to put in your garden. Very nice! Apparently 1200 ml (2 pints) holds 18,000 hungry ladybirds. A hungry ladybird can eat 40 to 50 aphids a day, which means that 18,000 ladybirds could eat a million aphids daily. Encourage ladybirds in your garden!

- You can whiten your teeth by rubbing them with sage leaves.

- Orange peel is said to repel cats from the garden.

- Fallen oak leaves are a good source of the trace element boron.

- Derris and Pyrethrum are reasonably safe commercial sprays. But remember, derris is deadly to fish.

- When wandering around the garden, pinch out the dead heads of flowering plants to extend their flowering period and conserve energy

- Goats will eat out small blackberry patches.

- Give yourself time to sit in your garden and become conscious of the garden as a whole, feel a conscious connection with it.

- Don't lose your late tomato crop to frost. Pull the whole plant out and hang it in a shed so the fruit can continue to ripen.

- To deter flies and mosquitoes from coming in the window, chop up some garlic cloves into a saucer, add a touch of olive oil, and place it on the window sill.

- If you are buying old hay or straw be careful not to inhale the mould dust when you are spreading it onto the garden. Inhaling the mould spores is a health hazard. Much like smoking!

- Derris dust mixed with jam and put where ants and the European wasp are active effectively kills them.

- Another European wasp trap: hang a jar containing some sugar solution on a branch from your fruit tree. Tie a piece of paper with a small hole in it over the top. The wasps will go in, but never come out. Also effective is a small plastic funnel with its spout shortened and pointing into the jar. The wasp can go down, and in, but not out.

- A cockroach trap: take some empty glass jars, smear the inside top 3–4 cm (1.5 inches) with Vaseline, and drop a piece of over-ripe banana inside. Place the jar outside near doors and windows. It is claimed to be very effective.

- A halved onion rubbed on your limbs will repel flies while you are working. This is a biological control that will do you no harm.

- To keep tomato seeds, select your biggest and best tomato. To extract the seed from the tomato it should be pulped in a fine sieve and washed under a jet of cold water. When the seeds are washed and separated, they can be dried on a piece of glass in a warm room.

- Do not kill the spiders in your home or garden, especially the garden. Unknown and unheralded, spiders kill and eat our insect pests. Arachnids are the world's number one predator of insects, estimated to account for about 90% of all insects consumed.

- Keep a few geckos in your house. They are more approachable than spiders. They come out at night and dine on cockroaches and spiders, then retire by day. We have a lot in our house, and they are so effective they are our total control for cockroaches. I like them!

- Studies in America have shown that artificially ripened tomatoes have one-third less vitamin C than vine-ripened tomatoes.

- Have a fish pond in the garden and make a place for frogs to breed in it. The larger varieties will take slugs and snails from your garden on damp nights, and you may be helping some endangered frogs to multiply. We have about seven varieties in our frog pond who sing to us on wet nights. I love 'em!

- There is a lot of evidence to suggest that evening watering in the vegetable garden increases the risk of fungal diseases. If this is your problem try watering quite early in the morning so the foliage is dry at night.

- When growing sweet corn in blocks, leave the stems standing when the crop is finished. The following spring sow your peas in the mulch between the rows of old corn stalks. Your peas then have their climbing supports ready and waiting. When the peas are finished, simply walk up the rows of corn and peas and flatten them to the ground, then mulch over them. There is no need to pull corn and peas out of the ground.

- Chickweed is a tasty and nutritious addition to salads and coleslaw.

- Use the hills of rich loamy mulch from your old cucumber and pumpkin crop to put in the tomato trenches for rich, fertile, living soil.

- Organic gardening is excellent therapy to calm nerves, and to relax the stress and pressure of modern living. Throw away those addictive tranquillisers; get out into the garden and feel the tensions flowing away.

- To make your own liquid fertiliser, suspend a sack (large bag) of cow, sheep or poultry manure in a drum of water for one week. Dilute one part fertiliser to two parts water. In a word, it's excellent.

- When using liquid fertilisers, always be sure that the soil is moist. Never pour or water liquid fertiliser onto a dry soil.

- Try doing a small and simple task in the garden, like dead-heading flowers with your whole attention on what you are doing. As the mind quietens, tune in to the flower plants, consciously aware and open.

- If you must, try pumpkin seeds as mousetrap bait. Mice love them.

- Cucumber peel is said to repel the tiny ants that invade the house. Sprinkle small pieces where the ants are a nuisance. However, the tiny ants are a natural predator to termites, so be careful how you treat them.

- To keep your house plants healthy and full of 'zing', mist them most evenings before going to bed. It follows the natural order. Add four drops of seaweed fertiliser to each 500 ml (18 fluid ounces) of water.

- Do you have woolly aphids on your potted plants? Saturate a cotton bud in methylated spirits and dab it onto them.

- If you are growing plants with variegated foliage, remember that the white, yellow and pale green foliage types require plenty of light, but little to no direct sun, while the red-leafed, ochre-leafed and orange-leafed species prefer full direct sun to maintain their colour.

Finally, there are many gardening magazines that require your questions, and, so that others may benefit from the answer, please do not write to me with your gardening questions.

CHAPTER 16

BEFORE I LEAVE YOU

BEFORE I LEAVE YOU, I would like to share a few more words about the potential of conscious gardening. As I have indicated, if you decide that this makes sense for you, or the timing is right for this inner development, and you practise conscious gardening, you will soon learn that conscious gardening becomes conscious living.

So, are there fairies at the bottom of your garden? People will generally respond to this question in one of three ways: they will skip the following pages as arrant nonsense, or they will realise that the unseen metaphysical energies of Nature are attracted to the practitioner of conscious gardening, or they will be curious and, hopefully, receptive.

Such a question can be abruptly confronting. Most people do not believe in fairies, but do they ever wonder if fairies believe in us? Most people would say that organic growing has nothing whatsoever to do with such nebulous entities as fairies. But how open are they to being wrong? How open are you to the vast aspects of Nature that express beyond the ability of your physical sense perception? How open are you to Nature energies, or Nature spirits that work within the physical and metaphysical framework of Nature? In fact, put bluntly, *how open are you?*

If you answer my questions truthfully and you are not open to my suggestions, then as an organic gardener you are going to stay within the strict limits of applied techniques. This does not imply that you cannot be a good organic gardener; it means that the 'garden of your mind' has a fence that will keep you contained.

If, however, you are as open to the intangible as to the tangible, to the invisible as to the visible, to the formless as to the form, then you are open to an exciting journey taking you deeper into the great energy of Nature that is expressing in your garden.

MEETING PLACE OR BATTLEFIELD

You cannot penetrate the mystery of which I write by merely paying lip service, or by intellectualising it as a concept; it must become actualised in your life and in your day-to-day living. Every time you go into the garden, your own attitude will determine whether your garden is a meeting place with Nature, or a battlefield, with Nature as the enemy. And it is you who make the choice.

If you reach for poison each time some bugs threaten your plants, you choose to make the garden a battlefield. You have become the antagonist within your consciousness, and you will be creating the battle. If, however, you study the condition of the plants under threat, checking to see if they are growing in adverse conditions, then by this act you are meeting with Nature as a student.

Almost always when a swarm of bugs attacks a plant or a group of plants, it is because the plants were under stress *before* the insects attacked. Disease is not in the natural order of life, so Nature seeks to eliminate it. We, with an artificial agricultural system, have never come to terms with this. Modern agribusiness farming is based on exploitation, manipulation and coercion of the soil, Nature, and humanity. We are the losers in this system. It is a design of sick, diseased crops that are chemically stimulated in a depleted, distressed soil system, and sprayed with fungicides, insecticides and herbicides in an effort to keep it all alive.

Dis-ease means out of balance, out of the natural order of life, although we have become so familiar with it we consider it normal.

Having spent nearly a decade as a practising organic farmer earlier in my life, followed by a few years as an Organic Farming consultant, I am aware of how this stressed system of farming has integrated its energy into the public. Stress is now the number one cause of disease in humans. Does it not seem likely that if we eat food with a stressed energy field, we also are going to be more inclined toward stress? This is simply an unwanted and unfortunate energetic connection between food and consumer. Fortunately, the current movement toward organic gardening and food grown by organic growers is the response by people who are more sensitive to their health, the environment, and the natural order of life. They see the connections.

A Question of Health

During my years as a farmer, I was literally forced to become more open to Nature. I had a dairy herd of a hundred cows that, basically, were sick, yet this state of ill health was considered normal for dairy cows. It was normal for the dairy farmer to constantly battle mastitis, bloat, grass tetany and milk fever, just to name the common ones, yet all were symptoms that something was seriously amiss with the cows.

I was regarded as 'odd' to question the whys and wherefores of normal bovine health. I wanted to reach the cause of the problems, not continually treat the effects. When I finally did trace the cause, I was in for a bit of a shock. All the evidence pointed to—me!

I was responsible for the health of the soil. Although it was obvious to me that healthy soil must equate with healthy pasture, in turn reflecting in the health of the cows, this thinking was not considered 'normal'. But it went deeper than that. My connection with the farm animals and the land had nonphysical, intangible links that were to have deeper repercussions. I looked for the connections of every living thing involved, but not once did I truly consider myself as part of the equation.

Gradually, over a period of years, I learned that the herd of dairy cows and I were connected in consciousness. I learned that my energy affected the cows. If I went to milk the cows in a bad mood, with a sense of frustration based on the sheer monotonous regularity of the job, then the cows would react to me accordingly. If I milked the cows feeling the fear and despair of financial problems, the cows would react in a negative way, often holding back on their flow of milk. If I felt angry and aggressive, the tails of the cows would lift high, and hot green liquid moo-poo would splatter all over the place. Equally, if I felt genuinely happy while milking, the cows would be quiet, letting the milk flow readily and easily. This, unfortunately, was rare! When I mentioned these observations to my farming friends, they laughed at me. It was around this time I became known as 'the mad Englishman on the hill'.

A COW OF A TEACHER

One incident I was involved in affected me more profoundly than any other single factor, resulting in an approach to Nature that is still growing and expanding. I had been milking the cows for about four years, slowly learning about my effect on them, but unable to make any real change. I really liked my cows, but I detested milking them, therefore my attitude was negative, filled as it was with frustration.

Be aware that all this happened thirty-something years ago. One afternoon I was in a particularly foul mood and, sensing this, one of the more temperamental cows kicked viciously at me as I bent down to put the milking cups on. She caught me very painfully on the large thigh muscle. I jumped back and, caught in an old mode of reaction, snatched up the leg chain with which to hit the cow. I swung the chain hard . . . and it all went horribly wrong. She kicked high at me again, and somehow the chain, wrapped harmlessly around her ankle, snatched out of my hand and spun through the air in a couple of rapidly accelerating arcs, which ended by wrapping around my left arm.

The pain was instantaneous and frightening. I felt physically sick. Yet, in the intensity of the shock and pain was an instant of perfect clarity—I had done this to myself. I was the author of my pain. And with that realisation, I changed. My whole attitude to the cows and milking changed completely. In that intense moment of pain was born respect and tolerance. My arrogance died, and a real humility was born. This change was not something that I did deliberately. It was an instantaneous change in my consciousness. Change only happens in perfect timing, so obviously the timing was perfect . . . if not the technique!

I was unable to milk the cows for several days, my arm bruised to the bone. It was to be four months before my arm was free of pain. However, when I returned to the dairy, the full effect of what had happened was revealed. Prior to this incident all the cows would be agitated by my presence in the milking shed—never anywhere else—reacting with nervous behaviour. Now, on my return, every cow was quiet and placid. All the old agitation was gone. But what really amazed me was that each and every cow clearly knew that I had changed. The herd's more highly strung cows—and every herd has them—that had always been more easily upset and jittery, were now calm and easy to milk. To my astonishment I was able to milk more quickly and easily, and the milk yield was greater. This was the way it continued for the next four years of my milking the cows, when our dairying finally came to an end.

Interestingly, every cow in that large herd knew that I had changed, and responded to that change the very next time I milked them. They did not stay locked in a four-year pattern of nervous hostility. Treenie and my children were aware of the dramatic change in me, for it affected my whole life, but other people, even my friends—all supposedly more intelligent than cows—knew nothing of it. I pondered this for years.

Today, I know how it happened. The consciousness of myself,

both as the farmer and the milker, was connected to the cow herd consciousness. I could not read their energy—although I did learn to—but they could easily read mine. I had to learn, but to animals, closer to the natural rhythm of Nature, it is within their natural ability. Wild animals easily read the conscious intent of predators and other herd animals. I learned that consciousness is a non-intellectual connection, and that our intellect deals far better with the illusion of separation than it does with the truth of holistic connections. Just as I had been the cause of stress in the herd of cows, so I had to experience the effect of that cause.

CAUSE AND EFFECT

Despite the story I have related, there is nothing mystical about cause and effect. If, during my public speaking, I mention the effect we are reaping by our increasing disassociation and disconnection from Nature, I feel the dismay of people. I often get the impression that people would rather not know.

Back in those farming years when speaking to a group of beef farmers, I told them that if they continued to apply the then high levels of herbicides and fungicides on their pasture, they would see their meat condemned as unfit for human consumption. I was ridiculed. The import ban on such meat came 15 years later—but we in Oz could eat it!

Cause and effect. Like it or not, in our three-dimensional reality we live with cause and effect. If, for example, we eat eggs laid by stressed and miserable battery hens, then we are the consumers of eggs containing stress and misery in their energetic resonance. If we sow discord, then discord is what we reap. There is no way around this. None of our physical senses or scientific instruments can detect the discord, but our bodies invariably have a negative reaction to it. We do not thrive on stress and discord, not in our eggs, our meat, or our grain, fruit, or vegetables. Nor do we thrive on the stress and discord of our thoughts.

I want you to realise that what we cannot see, or do not know about, or cannot measure *does* affect us. Every person on this planet is affected by energies that express beyond the physical, and not believing it makes no difference at all.

UNSEEN ENERGIES

When I was a farmer I became aware of Nature as being far more than merely physical. Treenie and I learned that we could communicate with our cows with our focussed thoughts. On this conscious level we were able to direct them into fields where we wanted them to graze. In fact, we became so proficient at this that our trained cattle dogs became redundant.

It was on our farm in Tasmania that I consciously became a student of Nature. Undergoing that dramatic shift in the milking shed, from an attitude of arrogance to one of humility, had the effect of changing my whole approach to Nature and to life. It was truly catalytic. I came to realise that there is a vast gulf between Nature and humanity, and in that realisation was born the longing to cross it. Crossing that gulf was a metaphysical journey that took me the next fifteen years. I learned that it is the intellect that fabricates and maintains the 'Gulf of Separation', while it is conscious intelligence which reveals a greater Truth.

When I was a young man my father said to me, "If you want to be a farmer, before you sow any seeds you must first sow your heart." He was speaking of a very powerful principle: *our heart/ love connects us with Nature.* There is no other connection. Exactly the same principle applies in the garden. If you love growing plants, then grow the plants that give you the most joy, satisfaction and fulfilment. If you prefer growing useful vegetables, then grow them in an organic permaculture design where the whole garden is devoted to growing a wide and diverse selection of food plants. Be true to yourself.

However, if you enjoy growing flowers exclusively, then grow flowers, or whatever gives you joy. There is no should and should not; there is just your relationship with Nature in the personal meeting place of your garden.

Bonsai Bonanza

I used to feel that bonsai was an art based on the exploitation of a tree. I regarded it as cruel and unnecessary. I often admired the little trees, but bonsai was not for me. Then one day I visited a Horticulture and Flower Show. I admired the usual displays of spectacular plants, colourful flowers, and all the new releases in the plant world. But, more significantly, I also encountered the unexpected.

I had entered a large marquee where many plant societies were exhibiting their most favoured plant species. The African violets displayed their usual shy, yet bold colours, while the Begonias dripped with huge flowers. The orchids were as exotic and exciting as ever—but there was something else. I sensed the presence of a strong energy, and I knew that it came from a plant. I was intrigued, for I could not identify it. Rather than chase around looking for the source of this enigmatic energy, I continued my way past stall after stall, deliberately delaying the moment of discovery, prolonging the thrill of anticipation. It was odd. I was in a large area among hundreds of other people, yet I knew that I was the only person who was aware of this powerful and unusual resonating plant energy.

Then, before me was a large stall with a display of bonsai. In the very centre of the stall, ancient, twisted and magnificent, stood a large black pine, about one metre (yard) tall. To me, the energy and power radiating from that plant was almost overwhelming. I stood staring at it, gasping. Everything and everyone else faded away; there was only the tree, and me.

Unfortunately, the tree and the stall owner both chose the same moment to communicate with me, one verbally, the other in the silence of consciousness.

"You obviously like our bonsai," said the human voice.

"Er, it's magnificent," I agreed.

The tree was brief. Very strongly I felt connection, recognition, and acceptance. I 'inner-heard' the words, *"Physically dwarfed, spiritually magnified."* With this came a dynamic and expansive 'inner cognition', and my awareness of the tree, the art of bonsai, and the potential synthesis between a tree Being and a human Being was rich, full, and instant. It was all to do with consciousness, connecting human and bonsai on other, inner-dimensions of reality. As my inner *knowing* clarified, the stall owner—who had no idea of what had taken place—continued our conversation.

"The big one takes your fancy, does it?"

"Very much," I replied.

"Of course, it's not for sale."

"I didn't expect it would be. How old is it?"

The man told me that as far as he knew the bonsai black pine was about three hundred years old. It was a valued family heirloom. He was rather vague about its ancestry, but very clear about his pride of ownership. As he talked, I realised that it was the power of directed and focussed love from him and his ancestors that had fostered the spiritual growth of the tiny giant. I felt no desire to own the tree. Ownership became meaningless. What mattered was the indefinable connection of spirit. No matter where that tree was, we were connected.

Many years have passed since then, but I have yet to experience a tree with a stronger energy than that black pine bonsai. I have seen and felt seven-hundred-year-old bonsai in Japan, and slept under gigantic Sequoia trees in America, but the black pine remains unique in my connection. As I have already stated several times, the meaning of fertilise is to enrich. The bonsai was fertilised each day by a focus of love, care, and appreciation.

Not unexpectedly, I became a bonsai enthusiast. However, I decided that I would cultivate my own bonsai, rather than buy them ready made. I made one stipulation: I would ask each tree if it wanted to become a bonsai under my care. Nevertheless, I was rather abashed when the first dozen or so seedling trees clearly indicated they wanted no part in it!

One afternoon I spotted a small fig, *Ficus*, struggling to grow beneath its massive parent tree. I asked this sapling to be a bonsai— and I got a strong and instant affirmation. Since then my collection has grown to eight trees, all different *Ficus*, and a single boabab, *Adansonia*. Although I prune the roots, I do not wire the branches; fig do not like it! I visualise how I would like them to grow, but allow them their own natural freedom of expression.

For me, it is all about the connection. I feel connected to them when I water them or prune them, and I feel as connected when I am travelling overseas. And it is a two-way connection.

Are You an Onlooker or Participant?

As an organic gardener, are you an onlooker of the expression of Nature in your garden, or are you a participant in this expression? If you sow your seeds and set your plants and that's that, you are most likely an onlooker. To participate in the cycles of growth that take place, you need to consciously observe the plants while *feeling* into their energy. In this way you *feel* the dynamic of change that moves constantly through the plants. If you do this and you feel discord in the energy of a plant, you will have an intuitive knowing of how to deal with it.

Our everyday reality has the same relationship with a holistic reality as does a flower seed with the beautiful flower it will become. *We, too, are becoming something greater than we are currently being.* I experience this because I made a conscious decision to expand and enrich my reality by learning the deeper secrets of life from a teacher within Nature. As a farmer I came to the realisation that I was an onlooker of both Nature and life, and I longed to be an active participant.

In the long working hours as a dairy farmer, it is paradoxical that when I gave myself time to sit in the fields of pasture and attune with Nature, I learned more in thirty minutes of silence than in my months of rational thinking. No matter how clever we are, we cannot intellectualise ourselves closer to Nature. We are required to become humble and silent, and to listen.

WHOLENESS

The approach that we need to develop is to recognise that all life is connected. What we do in our garden affects the whole. Your relationship with your family, friends, Nature, and most of all, your self, is our relationship with life. A wholistic approach to your garden means that your work and effort become love in action. A weed or bug is not an enemy, it is an envoy from Nature with a message; all is not well in the garden. A weed often denotes that some trace elements are either missing or overabundant, or that Nature dislikes bare soil. It may also mean that you have a drainage problem.

Wholeness means that nothing in Nature, or life, is in isolation. If you learn to see with the eyes of your heart, you, too, may see the universe in a flower. Yet if you look for the universe in a flower, you will very seldom see it. Metaphysical reality does not work this way. You simply learn to *see*, allowing life to reveal that which is appropriate in the moment.

Your garden is a potential interface between you and Nature. Every gardener knows that *the secret of a green thumb is love*. Therein lies the interface. Whenever we are working with plants, animals, or people we love, we connect with the greater whole. In these moments of wholeness we touch into an expanded view of life and Nature.

Nature is an expression of cycles. These cycles involve continual earth changes, changes which are expressing in Nature at this very time. Climates are changing; the very stability of the land is changing. The planet Earth is going through a period of change, which means, like it or not, we also are being subjected to major change. Our reaction will be to resist the change that visits our lives, yet we would be wiser to learn to ride the waves of change without all the emotional resistance. I suspect that our agricultural system will go through major change, changes that will enforce a system of cooperation with Nature, rather than the current system based in a forced coercion of Nature. Although we find it difficult to embrace change in our lives, change is a holistic and natural expression in the cycles of life. *Nature is change, not permanence;* we would do well to remember that.

ILLUSION OF SEPARATION

Every gardener is familiar with buying plants for the garden. When I buy a new plant, I walk around the garden looking for where to set it. If I am in a hurry then I put it where it seems suitable, and sometimes I make an error, like the fragrant *Oleander* near the rampant *Hibiscus*. If I buy a plant with a clear knowing of where to position it, I seldom make such an error. If I bring the unexpected plant home and, while looking for a place to set it I attune with the plant, then together we will always find the most perfect place, a position where it will thrive. You can almost feel and hear the plant, 'Over there, over there, yes there!' But you do need to be open and receptive.

If, as our physical senses suggest, we are separate from Nature, such a connection between plant and human would not be possible. The same is true with our pets. Our connection transcends our physical senses. There would be no way to make any connection with another life form because separation would deny it. Beyond the physical form, we connect with the life around us emotionally and spiritually. What we consider as a mental connection is really the thinking that accompanies our emotions. Emotions are a very powerful medium of communication.

Our five senses are unable to reveal the full truth of our reality, yet if they did we would have no real incentive to develop our extra-sensory perception. Our intellect and senses create the world of illusion in which we spend our whole lives, yet as holistic Beings we all have the ability to pierce this illusion. Very few try.

LATENT ABILITIES

While devoting many years of my life to exploring the metaphysical aspects of Nature and life, I have had frequent nonphysical experiences that most people would consider as impossible. I have written books about them. Among other things, I have learned how to *inner listen*. Very few people learn how to do this, yet the ability is latent within all of us. I listen to the silent messages of Nature. Nature speaks to us through the kingdoms of plants, rivers, animals, rocks, and waterfalls.

However, the inner voice does not just happen. We have to learn to 'inner listen'. We forget that although we hear with our ears, we *listen* from within. While we know how to 'look at' with our eyes, we have forgotten how to truly *see* from our hearts. As we grew away from the wonder and awe of our child self, we lost our ability to see *newness*. Instead, we have become stuck in sameness.

Nature is not exclusively physical. The physical Nature that surrounds us is no more than the physical reflection of a metaphysical Nature.

When you look in a mirror, you know perfectly well that the mirror image is not you. It is a flat, one-dimensional reflection of the physical, three-dimensional person you consider yourself to be. Not only that, but the mirror cannot reflect your emotional, mental, or spiritual selves. The mirror shows you only a fraction of your Self. So it is with Nature. The beautiful, wondrous Nature that fills our physical lives is just an echo of far greater ethereal realms of nonphysical realities. Lewis Carroll knew this: we have to do as Alice did and go through the 'looking glass'. Through the mirror, beyond the illusion of reflection, into a far greater, far richer, spiritual world in which we actually belong.

ATTUNING WITH NATURE

First, let us look at what attuning with Nature actually means. It is about bringing yourself into harmony with Nature, into accordance with natural energies, experiencing a rapport with Nature that transcends your usual, more ambivalent connections.

How can you attune with Nature in your garden if you are distracted by 'doing to' the garden? If you have a favourite tree or place in the garden, sit down, get comfortable, and close your eyes. Relax. Now listen. At first you will hear physical sounds; the breeze in the leaves of a tree, perhaps traffic, or birds singing, or even neighbours shouting, a dog barking. Most of these noises are distracting, aggravating. If this is so, you will find that in your thoughts you are having a dialogue about what a nuisance the sounds are. You will be resisting them, and by that resistance you will be attaching yourself to the very sounds you do not want to hear.

Not a good idea! Let go of the sounds, don't identify them or connect with them in your thinking, do not analyse them. Withdraw all resistance.

Listen. There is a good way to measure how effectively you are listening. You sit, relaxed; *if you are thinking then you are not listening.* You are hearing sounds, but you are not listening. Remember, you hear with your ears, but *you listen from within your heart.* Very few people know how to listen. Listening requires your total attention. *Listening takes you into the moment; thinking takes you out of the moment.*

Nature lives in, and expresses from, the moment. If you want to attune with Nature, then you also have to be in the moment. I will be honest, it takes a lot of dedicated practice to be consciously 'at one with' Nature in the moment.

When you sit quietly in your garden, or by a stream, or seashore, or even in a room with soft heart music, and listen, then—with practice—the metaphysical ears of the heart will open and an 'inner listening' will begin to take place. By being in the moment, you will become aware of the very pulse of life, *the movement in the moment.* Within this pulse, you are able to listen to the silent voice of Nature.

Equally, at this magical moment the metaphysical eyes of your heart begin to open, revealing a greater world of reality that is screened from our physical eyes. A few people see this naturally, very few. In this greater reality there are many types of Nature spirits, ranging from infinitely tiny Beings that, literally, impregnate universal forces of energy into the cells of plants, to great Beings that are the architects of Nature's forms, defining the shape and structure of all physical life on Earth.

We have lost our innate ability to be in touch with this greater reality.

We have abandoned our spiritual home, stepping into the world of mind. We have lost our holistic spiritual connection with life, while developing the material world of separation where cynicism and rationality have become our tools of trade to deal with the deceit of illusion.

We are spiritual Beings who have closed the door on our true and greater spiritual reality. It takes a fair journey, but the door can be reached and thrown open—that I know.

One of the most exciting aspects of being a human is that we have such a vast potential to explore and develop. Nothing excites me more than this. This is my passion, to explore the infinite dimensions and expressions of life, with Nature as my guide. Believe me, when you make the nonphysical connection with the consciousness of Nature, Nature is anything but impersonal.

This is why I have written this book. I want to offer you a door into a reality greater than anything you can imagine, so that you, too, can make that journey if you so choose. The speed you travel, and the distance, is entirely up to you. Oh, there are road signs!

If you are a practising conscious gardener, the journey has begun.

I wish you bon voyage.
–Michael J. Roads

INDEX

About Michael J. Roads

The deep wisdom contained in Michael's spiritual Enlightenment is the basis for his 5-Day Intensives, seminars and books, currently in thirteen languages. Michael's public speaking tours have included invitations to Australia, New Zealand, Norfolk Island, South Africa, the Netherlands, Italy, Switzerland, Austria, Belgium, Germany, UK, Denmark, Sweden, Norway, West Indies, U.S., Canada, and Japan.

An extraordinarily gifted communicator, Michael imparts and conveys Truth heart-to-heart, far beyond the reach of words, creating the space to awaken from a dream . . . to ignite the Truth alive within each person.

'The Power of Love' 5-Day Intensives are about Unconditional Love and emotional completeness.

For information about Michael's Intensives, seminars, international tour schedule, books, CDs, quarterly newsletter and more, please visit his web site:

www.michaelroads.com
email: carolyn@michaelroads.com for tour information
email: office@michaelroads.com for all product information.
Contact Michael directly:
michael@michaelroads.com
Roadsway International
PO Box 778
Nambour, QLD 4560
Australia

CPSIA information can be obtained at www.ICGtesting.com
Printed in the USA
BVOW08s0858221115

428052BV00003B/178/P

9 781942 497059